The Real History
of the Rosicrucians

ARTHUR EDWARD WAITE

The Real History of the Rosicrucians, A. E. Waite
Jazzybee Verlag Jürgen Beck
86450 Altenmünster, Loschberg 9
Deutschland

ISBN: 9783849675684

www.jazzybee-verlag.de
admin@jazzybee-verlag.de

Printed by Createspace, North Charleston, SC, USA

CONTENTS:

PREFACE.

BENEATH the broad tide of human history there flow the stealthy undercurrents of the secret societies, which frequently determine in the depths the changes that take place upon the surface. These societies have existed in all ages and among all nations, and tradition has invariably ascribed to them the possession of important knowledge in the religious scientific or political order according to the various character of their pretensions. The mystery which encompasses them has invested them with a magical glamour and charm that to some extent will account for the extravagant growth of legend about the Ancient Mysteries, the Templars, the Freemasons, and the Rosicrucians, above all, who were the most singular in the nature of their ostensible claims and in the uncertainty which envelopes them.

"A halo of poetic splendour," says Heckethorn, "surrounds the Order of the Rosicrucians; the magic lights of fancy play round their graceful daydreams, while the mystery in which they shrouded themselves lends additional attraction to their history. But their brilliancy was that of a meteor. It just flashed across the realms of imagination and intellect, and vanished for ever; not, however, without leaving behind some permanent and lovely traces of its hasty passage. . . . Poetry and romance are deeply indebted to the Rosicrucians for many a fascinating creation. The literature of every European country contains hundreds of pleasing fictions, whose machinery has been borrowed from their system of philosophy, though that itself has passed away."

The facts and documents concerning the Fraternity of the Rose Cross, or of the Golden and Rosy Cross, as it is called by Sigmund Richter, are absolutely unknown to English readers. Even well-informed people will learn with astonishment the extent and variety of the Rosicrucian literature which hitherto has lain buried in rare pamphlets, written in the old German tongue, and in the Latin commentaries of the later alchemists. The stray gleams of casual information which may be gleaned from popular encyclopædias cannot be said to convey any real knowledge, while the essay of Thomas De Quincey on the "Rosicrucians and Freemasons," though valuable as the work of a sovereign prince of English prose composition, is a mere transcript from an exploded German savant, whose facts are tortured in the interests of a somewhat arbitrary hypothesis. The only writer in this country who claims to have treated the subject seriously and at length is Hargrave Jennings, who, in "The Rosicrucians, their Rites and Mysteries," &c., comes forward as the historian of the Order. This book, however, so far from affording any information on the questions it professes to deal with, "keeps guard over " the secrets of the Fraternity, and is simply a mass of ill-digested erudition concerning Phallicism and Fire-Worship, the Round Towers of Ireland and Serpent Symbolism, offered

1

with a charlatanic assumption of secret knowledge as an exposition of Rosicrucian philosophy.The profound interest now manifested in all branches of mysticism, the tendency, in particular, of many cultured minds towards those metaphysical conceptions which are at the base of the alchemical system, the very general suspicion that other secrets than that of manufacturing gold are to be found in the Pandora's Box of Hermetic and Rosicrucian allegories, make it evident that the time has come to collect the mass of material which exists for the elucidation of this curious problem of European history, and to depict the mysterious Brotherhood as they are revealed in their own manifestos and in the writings of those men who were directly or indirectly in connection with them. Such a publication will take the subject out of the hands of unqualified writers, and of the self-constituted pontiffs of darkness and mystery who trade upon the ignorance and curiosity of their readers.

As the result of conscientious researches, I have succeeded in discovering several tracts and manuscripts in the Library of the British Museum, whose existence, so far as I am aware, has been unknown to previous investigators, while others, including different copies and accounts of the "Universal Reformation," as well as original editions of the "Chymical Marriage of Christian Rosy Cross," which are not in the Library Catalogue, though less generally obscure, I have met with in a long series of German pamphlets belonging to the first quarter of the seventeenth century. These, with all other important and available facts and documents, I have carefully collected and now publish them in the present volume, either summarised or *in extenso* according to their value, and I offer for the first time in the literature of the subject the Rosicrucians represented by themselves. I claim that I have performed my task in a sympathetic but impartial manner, purged from the bias of any particular theory, and above all uncontaminated by the pretension to superior knowledge, which claimants have never been able to substantiate.

INTRODUCTION.

"In cruce sub sphera venit sapientia vera."--*Hermetic Axiom.*

"La rose qui a été de tout temps l'emblême de la beauté, de la vie, de l'amour et du plaisir, exprimait mystiquement toutes les protestations manifestées à la renaissance. . . . Rénuir la rose, à la croix, tel était le problème posé par la Haute Initiation."--*Éliphas Lévi.*

THREE derivations are offered of the name Rosicrucian. The first, which is certainly the most obvious, deduces it from the ostensible founder of the order, Christian Rosenkreuze. I shall show, however, that the history of this personage is evidently mythical or allegorical, and therefore this explanation merely cakes the inquiry a step backward to the question, What is the etymology of Rosenkreuze? The second derivation proposed is from the Latin words *Ros*, dew, and *Crux*, cross. This has been countenanced by Mosheim, who is followed by Ree's Encyclopædia; and other publications. The argument in its favour may be fairly represented by the following quotation:--"Of all natural bodies, dew was deemed the most powerful dissolvent of gold; and the cross, in chemical language, was equivalent to light; because the figure of a cross exhibits at the same time the three letters of which the word lux, or light, is compounded. Now, lux is called . . . the seed or menstruum of the red dragon, or, in other words, that gross and corporeal light, which, when properly digested and modified, produces gold. Hence it follows, if this etymology be admitted, that a Rosycrucian philosopher is one who by the intervention and assistance of the dew, seeks for light, or, in other words, the substance called the Philosopher's Stone."This opinion exaggerates the importance attributed to the dew of the alchemists. The universal dissolvent has figured under various names, of which *ros* is by no means most general; the comprehensive "Lexicon Alchymiæ" does not mention it. According to Gaston le Doux, in his "Dictionnaire Hermétique," Dew, simply so called, signifies Mercury; Dew of the Philosophers is the matter of the stone when under the manipulation of the artist, and chiefly during its circulations in the philosophical egg. The White and Celestial Dew of the Wise is the philosophical stone perfected to the White. Mosheim derived his opinion from Peter Gassendi, and from a writer in Eusebius Renandot's "Conferences Publiques," who confesses that he knew nothing whatsoever of the Rosicrucians till the task of speaking on the subject was imposed on him by the *Bureau d'Addresse*. He says:--"Dew, the most powerful dissolvent of gold which is to be found among natural and non-corrosive substances, is nothing else but light coagulated and rendered corporeal; when it is artistically concocted and digested in its own vessel during a suitable period it is the true menstruum of the Red Dragon, *i.e.*, of gold, the true matter of the Philosophers. The society desiring to bequeath to posterity the ineffaceable sign of this secret, caused them to

3

adopt the name *Frères de la Rozée Cuite*." The mystic triad of the Society, F. R. C., has been accordingly interpreted *Fratres Roris Cocti*, the Brotherhood of the Concocted or Exalted Dew, but the explanation has little probability in itself.

"Several chemists," says Pernetz, in his "Dictionnaire Mytho-Hermétique," "have regarded the dew of May and September as the matter of the *Magnum Opus*, influenced doubtless by the opinion of various authors that dew was the reservoir of the universal spirit of Nature. . . . But when we seriously study the texts of the true philosophers, wherein they snake reference to dew, we are soon convinced that they only speak of it by a similitude, and that theirs is metallic, that is, it is the mercurial water sublimated into vapour within the vase, and precipitated at the bottom in the form of fine rain. Thus when they write of the dew of the month of May, they are referring to that of their philosophic Spring, which is governed by the gemini of the alchemical Zodiack, which differs from the ordinary astronomical Zodiack. Philalethes has positively said that their dew is their mercurial water rising from putrefaction."

The third derivation is that which was generally adopted, even from the beginning, by writers directly or indirectly connected with the Rosicrucians. It deduces the term in question from the words *rosa*, rose, and *crux*. This is sanctioned by various editions of the society's authoritative documents, which characterise it as the Broederschafft des Roosen Creutzes, that is, the Rose-Crucians, or *Fratres Rosatæ Crucis*, according to the "Confessio Recepta," terms quite excluding the conception of dew, which in German is Thau, while in Latin the Brothers of the Dewy Cross would be *Fratres Roratæ Crucis*. This derivation is also supported by the supposed symbol of the Order, whose "emblem, monogram, or jewel," says Godfrey Higgins, "is a Red Rose on a Cross, thus:--

When it can be done it is surmounted with a glory and placed on a calvary. When it is worn appended and made of cornelian, garnet, ruby, or red glass, the calvary and glory are generally omitted."Mr Hargrave Jennings, who borrows the whole of this passage without acknowledgment of any kind, also tells us that "the jewel of the Rosicrucians is formed of a transparent red stone with a red cross on one side and a red rose on the other--thus it is a crucified rose."

All derivations, however, are to some extent doubtful and tentative. The official proclamations of the Society are contained in the "Fama Fraternitatis," and in the "Confessio Fraternitatis," which, in their original editions, appear to describe it simply as the *Fraternitas de R. C.*, while the initials of its founder are given as C. R. "The Chemical Nuptials of Christian Rosen Kreuze," published anonymously at Strasbourg in 1616, and undeniably connected with the order, seem to identify it as the Brotherhood of the Rose-Cross, and its founder as Father Rosycross. These designations at any rate were immediately adopted in Germany, and they appear in the subsequent editions of both manifestos, though as early as 1618 I find Michael Maier, the alchemist, expressing a different opinion on this point in his "Themis Aurea, hoc est, De Legibus Fraternitatis R. C. Tractatus." "No long time elapsed, when the Society first became known by that which was written, before an interpreter came forward who conjectured those letters to signify the Rose Cross, in which opinion the matter remains till this present, notwithstanding that the Brothers in subsequent writings do affirm it to be erroneously so denominated, and testify that the letters R. C. denote the name of their first inaugurator. If the mind of one man could search that of another and behold formed therein the idea or sensible and intelligible form, there would be no necessity for speech or writing among men. But this being denied to us while we subsist in this corporeal nature, though doubtless granted to pure intelligences, we explain our rational conceptions one to another by the symbols of language and writing. Therefore letters are of high efficacy when they embrace a whole society and maintain order therein, nor is an opportunity afforded to the curious to draw omens from integral names, nor from families situations, nor from places persons, nor from persons the secrets of affairs."

Proposing his own definitions, he says:--"I am no augur nor prophet, notwithstanding that once I partook of the laurel, and reposed a few brief hours in the shadow of Parnassus; nevertheless, if I err not, I have unfolded the significance of the characters R. C. in the enigmas of the sixth book of the Symbols of the Golden Table. R signifies Pegasus, and C, if the sense not the sound be considered, *lilium*. Let the KNOWLEDGE OF THE ARCANA be the key to thee. Lo, I give thee the Arcanum! d. wmml. zii. w. sgqqhka. x. Open if thou canst. . . . Is not this the hoof of the Red Lion or the drops of the Hippocrene fountain?" Beneath this barbarous jargon we discern, however, an analogy with the Rose symbolism. Classical tradition informs us that the Red Rose sprang from the blood of Adonis, but Pegasus was a winged horse which sprang from the blood of Medusa, and the fountain of Hippocrene was produced by a stroke of the hoof of Pegasus.

In England the pseudonymous author of the "Summum Bonum," who is supposed to be Robert Fludd, gives a purely religious explanation of the Rose Cross symbol, asserting it to mean "the Cross sprinkled with the rosy blood of Christ." The general concensus of opinion is preferable to fanciful interpretations, and we may therefore safely take the words *Rosa* and *Crux* as explanatory of the name Rosicrucian, and by *Fratres R. C.* we may understand *Fratres Roseæ Crucis*, despite the silence of the manifestos and the protests of individual alchemists.

The next question which occurs is the significance of this curious emblem--a Red Rose affixed to a red, or, according to some authors, a golden cross. This question cannot be definitely answered. The-characteristic sign of a secret society will be naturally as mysterious as itself in the special meaning which the society may attach to it, but some intelligence concerning it can perhaps be gleaned from its analysis with universal symbolism. Now, the Rose and the Cross, in their separate significance, are emblems of the most palmary importance and the highest antiquity. There is a Silver Rose, called Tamara Pua, in the Paradise of the Brahmans. "This Paradise is a garden in heaven, to which celestial spirits are first admitted on their ascent from the terrestrial sphere. The Rose contains the images of two women, as bright and fair as a pearl; but these two are only one, though appearing as if distinct according to the medium, celestial or terrestrial, through which they are viewed. In the first aspect she is called the Lady of the Mouth, in the other, the Lady of the Tongue, or the Spirit of Tongues. In the centre of this Silver Rose, God has his permanent residence."

A correspondence will be readily recognised between this divine woman or virgin--two and yet one, who seems to typify the Logos, the Spirit of Wisdom, and the Spirit of Truth--and the two-edged sword of the Spirit in the Apocalypse, the *Sapientia quæ ex ore Altissimii prodiit*, as it is called in the sublime Advent antiphon of the Latin Church. The mystical Rose in the centre of the allegorical garden is continually met with in legend. Buddha is said to have been crucified for robbing a garden of a flower, and after a common fashion of mythology, the divine Avatar of the Indians is henceforth identified with the object for which he suffered, and he becomes himself "a flower, a Rose, a Padma, Lotus, or Lily." Thus he is the Rose crucified, and we must look to the far East for the origin of the Rosicrucian emblem. According to Godfrey Higgins, this is "the Rose of Isuren, of Tamul, and of Sharon, crucified for the salvation of men--crucified," he continues, "in the heavens at the vernal equinox." In this connection we may remember the Gnostic legend that Christ was crucified in the Empyrean; and as Nazareth, according to St Jerome, signified the flower, and was situated in Carmel, "the vineyard or garden of God," Jesus of Nazareth, by a common extension of the symbolism, is sometimes identified as this crucified flower. In classical fable, the garden of Midas, the King of the Phrygians, was situated at the foot of Mount Bermion, and was glorified by the presence of roses with sixty petals, which exhaled an extraordinary fragrance. Now, the rose was sacred to Dionysius, or Bacchus, and Bacchus endowed Midas with the power of transmuting everything into gold; so here is a direct connection between the Rose and Alchemy.

In the Metamorphoses of Apuleius, Lucius is restored to his human shape by devouring a chaplet of roses. Everywhere the same typology meets us. The Peruvian Eve sinned by plucking roses, which are also called *Frute del Arbor*. A messenger from heaven announces to the Mexican Eve that she will bear a Son who shall bruise the serpent's head; he presents her with a Rose, and this gift was followed by an Age of Roses, as in India there was the Age of the Lotus.

There are occasional allusions to the Rose in the Hebrew Scriptures, but it is used as a poetic image rather than an arcane symbol, and as such it has been always in high favour with poets. In the west it appears for the first time in allegorical literature as the central figure in the "four-square garden" of the ancient "Romance of the Rose." The first part of this poem was written by Guillaume de Lorris before the year 1260, and it was completed by Jean de Meung, whose death occurred in the year 1316, according to the general opinion. This extraordinary work, once of universal popularity, is supposed by some of its commentators to admit of an alchemical interpretation, and openly professes the principles of the *Magnum Opus*. The garden, or *vergier*, which contains the Rose, is richly sculptured on its outer walls with symbolical figures of Hatred, Treason, Meanness, Covetousness, Avarice, Envy, Sadness, Age, Hypocrisy, Poverty--all the vices and miseries of mortality. Idleness opens the gate to him, Merriment greets him and draws him into the dance, and then he beholds the God of Love, accompanied by *Dous-Regars*, a youth who carries his bows and arrows, by Beauty, Wealth, Bounty, Frankness, Courtesy, &c. The lover, while he is contemplating the loveliness of the Rose,

> Qui est si vermeille et si fine . . .
> Des foilles i ot quatre paire,
> Que Nature par grand mestire
> I ot assises tire à tire. Le coe ot droite comme jons,
> Et par dessus siet li boutons,
> Si qu 'il ne cline ne ne pent.
> L' odor de lui entor s' espent;
> La soatisme qui en ist,

7

Toute la place replenist,is pierced by the shafts of the deity, but he does not in spite of his sufferings abandon his project, which is to possess the Rose, and after imprisonment and various adventures,

> La conclusion du Rommant
> Est que vous voyez cy l'Amant
> Qui prent la Rose à son plaisir,
> En qui estoit tout son désir.

It will require no acquaintance with the methods of the symbolists to discern the significance of this allegory:--

La Rose c'est d'Amour le guerdon gracieux. But a little later the same emblem reappears in the sublime poem of Dante. The Paradise of the *Divina Commedia* consists, says Eliphas Lévi, of "a series of Kabbalistic circles divided by a Cross, like Ezekiel's pantacle; a Rose blossoms in the centre of this Cross, and it is for the first time that we find the symbol of the Rosicrucians publicly and almost categorically revealed."

The passage referred to, so far as regards the Rose, is as follows:--

> "There is in heaven a light, whose goodly shine
> Makes the Creator visible to all
> Created, that in seeing him alone
> Have peace; and in a circle spreads so far,
> That the circumference were too loose a zone
> To girdle in the sun. All is one beam,
> Reflected from the summit of the first,
> That moves, which being hence and vigour takes.
> And as some cliff; that from the bottom eyes
> His image mirror'd in the crystal flood,
> As if to admire his brave apparelling
> Of verdure and of flowers; so, round about,
> Eyeing the light, on more than million thrones,
> Stood, eminent, whatever from our earth
> Has to the skies return'd. How wide the leaves
> Extended to their utmost, of this ROSE,
> Whose lowest step embosoms such a space
> Of ample radiance! Yet, nor amplitude
> Nor height impeded, but my view with ease
> Took in the full dimension of that joy.
> Near or remote, what then avails, *where God*
> *Immediate rules*, and Nature, awed, suspends
> Her sway? Into the yellow of the Rose

Perennial, which, in bright expansiveness,
Lays forth its gradual blooming, redolent
Of praises to the never-wintering sun. . . .
Beatrice led me. . . . In fashion as a snow-white Rose lay then
Before my view the saintly multitude,
Which in his own blood Christ espoused. Meanwhile
That other host that soar aloft to gaze
And celebrate His glory whom they love,
Hovered around, and like a troop of bees
Amid the vernal sweets alighting now,
Now clustering where their fragrant labour glows,
Flew downward to the mighty flower; a rose
From the redundant petals streaming back
Unto the steadfast dwelling of their joy.
Faces had they of flame, and wings of gold:
The rest was whiter than the driven snow.
And as they flitted down into the flower,
From range to range fanning their plumy loins,
Whispered the peace and ardour which they won
From that soft winnowing. Shadow none, the vast
Interposition of such numerous flights
Cast from above, upon the flower, or view
Obstructed aught. For through the Universe
Wherever merited, Celestial Light
Glides freely, and no obstacle prevents.
CARY'S DANTE, "The Paradise," xxx., xxxi.

"Not without astonishment will it be discovered," continues Lévi, that the *Roman de la Rose* and the Divine Comedy are two opposite forms of the same work--initiation into intellectual independence, satire on all contemporary institutions and allegorical formulations of the great secrets of the Rosicrucian Society. These important manifestations of occultism coincide with the epoch of the downfall of the Templars, since Jean de Meung or Clopinel, contemporary of Dante's old age, flourished during his most brilliant years at the Court of Philippe le Bel. The 'Romance of the Rose' is the epic of ancient France. It is a profound work in a trivial guise, as learned an exposition of the mysteries of occultism as that of Apuleius. The Rose of Flamel, of Jean de Meung, and of Dante, blossomed on the same rose-tree." This is ingenious and interesting, but it assumes the point in question, namely, the antiquity of the Rosicrucian Fraternity, which, it is needless to say, cannot be proved by the mere existence of their symbols in the mystical poetry of a remote period. In the Paradise of Dante we find, however, the emblem whose history we are tracing, placed, and assuredly

9

not without reason, in the supreme, central heaven amidst the intolerable manifestation of the Untreated Light, the Shecinah of Rabbinical theosophy, the chosen habitation of God--"a sacred Rose and Flower of Light, brighter than a million suns, immaculate, inaccessible, vast, fiery with magnificence, and surrounding God as if with a million veils. This symbolic Rose is as common a hierogram throughout the vast temples and palaces of the Ancient East as it is in the immense ruins of Central America."From the time of the Guelphs and the Ghibellines a common device in heraldry is the Rose-Emblem. It figures on our English coins; it is used as a royal badge in the Civil War between the houses of York and Lancaster, it is associated above all with the great mediæval cultus of the Mother of God, being our Lady's flower *par excellence*, as the lily is characteristic of St Joseph. "As an emblem of the Virgin, the Rose, both white and red, appears at a very early period; it was especially so recognised by St Dominic, when he instituted the devotion of the rosary, with direct reference to St Mary. The prayers appear to have been symbolised as roses." In Scandinavia the same flower was sacred to the goddess Holda, who is called "Frau Rosa," and "it was partly transferred, as were other emblems of Holda, Freyja, and Venus, to the Madonna, who is frequently called by the Germans, Mariën-Röschen . . . But there has been a tendency to associate the White Rose with the Virgin Mary, that being chiefly chosen for her feast-days, while the more earthly feelings associated with the 'Frau Rosa,' are still represented in the superstitions connected with the Red Rose."

In Germany it appears as the symbol of silence. It was sculptured on the ceiling of the banquet hall to warn the guests against the repetition of what was heard beneath it. "The White Rose was especially sacred to silence. It was carved in the centre of the Refectory of the ancients for the same reason," and the expression *Sub Rosa*, which was equivalent among the Romans to an inviolable pledge, originated in the ancient dedication of the flower to Aphrodite, and its reconsecration by Cupid to Harpocrates, the tutelary deity of Silence, to induce him to conceal the amours of the goddess of love.

In mediæval alchemy Rosa signifies Tartarum, and in the twelfth Clavis of Basil Valentine there is a vase or yoni with a pointed lingam rising from its centre, and having on each side a sprig surmounted by a Rose. Above is the well-known emblem

which symbolises the accomplishment of the *Magnum Opus*, while through an open window the sun and moon shed down their benign influence and concur in the consummation of the ineffable act. The same Rose-symbol is to be found in the hieroglyphics of Nicholas Flamel—

The mystic Rose
Of Hermic lore, which issues bright and fair,
Strange virtues circling with the sap therein,
Beneath the Universal Spirit's breath,
From the Mercurial Stone.

Finally, in 1598, Henry Khunrath, a supreme alchemical adept, published his "Amphitheatrum Sapientiæ Æternæ," containing nine singular pantacles, of which the fifth is a Rose of Light, in whose centre there is a human form extending its arms in the form of a cross, and thus reversing the order.

The Cross is a hierogram of, if possible, still higher antiquity than the floral emblem. It is at any rate more universal and contains a loftier and more arcane significance. Its earliest form is the *Crux Ansata*,

which, according to some authorities, signified hidden wisdom, and the life of the world to come; according to others, it is the lingam; as the hieroglyphic sign of Venus it is an ancient allegorical figure, and represents the metal copper in alchemical typology. The *Crux Ansata* and the Tau

T

are met with on most Egyptian monuments. In the latter form it was an emblem of the creative and generative energy, and, according to Payne Knight, was, even in pre-Christian times, a sign of salvation. The Cross, "the symbol of symbols," was used also by the Chaldæans; by the Phoenicians, who placed it on their coins; by the Mexicans, who paid honour to it and represented their God of the Air, nailed and immolated thereon; by the Peruvians, who, in a sacred chamber of their palace, kept and venerated a splendid specimen carved from a single piece of fine jasper or marble; and by the British Druids. It was emblazoned on the banners of Egypt, and in that country, as in China, was used to indicate "a land of corn and plenty." When divided into four equal segments it symbolised the primeval abode of man, the traditional Paradise of Eden. It entered into the monograms of Osiris, of Jupiter Ammon, and of Saturn; the Christians subsequently adopted it, and the Labarum of Constantine is identical with the device of Osiris. It is equally common in India, and, according to Colonel Wilford, is exactly the Cross of the Manichees, with leaves, flowers, and fruits springing from it. It is called the divine tree, the tree of the gods, the tree of life and knowledge, and is productive of all things good and desirable. According to Godfrey Higgins we must go to the Buddhists for the origin of the Cross, "and to the Lama of Thibet, who takes his name from the Cross, called in his language Lamh." The Jamba, or cosmic tree, which Wilford calls, the tree of life and knowledge, figures in their maps of the "world as a cross 84 joganas (answering to the 84 years of the life of Him who was exalted upon the Cross), or 423 miles high, including the three steps of the Calvary, with which, after the orthodox Catholic fashion, it was invariably represented. The neophyte of the Indian Initiations was sanctified by the sign of a Cross, which was marked on every part of his

body. After his perfect regeneration it was again set upon his forehead ⊤ and inverted ⊥ upon his breast. The paschal lamb of the Jewish passover was roasted on a cross-shaped wooden spit, and with this sign Ezekiel ordered the people to be marked who were to be spared by the destroyer. Thus it figures as a symbol of salvation, but classical mythology attributes its invention to Ixion, who was its first victim. As an instrument of suffering and death, it is not, however, to be found on ancient monuments. It had no orthodox shape among the Romans when applied to this purpose, and the victims were either tied or nailed, "being usually left to perish by thirst and hunger." In the Christendom of both the East and West this divine symbol has a history too generally known to need recapitulation here. On this point the student may consult the "Dictionary of Christian Antiquities," where a mass of information is collected.

The following interesting passage will show the connection which exists between the Cross and alchemy. "In common chemistry," says Pernetz, crosses form characters which indicate the crucible, vinegar, and distilled vinegar. But as regards hermetic science, the Cross is . . . the symbol of the four elements. And as the philosophical stone is composed of the most pure substance of the grosser elements . . ., they have said, In *cruce salus*, salvation is in the Cross; by comparison with the salvation of our souls purchased by the blood of Jesus Christ who hung on the tree of the Cross. Some of them have even pushed their audacity further, and fear not to employ the terms of the New Testament to form their allegories and enigmas. Jean de Roquetaillade, known under the name of *Jean de Rupe Scissa*, and Arnaud de Villeneuve, say in their works on the composition of the Stone of the Philosophers:--It is needful that the Son of Man be lifted up on the Cross before being glorified; to signify the volatilisation of the fixed and igneous part of the matter."I have briefly traced the typological history of the Rose and Cross. It is obvious, as I have already remarked, that the antiquity of these emblems is no proof of the antiquity of a society which we find to be using them at a period subsequent to the Renaissance. It does not even suppose that society's initiation into the hieratic secrets which the elder world may have summarised in those particular symbols. In the case which is in question, such a knowledge would involve the antiquity of the Rosicrucians, because it is only at a time long subsequent to their first public appearance that the past has been sufficiently disentombed to uncover the significance of its symbols to uninitiated students. Can a correspondence be established between the meaning of the Rose and the Cross as they are used by the ancient hierogrammatists, and that of the Rose-Cross as it is used by the Rosicrucian Fraternity? This is the point to be ascertained. If a connection there be, then in some way, we may not know what, the secret has been handed down from generation to generation, and the mysterious brotherhood which manifested its existence spontaneously at the beginning of the seventeenth century, is affiliated with the hierophants of Egypt and India, who, almost in the night of time, devised their allegories and emblems for the blind veneration of the vulgar and as lights to those who knew.

In the fifth book of the "Histoire de la Magie," Eliphas Lévi provides the following commentary on the Rosicrucian symbol:--

"The Rose, which from time immemorial has been the symbol of beauty and life, of love and pleasure, expressed in a mystical manner all the protestations of the Renaissance. It was the flesh revolting against the oppression of the spirit, it was Nature declaring herself to be, like grace, the daughter of God, it was love refusing to be stifled by the celibate, it was life desiring to be no longer barren, it was humanity aspiring to a natural religion, full of love and reason, founded on the revelation of the harmonies of existence of which the Rose was for initiates the living and blooming symbol. The Rose, in fact, is a pantacle; its form is circular, the leaves of the corolla are heart-shaped, and are supported harmoniously by one another; its colour presents the most delicate shades of primitive hues; its calyx is purple and gold. . . . The conquest of the Rose was the problem offered by initiation to science, while religion toiled to prepare and establish the universal, exclusive, and definitive triumph of the Cross.

"The reunion of the Rose and the Cross, such was the problem proposed by supreme initiation, and, in effect, occult philosophy, being the universal synthesis, should take into account all the phenomena of Being."

This extremely suggestive explanation has the characteristic ingenuity of the hierophants of theosophical science, but it has no application whatsoever to the ostensible or ascertainable aims of the Rosicrucian adepts. It is the product of intellectual subtlety and the poetic gift of discerning curious analogies; it is quite beside the purpose of serious historical inquiry, and my object in quoting it here is to show by the mere fact of its existence that the whole question of the significance of the Crucified Rose, in its connection with the society, is one of pure conjecture, that no Rosicrucian manifestos and no acknowledged Brother have ever given any explanation concerning it, and that no presumption is afforded by the fact of its adoption for the antiquity of the society or for its connection with universal symbolism.

The researches of various writers, all more or less competent, have definitely established the *Crux Ansata* as typical of the male and female generative organs in the act of union, the Egyptian Tau, with its variants as typical of the masculine potency, and the Rose as the feminine emblem. Then by a natural typological evolution the Cross came to signify the divine creative energy which fecundated the obscure matrix of the primeval substance and caused it to bring forth the universe. The simple union of the Rose and the Cross suggests the same meaning as the *Crux Ansata*, but the crucified Buddhistic Rose may be a symbol of the asceticism which destroys natural desire. There is little correspondence, in either case, with known Rosicrucian tenets, and, therefore, the device of the Rose-Cross is separated from ancient symbolism, and is either a purely arbitrary and thus unexplainable sign, or its significance is to be sought elsewhere.

Now, I purpose to show that the Rosicrucians were united with a movement, which, originating in Germany, was destined to revolutionise the world of thought and to transform the face of Europe; that the symbols of the Rose and the Cross were prominently and curiously connected with this movement, and that the subsequent choice of these emblems by the secret society in question, followed naturally from the fact of this connection, and is easily explainable thereby. To accomplish this task satisfactorily, I must first lay before my readers the facts and documents which I have collected concerning the Fraternity.

CHAPTER I. ON THE STATE OF MYSTICAL PHILOSOPHY IN GERMANY AT THE CLOSE OF THE SIXTEENTH CENTURY.

THE traditions of the Neo-Platonic philosophy, with its elaborate theurgical system, were to some extent perpetuated through the whole period of the Middle Ages, for beside the orthodox theology of the great Latin Church, and amidst the clamour of scholastic philosophy, we find the secret theosophy of the magician, the Kabbalist, and the alchemical adept borrowing, directly or indirectly, from this prolific fountain of exalted mysticism. The traces of its influence are discoverable in Augustine, in Albertus Magnus, in St Thomas, the angel of the schools, and in other shining lights of western Christendom, while the metaphysical principles of Johannes Scotus Erigena, even so early as the close of the ninth century, were an actual revival of this philosophy. He translated the extraordinary works of Pseudo-Dionysius on the celestial hierarchies, the divine names, &c., which were an application of Platonism to Christianity, "and proved a rich mine to the mystics." This translation was largely circulated and held in the highest repute, more especially in Germany, where the Areopagite was appealed to as an authority by Eckhart at the beginning of the fourteenth century. At this time Germany was a stronghold of mysticism, which, according to Ueberweg, was at first chiefly developed in sermons by monks of the Dominican Order; its aim was to advance Christianity by edifying speculation, and to render it comprehensible by the transcendent use of the reason. "The author and perfecter of this entire development was Master Eckhart," who taught that the creature apart from the Absolute, that is, from God, was nothing, that "time, space, and the plurality which depends on them," are also nothing in themselves, and that "the duty of man as a moral being is to rise beyond this nothingness of the creature, and by direct intuition to place himself in immediate union with the Absolute." Eckhart was followed by Tauler, a great light of German mysticism, and one profoundly versed in the mysteries of the spiritual and interior life. A century later, with the revival of Platonism, came the Cardinal Nicolas Cusanus, "a man of rare sagacity, and an able mathematician, who arranged and republished the Pythagorean ideas, to which he was much inclined, in a very original manner, by the aid of his mathematical knowledge." This representative of the mysticism of Eckhart provided Giordano Bruno with the fundamental principles of his sublime and poetical conceptions. Bruno "renewed the theory of numbers, and gave a detailed explanation of the decadal system. With him, God is the great unity which is developed in the world and in humanity, as unity is developed in the indefinite series of numbers." The death of Giordano Bruno in the year 1600 brings us to a period of palmary importance and interest in the history of religion, science, and philosophy. The revival of learning had for some two centuries been illuminating and enlarging the intellectual horizon of Europe; the Reformation was slowly removing in several countries those checks which had hindered freedom of inquiry on most speculative subjects; that which had been practised in the privacy of the study might be displayed almost on the house top, that which had been whispered at the Sabbath of the Sorcerers could be canvassed with impunity in the market place. The spirit of the age which had dethroned the crucifix, burnt candles before the busts of Plato and Plotinus. The revolution in theology was followed by a general revolt against the old philosophical authorities, the seeds of which revolt must be looked for at the time when Aristotle and the Peripatetic successors were enthroned upon the ashes of the scholiasts, who pretending to follow Aristotle, had. perverted and disfigured his doctrines. As the birthplace of the Reformation, Germany enjoyed a greater share of intellectual unrestraint than any other country of Europe, and it was a chaos of conflicting opinions on all debateable topics. The old lines were loosened, the old tests failing, the chain of tradition was breaking at every point, a spirit of restless feverish inquiry was abroad, and daily new facts were exploding old methods. Copernicus had revolutionised astronomy by his discovery of the true solar system, Galileo already had invented the thermometer, and was on the threshold of a glorious future; a century previously Columbus had opened the still illimitable vistas of the western world; great minds were appearing in every country; amidst a thousand blunders, the independent study of the Bible was pursued with delight and enthusiasm, and in every city the hearts of an emancipated people were glowing with hope and expectation at the promise of the future.

Now, in an age of progress, of doubt, and of great intellectual activity, it is singular to remark the almost invariable prevalence of mysticism in one or other of its manifold phases, and the close of the sixteenth century beheld spreading over the whole of Germany and passing thence into Denmark, France, England, and Italy, a mighty school of mysticism in the great multitude of magicians, alchemists, &c., who directly or indirectly were followers of the renowned Paracelsus.

The sublime drunkard of Hohenheim, the contemporary of Agrippa, but grander in his aspirations, vaster in his capacities, and, if possible, still more unfortunate than the brilliant pupil of Trithemius, was the intellectual product of the great school of Kabbalism represented by Reuchlin and Picus de Mirandola. He united to his theoretical knowledge of theosophical mysteries an unrivalled practical acquaintance with every form of magic, and was as much an innovator in occult science as a reformer in medicine. For all orthodox alchemists, magicians, and professors of hidden knowledge, Paracelsus is a grand hierophant second only to the traditional Hermes. His brief and turbulent career closed tragically in the year 1541, but the works which he left secured him a vast posthumous audience, and the audacity of his speculations were undoubtedly instrumental in the emancipation of the German mind from the influence of traditional authority. At the close of the sixteenth century, then, we find the disciples of Parcelsus seeking, after the principles of their master and by the light of experimental research; 1. The secret of the transmutation of metals, or of the *magnum opus*, and applying to chemistry the usages of Kabbalism and ancient astrology. 2. The universal medicine, which included the Catholicon, or Elixir of Life and the Panacea, the first insuring to its possessor the prolongation or perpetuity of existence, the second restoring strength and health to debilitated or diseased organisms. 3. The Philosophic Stone, the great and universal synthesis which conferred upon the adept a sublimer knowledge than that of transmutation or of the Great Elixir, but on which both of these were dependent. "This stone," says a modern writer, who fairly interprets the more exalted and spiritual side of Hermetic traditions, "is the foundation of absolute philosophy; it is the supreme and immoveable reason. . . . To find the Philosophic Stone is to have discovered the Absolute," that is, the true *raison d'être* of all existences. Thus the initiate aspired to that infallible knowledge and wisdom which is afforded by divine illumination, his search for which is sometimes spoken of as the search for the quadrature of the circle, that is, for the extent or area of all sciences human and divine.

Among the concourse of inquirers, and the clamour of supposed and pretended discoverers, there rose gradually into deserved prominence an advanced school of illuminati, who, employing the terminology of the *turba philosophorum*, under the pretence of alchemical pursuits appear to have concealed a more exalted aim. The chief representative of this sect at the end of the sixteenth century was Henry Khunrath, and the work in which its principles are most adequately expressed is the "Amphitheatrum Sapientiæ Æternæ." The student is directed by these writers from the pursuit of material gold to the discovery of incorruptible and purely spiritual treasures, and they pretend to provide a mystical key or *Introitus apertus* to the "closed Palace of the King," in which these treasures are contained. Physical transmutation, the one and supreme end of the practical alchemist, sinks into complete insignificance; nevertheless, it is performed by the adept and is a landmark in his sublime progress. Rejecting the material theory even for this inferior process, they declare its attainment impossible for the unspiritual man, and just as the alchemical nomenclature is made use of in a transfigured sense, so the terminology of metaphysics appears to be pressed into the service of a conception far transcending the notions commonly conveyed by the words wisdom, spirituality, &c.

The result of this singular division in the camp of the alchemists was the inevitable mental confusion of that great crowd of inquirers into the secrets of nature who formed the audience of professional adepts. Every year books and pamphlets were issued from the German press, and purported to contain the secret of the *Magnum Opus*, expressed for the first time in plain, unmistakeable terms, but no writer proved more intelligible than his predecessors; the student, surrounded by authors whose search had been crowned with complete and unexampled success, could himself make no progress, new methods, though warranted infallible, were as barren as the old in their operation, and the universal interest in the subject was an incentive to innumerable impostors, who reaped large profits from the publication of worthless speculations and lying recipes. At such a juncture the isolated investigator naturally sought the assistance which is afforded by association; meetings of men like-minded took place for the discussion of different questions concerning the secret sciences; doctrines and practices were compared; men travelled far and wide to exchange opinions with distant workers in the same fields of experimental research, and the spirit of the time seemed ripe for the establishment of a society for the advancement of esoteric science and the study of natural laws. It was at this interesting period that the Rosicrucian Fraternity made public for the first time the fact of its existence, and attracted universal attention by its extraordinary history, and by the nature of its claims.

CHAPTER II. THE PROPHECY OF PARACELSUS, AND THE UNIVERSAL REFORMATION OF THE WHOLE WIDE WORLD.

PARACELSUS, in the eighth chapter of his "Treatise on Metals," gave utterance to the following prognostication:--*Quod utilius Deus patefieri sinet, quod autem majoris momenti est, vulgo adhuc latet usque ad Eliæ Artistæ adventum, quando is venerit.* "God will permit a discovery of the highest importance to be made, it must be hidden till the advent of the artist Elias." In the first chapter of the same work, he says:--*Hoc item verum est nihil est absconditum quod non sit retegendum; ideo, post me veniet cujus magnale nundum vivit qui multa revelabit.* "And it is true, there is nothing concealed which shall not be discovered; for which cause a marvellous being shall come after me, who as yet lives not, and who shall reveal many things." These passages have been claimed as referring to the founder of the Rosicrucian order, and as prophecies of this character are usually the outcome of a general desire rather than of an individual inspiration, they are interesting evidence that then as now many thoughtful people were looking for another saviour of society. At the beginning of the seventeenth century "a great and general reformation," says Buhle,--a reformation far more radical and more directed to the moral improvement of mankind than that accomplished by Luther,--"was believed to be impending over the human race, as a necessary forerunner to the day of judgment." The comet of 1572 was declared by Paracelsus to be "the sign and harbinger of the approaching revolution," and it will be readily believed that his innumerable disciples would welcome a secret society whose vast claims were founded on the philosophy of the master whom they also venerated, as a supreme factor in the approaching reformation. Paracelsus, however, had recorded a still more precise prediction, namely, that "soon after the decease of the Emperor Rudolph, there would be found three treasures that had never been revealed before that time." It is claimed that these treasures were the three works which I proceed to lay before my readers in this and in the two succeeding chapters.

Somewhere about the year 1614 a pamphlet was published anonymously in German, called "Die Reformation der Ganzen Weiten Welt," which, according to De Quincey, contained a distinct proposition to inaugurate a secret society, having for its object the general welfare of mankind. This description is simply untrue; the "Universal Reformation" is an amusing and satirical account of an abortive attempt made by the god Apollo to derive assistance towards the improvement of the age from the wise men of antiquity and modern times. It is a fairly literal translation of Advertisement 77 of Boccalini's "Ragguagli di Parnasso, Centuria Prima;" its internal connection with Rosicrucianism is not clear, but it has been generally reprinted with the society's manifestos, alchemical interpretations have been placed on it, and it is cited by various authors as the first publication of the Fraternity. I have determined to include it in this collection of authoritative documents, and have made use for this purpose three versions already existing in English. The literal translation from the Italian, made by Henry Earl of Monmouth, has been taken as the base. I have compared it with the original, and with the later versions which appeared in 1704 and 1706, and, where possible, I have abridged it by the elision of unnecessary and embarrassing prolixities.

It is needless to say that the unfortunate Trajano Boccalini had no connection himself with the Rosicrucian Brotherhood. The first "Centuria" appeared in 1612 at Venice, and he met his tragical and violent death in the following year.

A Universal Reformation of the Whole Wide World, by order of the God Apollo, is published by the Seven Sages of Greece and some other Litterati.

The Emperor Justinian, that famed compiler of the Digests and Code, the other day presented to Apollo, for the royal approbation, a new law against self-murder. Apollo was mightily astonished, and fetching a deep sigh, he said, "Is the good, government of mankind, Justinian, then fallen into so great disorder that men do voluntarily kill themselves? And whereas I have hitherto given pensions to an infinite number of moral philosophers, only that by their words and writings they may make men less apprehensive of death, are things now reduced to such calamity that even they will now live no longer, who could not formerly frame themselves to be content to die? And am I amongst all the disorders of my Litterati all this while supinely asleep?" To this Justinian answered, that the law was necessary, and that many cases of violent deaths having happened by many men having desperately made themselves away, worse was to be feared if some opportune remedy were not found out against so great a disorder.

Apollo then began diligently to inform himself, and found that the world was so impaired, that many valued not their lives nor estate, so they might be out of it. The disorders necessitated his Majesty to provide against them with all possible speed, and he absolutely resolved to institute a society of the men most famous in his dominions for wisdom and good life. But in the entrance into so weighty a business he met with insuperable difficulties, for amongst so many philosophers, and the almost infinite number of vertuosi, he could not find so much as one who was endowed with half the requisite qualifications to reform his fellow-creatures, his Majesty knowing well that men are better improved by the exemplary life of their reformers than by the best rules that can be given. In this penury of fitting personages, Apollo gave the charge of the Universal Reformation to the Seven Wise Men of Greece, who are of great repute in Parnassus, and are conceived by all men to have found the receipt of washing blackmoors white, which antiquity laboured after in vain. The Grecians were rejoiced at this news for the honour which Apollo had done their nation, but the Latins were grieved, thinking themselves thereby much injured. Wherefore Apollo, well knowing that prejudice against reformers hinders the fruit that is to be hoped by reformation, and being naturally given to appease his subjects' imbittered minds more by giving then satisfaction then by that legislative power with which men are not pleased withal, because they are bound to obey it, that he might satisfie the Romans, joined in commission with the Seven Sages of Greece, Marcus and Annæus Seneca, and in favour to the modern Italian philosophers, he made Jacopo Mazzoni da Cesena Secretary of the Congregation, and honoured him with a vote in their consultations.

On the fourteenth of the last month the seven wise men, with the aforesaid addition, accompanied by a train of the choicest vertuosi of this State, went to the Delfick Palace, the place appropriated for the Reformation. The Litterati were well pleased to see the great number of pedants, who, baskets in hands, went gathering up the sentences and apothegms which fell from those wise men as they went along. The day after the solemn entrance they assembled for the first time, and 'tis said that Thales the Milesian, the first of the Grecian sages, spake thus:--

"The business, most wise philosophers, about which we are met, is the greatest that can be treated on by human understanding; and though there be nothing harder then to set bones that have been long broken, wounds that are fistuled, and incurable cancers, yet difficulties which are able to affright others ought not to make us despair, for the impossibility will increase our glory, and I do assure you that I have already found out the true antydote against the poyson of these present corruptions. I am sure we do all believe that nothing hath more corrupted this age then hidden hatreds, feigned love, impiety, and the perfidiousness of double-dealers under the specious cloke of simplicity, love to religion, and charity. Apply yourselves to these, evils, gentlemen; make use of fire and razor, lay corrosive plasters to these wounds which I discover unto you, and mankind, which by reason of their vices, that lead them the highway to death, may be said to be given over by physitians, will soon be made whole, become sincere and plain in their proceedings, true in what they say, and such in their sanctity of life as they were in former times. The true and immediate cure, then, for these present evils consists in necessitating men to live with candour of mind and purity of heart, which cannot be better effected then by making that little window in men's breasts which his Majesty hath often promised to his most faithful vertuosi; for when those who use such art in their proceedings shall be forced to speak and act, having a window whereby one may see into their hearts, they will learn the excellent virtue of being, and not appearing to be; they will conform deeds to words, and their tongues to sincerity of heart; all men will banish lies and falsehood, and the diabolical spirit of hypocrisy will abandon many who are now possest with so foul a fiend."

The opinion of Thales was so well approved by the whole Congregation that it was unanimously voted just, and Secretary Mazzoni was commanded to give Apollo a sudden account thereof, who perfectly approved the opinion, and commanded that they should begin that very day to make windows in the breasts of mankind. But at the very instant that the surgeons took their instruments in hand, Homer, Virgil, Plato, Aristotle, Averroes, and other eminent Litterati went to Apollo, and said his Majesty must needs know that the prime means whereby men do govern the world with facility is the reputation of those who command, and they hoped his Majesty would be tender of the credit which the reverend Philosophical Synod and the honourable Colledg of Vertuosi had universally obtained for sanctity of life and manners. If his Majesty should unexpectedly open every man's breast, the philosophers who formerly were most highly esteemed ran evident hazard of being shamed, and that he might, peradventure, find fowlest faults in those whom he had held to be immaculate. Therefore, before a business of such importance should be taken in hand, they entreated that he would afford his vertuosi a competent time to wash and cleanse their souls. Apollo was greatly pleased by the advice of so famous poets and philosophers, and, by a publick edict, prorogued the day of incision for eight days, during which everyone did so attend the cleansing of their souls from all fallacies, hidden vice, hatred, and counterfeit love, that there was no more honey of roses, succory, cassia, scena, scamony, nor laxative syrups to be found in any grocer's or apothecary's shop in all Parnassus; and the more curious did observe that in the parts where the Platonicks, Peripateticks, and Moral Philosophers did live, there was then such a stink as if all the privies of the country had been emptied, whereas the quarters of Latin and Italian poets smelt only of cabbadg-porrage.

The time allotted for the general purging was already past, when, the day before the operation was to begin, Hippocrates, Galen, Cornelius, Celsus, and other the most skilful Physitians of this State, went to Apollo, and said:--"Is it possible, Sire, you that are the Lord of the Liberal Sciences, that this Microcosmos must be deformed, which is so nobly and miraculously framed, for the advantage of a few ignorant people? For not only the wiser sort of men, but even those of an indifferent capacity, who have conversed but four daies with any quack-salver, know how to penetrate even into the inmost bowels."

This memorandum of the physitians wrought so much with Apollo that he changed his former resolution, and by Ausonius Gallus bad the philosophers, of the Reformation proceed in delivering their opinions.

Then Solon thus began:--"In my opinion, gentlemen, that which hath put the present age into so great confusion is the cruel hatred and spiteful envy which is seen to reign generally amongst men. All hope then for these present evils is from the infusion of charity, reciprocal affection, and that sanctified love of our neighbour which is God's chiefest commandment to mankind. We ought, therefore, to employ all our skill in removing the occasions of those hatreds which reign in men's hearts, which, if we be able to effect, men will agree like other animals, who, by instinct, love their own species, and will, consequently, drive away all hatred and rancor of mind. I have been long thinking, my friends, what the true spring's head may be of all human hatred, and am still more established in my old opinion that it proceeds from the disparity of means, from the hellish custom of *meum* and *tuum*, which, if it were introduced among the beasts, even they would consume and waste themselves with the same hatred wherewith we so much disquiet ourselves, whereas the equality in which they live, and their having nothing of their own, are the blessings which preserve that peace among them which we have cause to envy. Men are likewise creatures, but rational; this world was created by Almighty God, that mankind might live thereon in peace, not that the avaritious should divide it amongst themselves, and should turn what was common into that *meum* and *tuum* which hath put us all into such confusion. So it clearly appears, that the depravation of men's souls by avarice, ambition, and tyranny, hath occasioned the present inequality, and if it be true, as we all confess it is, that the world is an inheritance left to mankind by one father and mother, from whom we are all descended like brethren, what justice is it that men should not all have a brother's share? What greater disproportion can be imagined then that this world should be such that some possess more than they can govern, and others have not so much as they could govern? But that which doth infinitely aggravate this disorder is, that usually vertuous men are beggars, whereas wicked and ignorant people are wealthy. From the root of this inequality it then ariseth, that the rich are injurious to the poor, and that the poor envy the rich.

"Now, gentlemen, that I have discovered the malady unto you, it is easie to apply the medicine. To reform the age no better course can be taken then to divide the world anew, allotting an equal part to everyone, and, that we may fall no more upon the like disorders, I advise, that, for the future, all buying and selling be forbidden, to the end that there may be established that parity of goods, the mother of publick peace, which my self and other lawmakers have formerly so much laboured to procure."

Solon's opinion suffered a long debate, and though it was not only thought good but necessary by Bias, Periander, and Pittacus, it was gainsaid by all the rest, and Seneca's opinion prevailed, who with substantial reasons convinced the assembly, that if they should come to a new division of the world, one great disorder would necessarily follow; that too much would fall to the share of fools, and too little to gallant men; and that plague, famine, and war were not God's severest scourges, for the affliction of mankind would be to enrich villains.

Solon's opinion being laid aside, Chilo argued as follows--"Which of you, most wise philosophers, doth not know that the immoderate thirst after gold hath now adaies filled the world with all the mischiefs which we see and feel. What wickedness, how execrable soever it be, will men not willingly commit, if thereby they may accumulate riches? Conclude, therefore, unanimously with me, that no better way can be found out, whereby to extirpate all the vices with which our age is opprest, then for ever to banish out of the world the two infamous mettals, gold and silver, for so the occasion of our present disorders being removed, the evils will necessarily cease."

Though Chilo's opinion had a very specious appearance, it would not bear the test, for it was said, that men took so much pains to get gold and silver because they are the measure and counterpoise of all things, and that it was requisite for man to have some mettals, or other thing of price, by which he might purchase what was fitting for him, that if there were no such thing as gold or silver, he would make use of something instead of them, which, rising in value, would be equally coveted, as was plainly seen in the Indies, where cockle-shells were made use of instead of money, and more vallued than either gold or silver. Cleobulus, particularly, being very hot in refuting this opinion, said, with much perturbation of mind: My Masters, banish iron out of the world, for that is the mettal which hath put us into the present condition. Gold and silver serve the purpose ordained by God, whereas iron, which Nature produced for the making of plow-shears, spades, and mattocks, is by the malice and mischief of men, forged into swords, daggers, and other deadly instruments."

Though Cleobolus his opinion was judged to be very true, yet it was concluded by the whole Assembly, that, it being impossible to expel iron but by grasping iron and putting on corslets, it was imprudent to multiply mischiefs, and to cure one wound with another. 'Twas, therefore, generally resolved, that the ore of gold and silver should be still kept, but that the refiners should be directed for the future to cleanse them well, and not to take them out of the fire till they had removed from both mettals that vein of turpentine which is the reason why gold and silver stick so close to the fingers even of good and honest men.

Then Pittachus, with extraordinary gravity, thus began:--"The world, most learned philosophers, is fallen into that deplorable condition which we labour to amend because men in these daies have given over travailing by the beaten roadway of vertue, and take the bye-waies of vice, by which, in this corrupted age, they obtain the rewards only due to vertue. Things are brought to such a woful state, that none can get entrance into the palace of dignity, honor, or reward by the gate of merit, but like thieves they climb

24

the windows with ladders of tergeversation, and some, by the force of gifts and favours, have even opened the roof to get thereby into the house of honour. If you would reform this corrupted age, my opinion is, that you should force men to walk by' the way of vertue, and make severe laws, that whosoever will take the laborsom journey which leads to supreme dignities must travail with the waggon of desert, and with the sure guide of vertue. Consequently, you should order the stopping up of all cross-paths and crooked lanes, discovered by ambitious men and modern hypocrites, who, multiplying faster then locusts in Africa, have filled the world with contagion. What greater affront can be put upon vertue then to see one of these rascals mounted on the throne of preferment when no man can guess what course he took to reach it? Which makes many think they have got it by the magick of hypocrisy, whereby these magicians do inchant the minds even of wise princes."

Pittacus his opinion was not only praised, but greatly admired by the whole Assembly, and certainly would have been approved as the most excellent, had not Periander changed their minds by the following discourse: "Gentlemen, the disorder mentioned by Pittacus is very true; but the thing we should chiefly consider is why princes, who are so quick-sighted and interested in their own State-affairs, do not bestow, in these our daies, their great places (as they were wont to do of old) on able and deserving men, by whose service they may receive advantage and reputation, but instead, make use of new fellows raised out of the mire, and without either worth or honor? The opinion of those who say that it is fatal for princes to love carrion is so false, that for the least interest of State they neglect their brethren, and wax cruel even against their own children, so far are they from ruining themselves by blind fondness for their servants. Princes do not act by chance, nor suffer themselves to be guided in their proceedings by their passions; whatsoever they do is out of interest, and those things which to private men appear errors and negligence are accurate politick precepts. All that have written of State-affairs freely confess that the best way to govern kingdoms well is to confer places of highest dignity upon men of great merit and known worth and valour. This is a truth very well known to princes; and though it be clearly seen that they do not observe it, he is a fool that believes they do not out of carelessness. I, who have long studied a point of so great weight, am perswaded that ignorant and raw men, and men of no merit, are preferred before learned and deserving persons, not out of any fault in the prince, but (I blush to say it) through default of the vertuosi. I acknowledge that princes stand in need of learned officers and men of experienced valor, but they likewise need faithful servants. If deserving men and men of valor were loyal in proportion to their capacity, we should not complain of the present disorders in seeing undeserving dwarfs become great giants in four daies' space, ignorance seated in the chair of vertue, and folly in valor's tribunal. 'Tis common to all men to overrate their own worth, but the vertuosi do presume so much upon their own good parts that they rather pretend to add to the prince's reputation by accepting preferments then to receive credit themselves by accepting his munificence. I have known many so foolishly enamoured of their own works that they have thought it a greater happiness for a prince to have an occasion of honouring them then good luck for the other to meet with so liberal a prince. Such men, acknowledging all favours conferred upon them as debts paid to their deserts, prove so ungrateful to their benefactors in their necessity that they are abhorred as perfidious, and are causes of this grievance, that princes seek fidelity instead of more shining accomplishments, that they may be secure of gratitude when they stand in need of it."

Periander having finished his discourse, Bias spake thus:--"Most wise philosophers, all of you sufficiently know that the reason of the world's depravity is only because mankind hath so shamefully abandoned those holy laws which God gave them to observe when he bestowed the whole world upon them for a habitation; nor did he place the French in France, the Spaniards in Spain, the Dutch in Germany, and bound up the fowl fiend in hell for any other reason but the advantage of that general peace which he desired might be observed throughout the whole world. But avarice and ambition (spurs which have alwaies egged on men to greatest wickedness), causing nations to pass into other men's countries, have caused these evils which we endeavour to amend. If it be true, as we all confess it is, that God hath done nothing in vain, wherefore, think you, hath His Divine Majesty placed the inaccessible Pyrenean mountains between the Spaniards and Italians, the rocky Alpes between the Italians and Germans, the dreadful English Channel between the French and English, the Mediterranean Sea between Africa and Europe? Why hath he made the infinite spacious rivers of Euphrates, Indus, Ganges, and the rest, save only that people might be content to live in their own countries by reason of the difficulties of fords and passages? And the Divine Wisdom, knowing that the harmony of universal peace would be out of tune, and that the world would be filled with incurable diseases, if men should exceed their allotted bounds, added the multitude and variety of languages to all the fore-mentioned impediments, without which all men would speak the same tongue, as all creatures of the same species sing, bark, or bray after one and the same manner. 'Tis then man's boldness in boaring through mountains, passing over the broadest and most rapid rivers, and even manifestly and rashly hazarding himself and all his substance by crossing the largest seas in a little wooden vessel, which caused the ancient Romans, not to mention any other nations, to ruine other men's affairs and discompose their own, not being satisfied with their dominion over the whole of Italy. The true remedy, then, for so great disorder is, first to force every nation to return to their own countreys, and then, to prevent the like confusion in future, I am of opinion that all bridges built for the more commodious passing of rivers should be absolutely broken down, that the ways over the mountains should be quite destroyed, and the mountains made more inaccessible by man's industry then originally by nature; and I would have all navigation forbidden upon severest penalty, not allowing so much as the least boats to pass over rivers."

Bias his opinion was regarded with unusual attention, but after being well examined by the best wits of the Assembly, it was found not to be good, for all those philosophers knew that the greatest enmities between nation and nation are not national, but occasioned by cunning princes, who are great masters in the proverb, *Divide et impera*, and that that perfection of manners being found in all nations joyned together which was not to be had in any particular one, travel is necessary to acquire the complete wisdom which adorned the Great Ulysses. Now, this is a benefit entirely owing to navigation, which is very necessary to mankind, were it onely for that God, having created this world of an almost incomprehensible greatness, having filled it with pretious things, and endowed every province with somewhat of particular navigation, 'tis by that wonderful art reduced to so small an extent that the aromatics of Molucca, though above fifteen thousand miles from Italy, seem to the Italians to grow in their own gardens. Thus the opinion of Bias was laid aside, when Cleobulus, rising up, and with a low bow, seeming to crave leave to speak, said thus:--"I clearly perceive, most wise gentlemen, that the reformation of the present age, a business of itself very easie, becomes by the diversity and extravagancy of our opinions rather impossible then difficult. And to speak with the freedom which becomes this place and the weight of the business which we have in hand, it grieves my heart to find, even amongst us, that common defect of ambitious and slight wits, who, getting up into publike pulpits, labor more to display their ingenuity by their new and curious conceits, then to profit their auditors by useful precepts and sound doctrines. To raise man out of the foul mire whereinto he has fallen, to what purpose is that dangerous operation of making little windows in their breasts, which Thales advised? And why should we undertake the laborious business of dividing the world into equal partitions according to Solon's proposition? Or the course mentioned by Chilo, of banishing gold and silver out of the world? Or that of Pittacus, of forcing men to walk in the way of merit and vertue? Or, lastly, that of Bias, that mountains should be raised higher and made more difficult then Nature hath made them, and that the miracle of navigation should be extirpated, the greatest proof of human ingenuity that was ever given? What are these but chimæras and sophistical fancies? The chief consideration which reformers ought to have is, that the remedy proposed be practicable, that it may work its effect soon and secretly, and that it may be chearfully received by those who are to be reformed, for, otherwise, we shall rather deform the world then improve it. There is great reason for this assertion, for that Physitian deserves to be blamed, who should ordain a medecine for his impatient which is impossible to be used, and which would afflict him more then his disease. Therefore is it the requisite duty of reformers to provide a sure remedy before they take notice of the wound; it is not onely foolishness but impiety to defame men by publishing their vices, and to shew the world that their maladies are grown to such a height that they are past cure. Therefore the Great Tacitus, who always speaks to the purpose if he be rightly understood, doth in this particular advise men. *Omittere potius prævalida et adulta vitia, quam hoc assequi, ut palam fieret, quibus flagittiis impares essemus.* Those who would fell an old oak are ill-advised if they begin with lopping the top boughs; our true method, gentlemen, is to lay the axe to the root, as I do now, in affirming that the reformation of the present age consists wholly in these few words-- REWARD THE GOOD AND PUNISH THE BAD."

Here Cleobulus held his peace, whose opinion Thales Milesius did with such violence oppose as showed how dangerous a thing it is to offend, though by speaking the truth, those who have the repute to be good and wise, for he with a fiery countenance broke forth into these words:-- "Myself, and these gentlemen, most wise Cleobulus, whose opinions you have been pleased to reject as sophistical and meer chimeras, did expect from your rare wisdom that you had brought some new and miraculous Bezoar from the Indies for cure of these present evils, whereas you have propounded that for the easiest remedy which is the hardest and most impossible that could ever be fancied by the prime pretenders to high mysteries, Caius Plinius and Albertus Magnus. There is not any of us, my Cleobulus, that did not know, before you were pleased to put us in mind of it, that the reformation of the world depends wholly upon rewarding such as are good and punishing the wicked. But give me leave to ask you, who are those that in this our age are perfectly good, and who exactly ill? I would also know whether your eye can discern that which could never yet be found out by any man living, how to know true goodness from that which is counterfeit. Do not you know that modern hypocrites are arrived at that height of cunning that, in this our unhappy age, those are accounted to be cunningest in their wickedness who seem most exactly good, and that really perfect men, who live in sincerity and singleness of soul, with an undisguised and unartificial goodness, are thought to be scandalous and silly? Every one by natural instinct loves those that are good and hates those that are wicked, but princes do it both out of instinct and interest, and when hypocrites or other cunning cheaters are listened unto by great men, while good men are suppressed and undervalued, it is not by the princes' own election but through the abuse of others. True vertue is known onely and rewarded by God, by whom also vices are discovered and punished. He onely penetrates into the depths of men's hearts, and we, by means of the window I proposed, might also have looked therein had not the enemy of mankind sown tares in the field where I sowed the grain of good advice. But new laws, how good and wholesome soever, have alwaies been and ever will be withstood by those vitious people who are thereby punished."

The reasoning of Thales gave mighty satisfaction to the Assembly, and all of them turned their eyes upon Periander, who, thinking himself thereby desired to speak his opinion, began thus: The variety of opinions which I have heard confirms me in my former tenet, that four parts of five who are sick perish because the physitians know not their disease; such errors are indeed excusable, because men are easily deceived in matters of mere conjecture, but that we, who are judged by Apollo to be the salt of the earth, should not know the evil under which the present age labours, redounds much to our shame, since the malady which we ought to cure lies not hidden in the veins, but is so manifestly known to all men that it self cries aloud for help. And yet, by all the reasons I have heard alledged, methinks you go about to mend the arm when it is the heart that is fistula'd. Gentlemen, since it is Apollo's pleasure that we should do so, since our reputation stands upon it, and charity to our so afflicted age requires it at our hands, let us, I beseech you, take from our faces the mask of respect, which hath been hitherto worn by us all, and let us speak freely. The fatal error then which has so long confirmed mankind in their unhappiness is this, that while the vices of the great have brought the world into confusion, a reformation of private men's faults has been thought sufficient to retrieve it. But the falshood, avarice, pride and hypocrisie of private men are not the vices (though I confess them to be hanious evils, which have so much depraved our age, for fitting punishments being by the law provided for every fault and foul action, man is so obedient to the laws and so apprehensive of justice that a few ministers thereof make millions of men tremble, and men live in such peace that the rich cannot, without much danger to themselves, oppress the poor, and every one may walk safely both by day and night with gold in their hand, not onely in the streets but even in the highways. But the world's most dangerous infirmities are discovered when publique peace is disturbed, and we must all of us confess that the ambition, avarice, and diabolical engagement which the swords of some powerful princes have usurped over the states of those less powerful is the great scandal of the present times. 'Tis this, gentlemen, which hath filled the world with hatred and suspicion, and hath defiled it with so much blood, that men, who were created by God with humane hearts and civil inclinations, are become ravenous wilde beasts, tearing one another in pieces with all sorts of inhumanity. The ambition of these men hath changed publike peace into most cruel war, vertue into vice, the love which we ought to bear our neighbours into such intestine hatred, that, though lyons appear lyons to their own species, yet the Scotch to the English, the Italians to the Germans, the French to the Spaniards, and every nation to another, appear not men and brethren but creatures of another kind, so that justice being oppressed by the inexplicable ambition of potent men, our race, which was born, brought up, and did live long under the government of wholesome laws, waxing now cruel to itself, lives with the instinct of beasts, ready to oppress the weaker. Theft which is undoubtedly base, is so persecuted by the laws that the stealing of an egg is a capital fault, yet powerful men are so blinded with ambition as to rob another man perfidiously of his whole state, which is not thought to be an execrable mischief but an noble occupation, and onely fit for kings. Tacitus, the master of policy, that he may win the good will of princes, is not ashamed to say, *In summa Fortuna id æquis quod vallidius, et sua retinere privatæ domus, de alienis certare, regiam laudem esse.* If it be true, as all politicians agree, that people are the prince's apes, how can those who obey live vertuously quiet when their commanders do so abound in vice. To bereave a powerful prince of a kingdome is a weighty business which is not to be done by one man alone. To effect so foul an intent they muster a multitude of men, who, that they may not fear the shame of stealing their neighbours' goods, of murthering men, and of firing cities, change the name of base thief into that of gallant souldier and valiant commander. And that which aggravates this evil is that even good princes are forced to run upon the same rocks to defend their own estates from the ravenousness of these harpyes, and to regain what they have lost, and to revenge themselves of those that have injured them, have in reprizal got possession of their dominions, till, lured on by gain, they betake themselves to the same shameful trade. Thus the method of plundering others of their kingdomes is become a reputable art, and humane wit, made to admire and contemplate the miracles of Heaven and the wonders of the earth, is wholly turned to invent stratagems and to plot treasons, while the hands, which were made to cultivate the earth that feeds us, are employed in the exercise of arms that we may kill one another. This is the wound which hath brought our age to its last gasp, and the true way to remedy it is for princes who use such dealings to amend themselves, and to be content with their own fortunes, for, certainly, it appears very strange that there should be any king who cannot satisfie his ambition with the absolute command over twenty millions of men. Princes, as you all know, were ordained by God on earth for the good of mankind; therefore, it would do well not onely to bridle their ambitious lust after the possessions of others, but I think it necessary that the peculiar engagement which some men pretend their swords have over all estates, be cut up by the root, and I advise above all things that the greatness of principalities be

30

limited, it being impossible that overgrown kingdoms should be governed with that exact care and justice which is requisite to the people's good, and which princes are bound to observe. There never was a vast monarchy which was not in a short time lost by the negligence of its governors."

Here Periander ended, whom Solon thus opposed:--"The true cause, Periander, of our present mischiefs which you have mentioned with such liberty of speech was not omitted by us out of ignorance, but out of prudence. The disorders you speak of began when the world was first peopled, and you know that the most skilful physitian cannot restore sight to one born blind. I mention this because it is much the same thing to cure an infirm eye as to reform antiquated errors. For as the skilful physitian betakes himself to his canters the first day he sees the distempered eye water, but is forced to leave that patient in deserved blindness who neglected to seek a cure till his sight was quite lost, so reformers should oppose abuses with severe remedies the very first hour that they commence, for when vice and corruption have got deep rooting, it is wiselier done to tolerate the evil, then to go about to remedy it out of time, with danger to occasion worse inconveniences, it being more dangerous to cut an old wen then it is misbecoming to let it stand. Moreover, we are here to call to mind the disorders of private men, and to use modesty in so doing, but to be silent in what concerns princes, for they having no superiours in this world it belongs only to God to reform them, He having given them the prerogative to command, us the glory to obey. Subjects, therefore, should correct the faults of their rulers onely by their own godly living, for the hearts of princes being in the hands of the Almighty, when people deserve ill from His Divine Majestie he raiseth up Pharoahs against them, and, on the contrary, makes princes tender-hearted, when people by their fidelity and obedience deserve God's assistance."

What Solon said was much commended by all the hearers, and then Cato began thus:--"Your opinions, most wise Grecians, are much to be admired, and have abundantly justified the profound esteem which all the Litterati have of you; the vices, corruptions, and ulcerated wounds under which the age languishes could not be better discovered and pointed out. Nor are your opinions, which are full of humane knowledge, gain-said here for that they are not excellent, but for that the malady is so habituated in the veins, and is even so grounded in the bones, that the constitution of mankind is worn out, and their vital vertue yields to the strength of the distemper; in short, the patient spits nothing but blood and putrefaction, and the hair falls from his head. The physitian, gentlemen, hath a hard part to play when the sick man's maladies are many, and one so far differing from another that cooling medicines, and such as are good for a hot liver, are nought for the stomach, and weaken it too much. Truly this is just our case, for the maladies which molest our age equal the stars of heaven, and are more various than the flowers of the field. I, therefore, think this cure desperate, and that the patient is totally incapable of humane help. We must have recourse to prayers and to other divine helps, which in like case are usually implored from God; this is the true north-star, which, in the greatest difficulties, leads men into the harbour of perfection, for *Pauci prudentia, honesta ab deterioribus, utilia ab noxiis discernunt; plures aliorum eventis docentur.* If we approve this consideration, we shall find that when the world was formerly sunk into the same disorders, it was God's care that did help it by sending a universal deluge to raze mankind, full of abominable and incorrigible vice, from off the world. And, gentlemen, when a man sees the walls of his house all gaping and ruinous, and its foundations so weakened that, in all appearance, it is ready to fall, certainly it is more wisely done to pull down the house and build it anew, then to lose money and time in piecing and patching it. Therefore, since man's life is so foully depraved with vice that it is past all human power to restore it to its former health, I do with all my heart beseech the Divine Majestie, and counsel you to do the like, that He will again open the cataracts of Heaven, and pour down upon the earth another deluge, with this restriction, that a new Ark may be made, wherein all boys not above twelve years of age may be saved, and that all the female sex, of whatsoever age, be so wholly consumed, that nothing but their unhappy memory may remain. And I beseech the same Divine Majestie that as He hath granted the singular benefit to bees, fishes, beetles, and other animals, to procreate without the female sex, so He will think men worthy of the like favour. I have learnt for certain that as long as there shall be any women in the world men will be wicked."

It is not to be believed how much Cato's discourse displeased the whole Assembly, who did all so abhor the harsh conceit of a deluge, that, casting themselves upon the ground, with their hands held up to heaven, they humbly beseeched Almighty God that He would preserve the excellent female sex, that He would keep mankind from any more deluges, or that He would send them on the earth onely to extirpate those discomposed and wilde wits, those untunable and bloodthirsty souls, those heterodox and phantastick brains, who, being of a depraved judgment, are nothing but mad men, whose ambition was boundless, and pride without end, and that when mankind should, through their demerits, become unworthy of any mercy from the Almighty, He would be pleased to punish them with the scourges of plague, sword, and famine, rather than to deliver mankind unto the good will and pleasure of those insolent and wicked rulers, who, being composed of nothing but blind zeal and diabolical folly, would pull the world in pieces if they could compass the bestial caprices they hourly hatch in their heads.

Cato's Opinion had this unlucky end, when Seneca thus began:--"Rough dealing is not so greatly requisite in reformation as would seem by many of your discourses, especially when disorders have grown to so great a height; on the contrary, they ought, like wounds which are subject to convulsions, to be Brest with a light hand. It is a scandal to the physitian that the patient should die with his prescriptions in his body, since all men will conclude that the medecine hath done him more harm then his I malady. It is a rash advice to go from one extreme to another, passing by the due medium; man's nature is not capable of violent mutations, and if it be true that the world hath been falling many thousand years into the present infirmities, he is a very fool who thinks to restore it to health in a few days. Moreover, in reformation the conditions of those who do reform, and the qualities of those that are to be reformed, ought to be exactly considered. We that are the reformers are philosophers and men of learning, and if those to be reformed be onely stationers, printers, such as sell paper, pens, and ink, or other such things appertaining to learning, we may very well correct their errors, but if we offer to rectify the faults of other trades, we shall commit worse errors, and become more ridiculous then the shoemaker who would judge of colours, and durst censure Apelles his pictures. This, I must say, is a defect frequent in us Litterati, who, for four *cujus* that we have in our heads, pretend to know all things, and are not aware that when we first swerve from our books we run riot, and say a thousand things from the purpose. I say this, gentlemen, because nothing more obviates reformations then to walk therein in the dark, which happens when reformers are not well acquainted with the vices of those with whom they have to deal. The reason is apparent, for nothing makes men more obstinate in their errors then when they find their reformers ill-informed of their defects. Now, which of us is acquainted with the falsehood of notaries, the prevarications of advocates, the simony of judges, the tricks of attorneys, the cheats of apothecaries, the filching of tailors, the roguery of butchers, and the cheating tricks of a thousand other artificers? And yet all these excesses must be by us corrected, which are so far from our profession that we shall appear like so many blind fellows fumbling to stop a leaky cask which spills the wine on every side. This, gentlemen, is enough to convince you that reformation is only likely to proceed well when marinors discourse of navigation, souldiers of war, shepherds of sheep, and herdsmen of bullocks. It is manifest presumption in us to pretend to know all things, and meer malice to believe that in every occupation there are not three or four honest men. My opinion, therefore, is, that we ought to send for a few of each profession of known probity and worth, and that every one should correct his own trade; by this means, we shall publish to the world a reformation worthy of ourselves and of the present exigencies."

Pittachus and Chilo extolled this speech to the skies, and seeing the other philosophers of a contrary sentiment, protested before God and the world that they believed it was impossible to find out a better means for the reformation of mankind, yet did the rest of their companions abhor it more than Cato's proposition, and with great indignation I told Seneca they much wondered that he, by taking more reformers into their number, should so far dishonour Apollo, who had thought them not only sufficient but excellently fit for that business. It was not wisely advised to begin the general reformation by publishing their own weakness, for all resolutions which detract from the credit of the publishers want that reputation which is the very soul of business. It was strange a man who was the very prime sage of Latin writers should be so lavish of authority, which should be guarded more jealously then women's honor, since the wisest men did all agree that twenty pound of blood taken from the life-vain was well imployed to gain but one ounce of jurisdiction.

The whole Assembly were mightily afflicted when, by the reputation of Seneca's opinion, they found smal hopes of effecting the reformation, for they relyed little on Mazzoni, who was but a novice; which though Mazzoni did by many signs perceive, yet, no whit discouraged, he spoke thus:--"It was not for any merit of mine, most wise philosophers, that I was admitted by Apollo into this reverend congregation, but out of his Majestie's special favour; and I very well know that it better becomes me to use my ears than my tongue, and certainly I should not dare to open my mouth upon any other occasion; but reformation being the business in hand, and I lately coming where nothing is spoken of but reformation and reformers, I desire that every one may hold their peace, and that I alone may be heard to speak in a business which I am so verst in that I may boast myself to be the onely Euclid of this mathematick. Give me leave, I beseech you, to say that you, in relating your opinions, seem to me to be like those indiscrete physitians who lose time in consulting and disputing without having seen the sick party, or heard from his own mouth the account of his disease. Our business, gentlemen, is to cure the present age of the foul infirmities under which she labours; we have all laboured to find out the reasons of the maladies and its proper remedys, but none of us hath been so wise as to visit the sick party. I therefore advise that we send for the present Age to come hither and be examined, that we interrogate it of its sickness, and that we see the ill-affected parts naked, for this will make the cure easie, which you now think desperate."

The whole Assembly was so pleased at Mazzoni's motion, that the reformers immediately commanded the Age to be sent for, who was presently brought in a chair to the Delphick Palace by the four Seasons of the year. He was a man full of years, but of so great and strong a complexion that he seemed likely to live yet many ages, onely he was short breathed, and his voyce was very weak, at which the philosophers, much wondering, asked him what was the reason that he, whose ruddy face was a sign of much natural heat and vigor, and of a good stomach, was nevertheless so feeble? And they told him that a hundred years before his face was so yellow that he seemed to have the jaundice, yet he spoke freely, and seemed to be stronger then he was now, and since they had sent for him to cure his infirmity, he should speak freely of his griefs.

The Age answered thus:--"Soon after I was born, gentlemen, I fell into these maladies under which I now labour. My face is fresh and ruddy because people have petered it and coloured it with lakes; my sickness resembles the ebbing and flowing of the sea, which alwaies contains the same water, though it rises and fals, with this variation notwithstanding, that when my looks are outwardly good, my malady is more grievous inwardly (as at this present), but when my face looks ill, I am best within. As for the infirmities which torment me, do but take off this gay jacket, wherewith some good people have covered a rotten carcass, and view me naked as I was made by Nature."

At these words the philosophers stript him in a trice, and found that this miserable wretch was covered all over four inches thick with a scurf of appearances. They caused ten razors to be forthwith brought unto them, and fell to shaving it off with great diligence, but they found it so far eaten into his very bones that in all the huge colossus there was not one inch of good live flesh, at which, being struck with horror and despair, they put on the patient's cloaths again, and dismist him. Then, convinced that the disease was incurable, they shut themselves up together, and abandoning the case of publike affairs, they resolved to provide for the safety of their own reputations. Mazzoni writ what the rest of the reformers dictated, a Manifesto, wherein they witnessed to the world the great care Apollo ever had of the virtuous lives of his Litterati, and of the welfare of all mankind, also what pains the Reformers had taken in compiling the General Reformation. Then, coming to particulars, they fixt the prices of sprats, cabbiges, and pumpkins. The Assembly had already underwritten the Reformation when Thales put them in mind that certain higlers, who sold pease and black-cherryes, vinted such small measures that it was a shame not to take order therein. The Assembly thankt Thales for his advertisement, and added to their reformation that the measures should be made greater. Then the palace gates were thrown open, and the General Reformation was read, in the place appointed for such purposes, to the people assembled in great numbers in the market-place, and was so generally applauded by every one that all Parnassus rang with shouts of joy, for the rabble are satisfied with trifles, while men of judgment know that *vitia erunt donec homines* --as long as there be men there will be vices--that men live on earth not indeed well, but as little ill as they may, and that the height of human wisdom lies in the discretion to be content with leaving the world as they found it.

CHAPTER III. THE FAMA FRATERNITATIS OF THE MERITORIOUS ORDER OF THE ROSY CROSS, ADDRESSED TO THE LEARNED IN GENERAL, AND THE GOVERNORS OF EUROPE.

THE original edition of the "Universal Reformation" contained the manifesto bearing the above title, but which the notary Haselmeyer declares to have existed in manuscript as early as the year 1610, as would also appear from a passage in the Cassel edition of 1614, the earliest which I have been able to trace. It was reprinted with the "Confessio Fraternitatis" and the "Allgemeine Reformation der Ganzen Welt" at Franckfurt-on-the-Mayne in 1615. A Dutch translation was also published in this year, and by 1617 there had been four Franckfurt editions, the last omitting the "Universal Reformation," which, though it received an elaborate alchemical elucidation by Brotoffer, seems gradually to have dropped out of notice. "Other editions," says Buhle, "followed in the years immediately succeeding, but these it is unnecessary to notice. In the title-page of the third Franckfurt edition stands--*First printed at Cassel* in the year 1616. But the four first words apply to the original edition, the four last to this. *Fama Fraternitatis; or, a Discovery of the Fraternity of the most Laudable Order of the Rosy Cross.*

Seeing the only wise and merciful God in these latter days hath poured out so richly His mercy and goodness to mankind, whereby we do attain more and more to the perfect knowledge of His Son Jesus Christ and of Nature, that justly we may boast of the happy time wherein there is not only discovered unto us the half part of the world, which was heretofore unknown and hidden, but He hath also made manifest unto us many wonderful and never-heretofore seen works and creatures of Nature, and, moreover, hath raised men, indued with great wisdom, which might partly renew and reduce all arts (in this our spotted and imperfect age) to perfection, so that finally man might thereby understand his own nobleness and worth, and why he is called *Microcosmos*, and how far his knowledge extendeth in Nature.

Although the rude world herewith will be but little pleased, but rather smile and scoff thereat; also the pride and covetousness of the learned is so great, it will not suffer them to agree together; but were they united, they might, out of all those things which in this our age God doth so richly bestow on us, collect *Librum Naturæ*, or, a Perfect Method of all Arts. But such is their opposition that they still keep, and are loth to leave, the old course, esteeming Porphyry, Aristotle, and Galen, yea, and that which hath but a meer show of learning, more than the clear and manifested Light and Truth. Those, if they were now living, with much joy would leave their erroneous doctrines; but here is too great weakness for such a great work. And although in Theologie, Physic, and the Mathematic, the truth doth oppose it itself, nevertheless, the old Enemy, by his subtilty and craft, doth shew himself in hindering every good purpose by his instruments and contentious wavering people.

To such an intention of a general reformation, the most godly and highly-illuminated Father, our Brother, C. R. C., a German, the chief and original of our Fraternity, hath much and long time laboured, who, by reason of his poverty (although descended of noble parents), in the fifth year of his age was placed in a cloyster, where he had learned indifferently the Greek and Latin tongues, and (upon his earnest desire and request), being yet in his growing years, was associated to a Brother, P. A. L., who had determined to go to the Holy Land. Although this Brothers dyed in Ciprus, and so never came to Jerusalem, yet our Brother C. R. C. did not return, but shipped himself over, and went to Damasco, minding from thence to go to Jerusalem. But by reason of the feebleness of his body he remained still there, and by his skill in physic he obtained much favour with the Turks, and in the meantime he became acquainted with the Wise Men of Damcar in Arabia, and beheld what great wonders they wrought, and how Nature was discovered unto them.

Hereby was that high and noble spirit of Brother C. R. C. so stired up, that Jerusalem was not so much now in his mind as Damasco; also he could not bridle his desires any longer, but made a bargain with the Arabians that they should carry him for a certain sum of money to Damcar. He was but of the age of sixteen years when he came thither, yet of a strong Dutch constitution. There the Wise Men received him not as a stranger (as he himself witnesseth), but as one whom they had long expected; they called him by his name, and shewed him other secrets out of his cloyster, whereat he could not but mightily wonder.

He learned there better the Arabian tongue, se that the year following he translated the book M into good Latin, which he afterwards brought with him. This is the place where he did learn his Physick and his Mathematics, whereof the world hath much cause to rejoice, if there were more love and less envy.

After three years he returned again with good consent, shipped himself over *Sinus Arabicus* into Egypt, where he remained not long, but only took better notice there of the plants and creatures. He sailed over the whole Mediterranean Sea for to come unto Fez, where the Arabians had directed him.

It is a great shame unto us that wise men, so far remote the one, from the other, should not only be of one opinion, hating all contentious writings, but also be so willing and ready, under the seal of secresy, to impart their secrets to others. Every year the Arabians and Africans do send one to another, inquiring one of another out of their arts, if happily they had found out some better things, or if experience had weakened their

37

reasons. Yearly there came something to light whereby the Mathematics, Physic, and Magic (for in those are they of Fez most skilful) were amended. There is now-a-days no want of learned men in Germany, Magicians, Cabalists, Physicians, and Philosophers, were there but more love and kindness among them, or that the most part of them would not keep their secrets close only to themselves.

At Fez he did get acquaintance with those which are commonly called the Elementary inhabitants, who revealed unto him many of their secrets, as we Germans likewise might gather together many things if there were the like unity and desire of searching out secrets amongst us.

Of these of Fez he often did confess, that their Magia was not altogether pure, and also that their Cabala was defiled with their Religion; but, notwithstanding, he knew how to make good use of the same, and found still more better grounds for his faith, altogether agreeable with the harmony of the whole world, and wonderfully impressed in all periods of time. Thence proceedeth that fair Concord, that as in every several kernel is contained a whole good tree or fruit, so likewise is included in the little body of man, the whole great world, whose religion, policy, health, members, nature, language, words, and works, are agreeing, sympathizing, and in equal tune and melody with God, Heaven, and Earth; and that which is disagreeing with them is error, falsehood, and of the devil, who alone is the first, middle, and last cause of strife, blindness, and darkness in the world. Also, might one examine all and several persons upon the earth, he should find that which is good and right is always agreeing with itself, but all the rest is spotted with a thousand erroneous conceits.

After two years Brother R. C. departed the city Fez, and sailed with many costly things into Spain, hoping well, as he himself had so well and profitably spent his time in his travel, that the learned in Europe would highly rejoyce with him, and begin to rule and order all their studies according to those sure and sound foundations. He therefore conferred with the learned in Spain, shewing unto them the errors of our arts, and how they might be corrected, and from whence they should gather the true *Inditia* of the times to come, and wherein they ought to agree with those things that are past; also how the faults of the Church and the whole *Philosophia Moralis* were to be amended. He shewed them new growths, new fruits, and beasts, which did concord with old philosophy, and prescribed them new Axiomata, whereby all things might fully be restored. But it was to them a laughing matter, and being a new thing unto them, they feared that their great name would be lessened if they should now again begin to learn, and acknowledge their many years' errors, to which they were accustomed, and wherewith they had gained them enough. Who so loveth unquietness, let him be reformed (they said). The same song was also sung to him by other nations, the which moved him the more because it happened to him contrary to his expectation, being then ready bountifully to impart all his arts and secrets to the learned, if they would have but undertaken to write the true and infallible Axiomata, out of all faculties, sciences, and arts, and whole nature, as that which he knew would direct them, like a globe or circle, to the onely middle point and *centrum*, and (as it is usual among the Arabians) it should onely serve to the wise and learned for a rule, that also there might be a society in Europe which might have gold, silver, and precious stones, sufficient for to bestow them on kings for their necessary uses and lawful purposes, with which [society] such as be governors might be brought up for to learn all that which God hath suffered man to know, and thereby to be enabled in all times of need to give their counsel unto those that seek it, like the Heathen Oracles.

Verily we must confess that the world in those days was already big with those great commotions, labouring to be delivered of them, and did bring forth painful, worthy men, who brake with all force through darkness and barbarism, and left us who succeeded to follow them. Assuredly they have been the uppermost point in *Trygono igneo*, I whose flame now should be more and more brighter, and shall undoubtedly give to the world the last light.

Such a one likewise hath Theophrastus been in vocation and callings, although he was none of our Fraternity, yet, nevertheless hath he diligently read over the Book M, whereby his sharp ingenium was exalted; but this man was also hindered in his course by the multitude of the learned and wise-seeming men, that he was never able peaceably to confer with others of the knowledge and understanding he had of Nature. And therefore in his writings he rather mocked these busie bodies, and doth not shew them altogether what he was; yet, nevertheless, there is found with him well grounded the afore-named Harmonia, which without doubt he bad imparted to the learned, if he had not found them rather worthy of subtil vexation then to be instructed in greater arts and sciences. He thus with a free and careless life lost his time, and left unto the world their foolish pleasures.

But that we do not forget our loving Father, Brother C. R., he after many painful travels, and his fruitless true instructions, returned again into Germany, the which he heartily loved, by reason of the alterations which were shortly to come, and of the strange and dangerous contentions. There, although he could have bragged with his art, but specially of the transmutations of metals, yet did he esteem more Heaven, and men, the citizens thereof, than all vain glory and pomp.

Nevertheless, he builded a fitting and neat habitation, in the which he ruminated his voyage and philosophy, and reduced them together in a true memorial. In this house he spent a great time in the mathematics, and made many fine instruments, *ex omnibus hujus artis partibus*, whereof there is but little remaining to us, as hereafter you shall understand.

After five years came again into his mind the wished for Reformation; and in regard [of it] he doubted of the ayd and help of others, although he himself was painful, lusty, and unwearisom; howsoever he undertook, with some few adjoyned with him, to attempt the same. Wherefore he desired to that end to have out of his first cloyster (to the which he bare a great affection) three of his brethren, Brother G. V., Brother I. A., and Brother I. O., who had some mere knowledge of the arts than at that time many others had. He did bind those three unto himself, to be faithful, diligent, and secret, as also to commit carefully writing all that which he should direct and instruct them in, to the end that those which were to come, and through especial revelation should be received into this Fraternity, might not be deceived of the least sillable and word.

After this manner began the Fraternity of the Rosie Cross--first, by four persons onely, and by them was made the magical language and writing, with a large dictionary, which we yet dayly use to God's praise and glory, and do finde great wisdom therein. They made also the first part of the Book M, but in respect that that labour was too heavy, and the unspeakable concourse of the sick hindred them, and also whilst his new building (called *Sancti Spiritus*) was now finished, they concluded to draw and receive yet others more into their Fraternity. To this end was chosen Brother R. C., his deceased father's brother's son; Brother B., a skilful painter; G. G., and. P. D., their secretary, all Germains except I. A., so in all they were eight in number, all batchelors and of vowed virginity, by whom was collected a book or volumn of all that which man can desire, wish, or hope for.

Although we do now freely confess that the world is much amended within an hundred years, yet we are assured that our Axiomata shall immovably remain unto the world's end, and also the world in her highest and last age shall not attain to see anything else; for our ROTA takes her beginning from that day when God spake *Fiat* and shall end when he shall speak *Pereat*; yet God's clock striketh every minute, where ours scarce striketh perfect hours. We also stedfastly beleeve, that if our Brethren and Fathers had lived in this our present and clear light, they would more roughly have handled the Pope, Mahomet, scribes, artists, and sophisters, and showed themselves more helpful, not simply with sighs and wishing of their end and consummation.

When now these eight Brethren had disposed and ordered all things in such manner, as there was not now need of any great labour, and also that every one was sufficiently instructed and able perfectly to discourse of secret and manifest philosophy, they would not remain any longer together, but, as in the beginning they had agreed, they separated themselves into several countries, because that not only their Axiomata might in secret be more profoundly examined by the learned, but that they themselves, if in some country or other they observed anything, or perceived some error, might inform one another of it. Their agreement was this:--

First, That none of them should profess any other thing then to cure the sick, and that gratis.

Second, None of the posterity should be constrained to wear one certain kind of habit, but therein to follow the custom of the country.

Third, That every year, upon the day C., they should meet together at the house *Sancti Spiritus*, or write the cause of his absence.

Fourth, Every Brother should look about for a worthy person who, after his decease, might succeed him.

Fifth, The word R. C. should be their seal, mark, and character.

Sixth, The Fraternity should remain secret one hundred years.

These six articles they bound themselves one to another to keep; five of the Brethren departed, onely the Brethren B. and D. remained with the Father, Brother R. C., a whole year. When these likewise departed, then remained by him his cousen and Brother I. O., so that he hath all the days of his life with him two of his Brethren. And although that as yet the Church was not cleansed, nevertheless, we know that they did think of her, and what with longing desire they looked for. Every year they assembled together with joy, and made a full resolution of that which they had done. There must certainly have been great pleasure to hear truly and without invention related and rehearsed all the wonders which God hath poured out here and there throughout the world. Every one may hold it out for certain, that such persons as were sent, and joyned together by God and the Heavens, and chosen out of the wisest of men as have lived in many ages, did live together above all others in highest unity, greatest secresy, and most kindness one towards another.

After such a most laudable sort they did spend their lives, but although they were free from all diseases and pain, yet, notwithstanding, they could not live and pass their time appointed of God. The first of this Fraternity which dyed, and that in England, was I. O., as Brother C. long before had foretold him; he was very expert, and well learned in Cabala, as his Book called H witnesseth. In England he is much spoken of, and chiefly because he cured a young Earl of Norfolk of the leprosie. They had concluded, that, as much as possibly could be, their burial place should be kept secret, as at this day it is not known unto us what is become of some of them, yet every one's place was supplied with a fit successor. But this we will confesse publickly by these presents, to the honour of God, that what secret soever we have learned out of the book M, although before our eyes we behold the image and pattern of all the world, yet are there not shewn unto us our misfortunes, nor hour of death, the which only is known to God Himself, who thereby would have us keep in a continual readiness. But hereof more in our Confession, where we do set down thirty-seven reasons wherefore we now do make known our Fraternity, and proffer such high mysteries freely, without constraint and reward. Also we do promise more gold then both the Indies bring to the King of Spain, for Europe is with child, and will bring forth a strong child, who shall stand in need of a great godfather's gift.

After the death of I. O., Brother R. C. rested not, but, as soon as he could, called the rest together, and then, as we suppose, his grave was made, although hitherto we (who were the latest) did not know when our loving Father R. C. died, and had no more but the bare names of the beginners, and all their successors to us. Yet there came into our memory a secret, which, through dark and hidden words and speeches of the hundred years, Brother A., the successor of D. (who was of the last and second row of succession, and had lived amongst many of us), did impart unto us of the third row and succession; otherwise we must confess, that after the death of the said A., none of us had in any manner known anything of Brother C. R., and of his first fellow-brethren, then that which was extant of them in our philosophical BIBLIOTHECA, amongst which our AXIOMATA was held for the chiefest, ROTA MUNDI for the most artificial, and PROTHEUS for the most profitable. Likewise, we do not certainly know if these of the second row have been of like wisdom as the first, and if they were admitted to all things.

It shall be declared hereafter to the gentle reader not onely what we have heard of the burial of Brother R. C., but also it shall be made manifest publicly, by the foresight, sufferance, and commandment of God, whom we most faithfully obey, that if we shall be answered discreetly and Christian-like, we will not be ashamed to set forth publickly in print our names and surnames, our meetings, or anything else that may be required at our hands.

Now, the true and fundamental relation of the finding out of the high-illuminated man of God, *Fra: C. R. C.*, is this:--After that A. in *Gallia Narbonensi* was deceased, there succeeded in his place our loving Brother N. N. This man, after he had repaired unto us to take the solemn oath of fidelity and secresy, informed us *bona fide*, that A. had comforted him in telling him, that this Fraternity should ere long not remain so hidden, but should be to all the whole German nation helpful, needful, and commendable, of the which he was not in anywise in his estate ashamed. The year following, after he had performed his school right, and was minded now to travel, being for that purpose sufficiently provided with Fortunatus' purse, he thought (he being a good architect) to alter something of his building, and to make it more fit. In such renewing, he lighted upon the Memorial Table, which was cast of brasse, and containeth all the names of the Brethren, with some few other things. This he would transfer into another more fitting vault, for where or when Brother R. C. died, or in what

42

country he was buried, was by our predecessors concealed and unknown unto us. In this table stuck a great naile somewhat strong, so that when it was with force drawn out it took with it an indifferent big stone out of the thin wall or plaistering of the hidden door, and so unlooked for uncovered the door, whereat we did with joy and longing throw down the rest of the wall and cleared the door, upon which was written in great letters--

Post CXX Annos Patebo,

with the year of the Lord under it. Therefore we gave God thanks, and let it rest that same night, because first we would overlook our *Rota*--but we refer ourselves again to the Confession, for what we here publish is done for the help of those that are worthy, but to the unworthy, God willing, it will be small profit. For like as our door was after so many years wonderfully discovered, also there shall be opened a door to Europe (when the wall is removed), which already doth begin to appear, and with great desire is expected of many. In the morning following we opened the door, and there appeared to our sight a vault of seven sides and seven corners, every side five foot broad, and the height of eight foot. Although the sun never shined in this vault, nevertheless, it was enlightened with another sun, which had learned this from the sun, and was situated in the upper part in the center of the siding. In the midst, instead of a tomb-stone, was a round altar, covered with a plate of brass, and thereon this engraven:--

A. C. R. C. *Hoc universi compendium unius mihi sepulchram feci.*

Round about the first circle or brim stood,

Jesus mihi omnia.

In the middle were four figures, inclosed in circles, whose circumscription was,

1. *Nequaquam Vacuum.*
2. *Legis Jugum.*
3. *Libertas Evangelii.*
4. *Dei Gloria Intacta.*

This is all clear and bright, as also the seventh side and the two heptagons. So we kneeled down altogether, and gave thanks to the sole wise, sole mighty, and sole eternal God, who hath taught us more than all men's wits could have found out, praised be His holy name. This vault we parted in three parts, the upper part or siding, the wall or side, the ground or floor. Of the upper part you shall understand no more at this time but that it was divided according to the seven sides in the triangle which was in the bright center; but what therein is contained you (that are desirous of our Society) shall, God willing, behold the same with your own eyes. Every side or wall is parted into ten squares, every one with their several figures and sentences, as they are truly shewed and set forth *concentratum* here in our book. The bottom again is parted in the triangle, but because therein is described the power and rule of the Inferior Governors, we leave to

43

manifest the same, for fear of the abuse by the evil and ungodly world. But those that are provided and stored with the Heavenly Antidote, do without fear or hurt, tread on and bruise the head of the old and evil serpent, which this our age is well fitted for. Every side or wall had a door for a chest, wherein there lay divers things, especially all our books, which otherwise we had, besides the *Vocabulario* of Theophrastus Paracelsus of Hohenheim, and these which daily unfalsifieth we do participate. Herein also we found his *Itinerarium* and *Vita*, whence this relation for the most part is taken. In another chest were looking-glasses of divers virtues, as also in other places were little bells, burning lamps, and chiefly wonderful artificial songs-- generally all was done to that end, that if it should happen, after many hundred years, the Fraternity should come to nothing, they might by this onely vault be restored again.

Now, as we had not yet seen the dead body of our careful and wise Father, we therefore removed the altar aside; then we lifted up a strong plate of brass, and found a fair and worthy body, whole and unconsumed, as the same is here lively counterfeited, with all the ornaments and attires. In his hand he held a parchment called T, the which next unto the Bible is our greatest treasure, which ought not to be delivered to the censure of the world. At the end of this book standeth this following *Elogium*.

Granum pectori Jesu insitum.

C. R. C. ex nobili atque splendida Germaniæ R. C. familia oriundus, vir sui seculi divinis revelationibus, subtilissimis imaginationibus, indefessis laboribus ad cœlestia atque humana mysteria; arcanavè admissus postquam suam (quam Arabico at Africano itineribus collejerat) plus quam regiam, atque imperatoriam Gazam suo seculo nondum convenientem, posteritati eruendam custodivisset et jam suarum Artium, ut et nominis, fides ac conjunctissimos heredes instituisset, mundum minutum omnibus motibus magno illi respondentem fabricasset hocque tandem preteritarum, præsentium, et futurarum, rerum compendio extracto, centenario major, non morbo (quem ipse nunquam corpore expertus erat, nunquam alios infestare sinebat) ullo pellente sed Spiritis Dei evocante, illuminatam animam (inter Fratrum amplexus et ultima oscula) fidelissimo Creatori Deo reddidisset, Pater delictissimus, Frater suavissimus, præceptor fidelissimus, amicus integerimus, a suis ad 120 annos hic absconditus est.

Underneath they had subscribed themselves,

1. *Fra.* I. A. *Fra.* C. H. *electione Fraternitatis caput.*
2. *Fra.* G. V. M. P. C.
3. *Fra.* F. R. C., *Junior hæres S. Spiritus.*
4. *Fra.* F. B. M. P. A., *Pictor et Architectus.*
5. *Fra.* G. G. M. P. I., *Cabalista.*

Secundi Circuli.

1. *Fra.* P. A. *Successor, Fra.* I. O., *Mathematicus.*

2. *Fra.* A. *Successor, Fra.* P. D. 3. *Fra.* R. *Successor Patris* C. R. C., *cum Christo triumphantis.*

At the end was written,

Ex Deo nascimur, in Jesu morimur, per Spiritum Sanctum reviviscimus.

At that time was already dead, Brother I. O. and Brother D., but their burial place where is it to be found? We doubt not but our *Fra. Senior* hath the same, and some especial thing layd in earth, and perhaps likewise hidden. We also hope that this our example will stir up others more diligently to enquire after their names (which we have therefore published), and to search for the place of their burial; the most part of them, by reason of their practice and physick, are yet known and praised among very old folks; so might perhaps our GAZA be enlarged, or, at least, be better cleared.

Concerning *Minutum Mundum*, we found it kept in another little altar, truly more finer then can be imagined by any understanding man, but we will leave him undescribed untill we shall be truly answered upon this our true-hearted FAMA. So we have covered it again with the plates, and set the altar thereon, shut the door and made it sure with all our seals. Moreover, by instruction, and command of our ROTA, there are come to sight some books, among which is contained M (which were made instead of household care by the praiseworthy M. P.). Finally, we departed the one from the other, and left the natural heirs in possession of our jewels. And so we do expect the answer and judgment of the learned and unlearned.

Howbeit we know after a time there will now be a general reformation, both of divine and humane things, according to our desire and the expectation of others; for it is fitting, that before the rising of the Sun there should appear and break forth *Aurora*, or some clearness, or divine light in the sky. And so, in the meantime, some few, which shall give their names, may joyn together, thereby to increase the number and respect of our Fraternity, and make a happy and wished for beginning of our PHILOSOPHICAL CANONS, prescribed to us by our Brother R. C., and be partakers with us of our treasures (which never can fail or be wasted) in all humility and love, to be eased of this world's labours, and not walk so blindly in the knowledge of the wonderful works of God.

But that also every Christian may know of what Religion and belief we are, we confess to have the knowledge of Jesus Christ (as the same now in these last days, and chiefly in Germany, most clear and pure is professed, and is now adays cleansed and voyd of all swerving people, hereticks, and false prophets), in certain and noted countries maintained, defended, and propagated. Also we use two Sacraments, as they are instituted with all Formes and Ceremonies of the first and renewed Church. In *Politia* we acknowledge the Roman Empire and *Quartam Monarchiam* for our Christian head, albeit we know what alterations be at hand, and would fain impart the same with all our hearts to other godly learned men, notwithstanding our handwriting which is in our hands, no man (except God alone) can make it common, nor any unworthy person is able to bereave us of it. But we shall help with secret aid this so good a cause, as God shall permit or hinder us. For our God is not blinde, as the heathen's Fortuna, but is the Churches' ornament and the honour of the Temple. Our Philosophy also is not a new invention, but as Adam after his fall hath received it, and as Moses and Solomon used it, also it ought not much to be doubted of, or contradicted by other opinions, or meanings; but seeing the truth is peaceable, brief, and always like herself in all things, and especially accorded by with *Jesus in omni parte* and all members, and as He is the true image of the Father, so is she His image, so it shal not be said, This is true according to Philosophy, but true according to Theologie; and wherein Plato, Aristotle, Pythagoras, and others did hit the mark, and wherein Enoch, Abraham, Moses, Solomon, did excel, but especially wherewith that wonderful book the Bible agreeth. All that same concurreth together, and maketh a sphere or globe whose total parts are equidistant from the center, as hereof more at large and more plain shal be spoken of in Christianly Conference (in den Boecke des Levens).

But now concerning, and chiefly in this our age, the ungodly and accursed gold-making, which hath gotten so much the upper hand, whereby under colour of it, many runagates and roguish people do use great villainies, and cozen and abuse the credit which is given them; yea, now adays men of discretion do hold the transmutation of metals to be the highest point and *fastigium* in philosophy. This is all their intent and desire, and that God would be most esteemed by them and honoured which could make great store of gold, the which with unpremeditate prayers they hope to obtain of the alknowing God and searcher of all hearts; but we by these presents publickly testifie, that the true philosophers are far of another minde, esteeming little the making of gold, which is but a *paragon*, for besides that they have a thousand better things. We say with our loving Father C. R. C., *Phy. aurium nisi quantum aurum*, for unto him the whole nature is detected; he doth not rejoice that he can make gold, and that, as saith Christ, the devils are obedient unto him, but is glad that he seeth the Heavens open, the angels of God ascending and descending, and his name written in the book of life.

Also we do testifie that, under the name of *Chymia*, many books and pictures are set forth in *Contumeliam gloriæ Dei*, as we wil name them in their due season, and wil give to the pure-hearted a catalogue or register of them. We pray all learned men to take heed of these kinde of books, for the Enemy never resteth, but soweth his weeds til a stronger one doth root them out.

So, according to the wil and meaning of *Fra*. C. R. C., we his brethren request again all the learned in Europe who shal read (sent forth in five languages) this our *Fama* and *Confessio*, that it would please them with good deliberation to ponder this our offer, and to examine most nearly and sharply their arts, and behold the present time with all diligence, and to declare their minde, either *communicato consilio*, or *singulatim* by print. And although at this time we make no mention either of our names or meetings, yet nevertheless every one's opinion shal assuredly come to our hands, in what language so ever it be, nor any body shal fail, whoso gives but his name, to speak with some of us, either by word of mouth, or else, if there be some lett, in writing. And this we say for a truth, that whosoever shal earnestly, and from his heart, bear affection unto us, it shal be beneficial to him in goods, body, and soul; but he that is false-hearted, or onely greedy of riches, the same first of all shal not be able in any manner of wise to hurt us, but bring himself to utter ruine and destruction. Also our building, although one hundred thousand people had very near seen and beheld the same, shal for ever remain untouched, undestroyed, and hidden to the wicked world.

Sub umbra alarum tuarum, Jehova.

CHAPTER IV. THE CONFESSION OF THE ROSICRUCIAN FRATERNITY, ADDRESSED TO THE LEARNED OF EUROPE.

THE translation of this manifesto which follows the Fama in the edition accredited by the great name of Eugenius Philalethes is prolix and careless: being made not from the Latin original but from the later German version. As a relic of English Rosicrucian literature I have wished to preserve it, and having subjected it to a searching revision throughout, it now represents the original with sufficient fidelity for all practical purposes. The "Confessio Fraternitatis" appeared in the year 1615 in a Latin work entitled "Secretioris Philosophiæ Consideratio Brevio à Philippo à Gabella, Philosophiæ studioso, conscripta; et nunc primum unà cum Confessione Fraternitatis R. C.," in lucem edita, Cassellis, excudebat G. Wesselius, a 1615, Quarto." It was prefaced by the following advertisement:--

"Here, gentle reader, you shall finde incorporated in our Confession thirty-seven reasons of our purpose and intention, the which according to thy pleasure thou mayst seek out and compare together, considering within thyself if they be sufficient to allure thee. Verily, it requires no small pains to induce any one to believe what doth not yet appear, but when it shall be revealed in the full blaze of day, I suppose we should be ashamed of such questionings. And as we do now securely call the Pope Antichrist, which was formerly a capital offence in every place, so we know certainly that what we here keep secret we shall in the future thunder forth with uplifted voice, the which, reader, with us desire with all thy heart that it may happen most speedily.

"FRATRES R. C."

Confessio Fraternitatis R. C. ad Eruditos Europæ.

CHAPTER I.

Whatsoever you have heard, O mortals, concerning our Fraternity by the trumpet sound of the Fama R. C., do not either believe it hastily, or wilfully suspect it. It is Jehovah who, seeing how the world is falling to decay, and near to its end, doth hasten it again to its beginning, inverting the course of Nature, and so what heretofore hath been sought with great pains and dayly labor He doth lay open now to those thinking of no such thing, offering it to the willing and thrusting it on the reluctant, that it may become to the good that which will smooth the troubles of human life and break the violence of unexpected blows of Fortune, but to the ungodly that which will augment their sins and their punishments.

Although we believe ourselves to have sufficiently unfolded to you in the *Fama* the nature of our order, wherein we follow the will of our most excellent father, nor can by any be suspected of heresy, nor of any attempt against the commonwealth, we hereby do condemn the East and the West (meaning the Pope and Mahomet) for their blasphemies against our Lord Jesus Christ, and offer to the chief head of the Roman Empire our prayers, secrets, and great treasures of gold. Yet we have thought good for the sake of the learned to add somewhat more to this, and make a better explanation, if there be anything too deep, hidden, and set down over dark, in the Fama, or fur certain reasons altogether omitted, whereby we hope the learned will be more addicted unto us, and easier to approve our counsel.

CHAPTER II.

Concerning the amendment of philosophy, we have (as much as at this present is needful) declared that the same is altogether weak and faulty; nay, whilst many (I know not how) alledge that she is sound and strong, to us it is certain that she fetches her last breath.

But as commonly even in the same place where there breaketh forth a new disease, nature discovereth a remedy against the same, so amidst so many infirmities of philosophy there do appear the right means, and unto our Fatherland sufficiently offered, whereby she may become sound again, and new or renovated may appear to a renovated world.

No other philosophy we have then that which is the head of all the faculties, sciences, and arts, the which (if we behold our age) containeth much of Theology and Medicine, but little of Jurisprudence; which searcheth heaven and earth with exquisite analysis, or, to speak briefly thereof, which doth sufficiently manifest the Microsmus man, whereof if some of the more orderly in the number of the learned shall respond to our fraternal invitation, they shall find among us far other and greater wonders then those they heretofore did believe, marvel at, and profess.

CHAPTER III.

Wherefore, to declare briefly our meaning hereof, it becomes us to labor carefully that the surprise of our challenge may be taken from you, to shew plainly that such secrets are not lightly esteemed by us, and not to spread an opinion abroad among the vulgar that the story concerning them is a foolish thing. For it is not absurd to suppose many are overwhelmed with the conflict of thought which is occasioned by our unhoped graciousness, unto whom (as yet) be unknown the wonders of the sixth age, or who, by reason of the course of the world, esteem the things to come like unto the present, and, hindered by the obstacles of their age, live no otherwise in the world then as men blind, who, in the light of noon, discern nothing onely by feeling.

CHAPTER IV.

Now concerning the first part, we hold that the meditations of our Christian father on all subjects which from the creation of the world have been invented, brought forth, and propagated by human ingenuity, through God's revelation, or through the service of Angels or spirits, or through the sagacity of understanding, or through the experience of long observation, are so great, that if all books should perish, and by God's almighty sufferance all writings and all learning should be lost, yet posterity will be able thereby to lay a new foundation of sciences, and to erect a new citadel of truth; the which perhaps would not be so hard to do as if one should begin to pull down and destroy the old, ruinous building, then enlarge the fore-court, afterwards bring light into the private chambers, and then change the doors, staples, and other things according to our intention.

Therefore, it must not be expected that new comers shall attain at once all our weighty secrets. They must proceed step by step from the smaller to the greater, and must not be retarded by difficulties.

Wherefore should we not freely acquiesce in the onely truth then seek through so many windings and labyrinths, if onely it had pleased God to lighten unto us the sixth Candelabrum? Were it not sufficient for us to fear neither hunger, poverty, diseases, nor age? Were it not an excellent thing to live always so as if you had lived from the beginning of the world, and should still live to the end thereof? So to live in one place that neither the people which dwel beyond the Ganges could hide anything, nor those which live in Peru might be able to keep secret their counsels from thee? So to read in one onely book as to discern, understand, and remember whatsoever in all other books (which heretofore have been, are now, and hereafter shal come out) hath been, is, and shal be learned out of them? So to sing or to play that instead of stony rocks you could draw pearls, instead of wild beasts spirits, and instead of Pluto you could soften the mighty princes of the world? O mortals, diverse is the counsel of God and your convenience, Who hath decreed at this time to encrease and enlarge the number of our Fraternity, the which we with such joy have undertaken, as we have heretofore obtained this great treasure without our merits, yea, without any hope or expectation; the same we purpose with such fidelity to put in practice, that neither compassion nor pity for our own children (which some of us in the Fraternity have) shal move us, since we know that these unhoped for good things cannot be inherited, nor be conferred promiscuously. CHAPTER V.

If there be any body now which on the other side wil complain of our discretion, that we offer our treasures so freely and indiscriminately, and do not rather regard more the godly, wise, or princely persons then the common people, with him we are in no wise angry (for the accusation is not without moment), but withall we affirm that we have by no means made common property of our arcana, albeit they resound in five languages within the ears of the vulgar, both because, as we well know, they will not move gross wits, and because the worth of those who shal be accepted into our Fraternity will not be measured by their curiosity, but by the rule and pattern of our revelations. A thousand times the unworthy may clamour, a thousand times may present themselves, yet God hath commanded our ears that they should hear none of them, and hath so compassed us about with His clouds that unto us, His servants, no violence can be done; wherefore now no longer are we beheld by human eyes, unless they have received strength borrowed from the eagle.

For the rest, it hath been necessary that the Fama should be set forth in everyone's mother tongue, lest those should not be defrauded of the knowledge thereof; whom (although they be unlearned) God hath not excluded from the happiness of this Fraternity, which is divided into degrees; as those which dwell in Damcar, who have a far different politick order from the other Arabians; for there do govern onely understanding men, who, by the king's permission, make particular laws, according unto which example the government shall also be instituted in Europe (according to the description set down by our Christianly Father), when that shal come to pass which must precede, when our Trumpet shall resound with full voice and with no prevarications of meaning, when, namely, those things of which a few now whisper and darken with enigmas, shall openly fill the earth, even as after many secret chafings of pious people against the pope's tyranny, and after timid reproof, he with great violence and by a great onset was cast down from his seat and abundantly trodden under foot, whose final fall is reserved for an age when he shall be torn in pieces with nails, and a final groan shall end his ass's braying, the which, as we know, is already manifest to many learned men in Germany, as their tokens and secret congratulations bear witness.

CHAPTER VI.

We could here relate and declare what all the time from the year 1378 (when our Christian father was born) till now hath happened, what alterations he hath seen in the world these one hundred and six years of his life, what he left after his happy death to be attempted by our Fathers and by us, but brevity, which we do observe, will not permit at this present to make rehearsal of it; it is enough for those which do not despise our declaration to have touched upon it, thereby to prepare the way for their more close union and association with us. Truly, to whom it is permitted to behold, read, and thenceforward teach himself those great characters which the Lord God hath inscribed upon the world's mechanism, and which He repeats through the mutations of Empires, such an one is already ours, though as yet unknown to himself; and as we know he will not neglect our invitation, so, in like manner, we abjure all deceit, for we promise that no man's uprightness and hopes shall deceive him who shall make himself known to us under the seal of secresy and desire our familiarity. But to the false and to impostors, and to those who seek other things then wisdom, we witness by these presents publikely, we cannot be betrayed unto them to our hurt, nor be known to them without the will of God, but they shall certainly be partakers of that terrible commination spoken of in our Fama, and their impious designs shall fall back upon their own heads, while our treasures shall remain untouched, till the Lion shall arise and exact them as his right, receive and imploy them for the establishment of his kingdom.

CHAPTER VII.

One thing should here, O mortals, be established by us, that God hath decreed to the world before her end, which presently thereupon shall ensue, an influx of truth, light, and grandeur, such as he commanded should accompany Adam from Paradise and sweeten the misery of man: Wherefore there shall cease all falshood, darkness, and bondage, which little by little, with the great globe's revolution, hath crept into the arts, works, and governments of men, darkening the greater part of them. Thence hath proceeded that innumerable diversity of persuasions, falsities, and heresies, which makes choice difficult to the wisest men, seeing on the one part they were hindered by the reputation of philosophers and on the other by the facts of experience, which if (as we trust) it can be once removed, and instead thereof a single and self-same rule be instituted, then there will indeed remain thanks unto them which have taken pains therein, but the sum of the so great work shall be attributed to the blessedness of our age. As we now confess that many high intelligences by their writings will be a great furtherance unto this Reformation which is to come, so do we by no means arrogate to ourselves this glory, as if such a work were onely imposed on us, but we testify with our Saviour Christ, that sooner shall the stones rise up and offer their service, then there shall be any want of executors of God's counsel.

CHAPTER VIII.

God, indeed, hath already sent messengers which should testifie His will, to wit, some new stars which have appeared in *Serpentarius* and *Cygnus*, the which powerful signs of a great Council shew forth how for all things which human ingenuity discovers, God calls upon His hidden knowledge, as likewise the Book of Nature, though it stands open truly for all eyes, can be read or understood by only a very few.

As in the human head there are two organs of hearing, two of sight, and two of smell, but onely one of speech, and it were but vain to expect speech from the ears, or hearing from the eyes, so there have been ages which have seen, others which have heard, others again that have smelt and tasted. Now, there remains that in a short and swiftly approaching time honour should be likewise given to the tongue, that what formerly saw, heard, and smelt shall finally speak, after the world shall have slept away the intoxication of her poisoned and stupefying chalice, and with an open heart, bare head, and naked feet shall merrily and joyfully go forth to meet the sun rising in the morning. CHAPTER IX.

These characters and letters, as God hath here and there incorporated them in the Sacred Scriptures, so hath He imprinted them most manifestly on the wonderful work of creation, on the heavens, the earth, and on all beasts, so that as the mathematician predicts eclipses, so we prognosticate the obscurations of the church, and how long they shall last. From these letters we have borrowed our magick writing, and thence have made for ourselves a new language, in which the nature of things is expressed, so that it is no wonder that we are not so eloquent in other tongues, least of all in this Latin, which we know to be by no means in agreement with that of Adam and of Enoch, but to have been contaminated by the confusion of Babel.

CHAPTER X.

But this also must by no means be omitted, that, while there are yet some eagle's feathers in our way, the which do hinder our purpose, we do exhort to the sole, onely, assiduous, and continual study of the Sacred Scriptures, for he that taketh all his pleasures therein shall know that he hath prepared for himself an excellent way to come into our Fraternity, for this is the whole sum of our Laws, that as there is not a character in that great miracle of the world which has not a claim on the memory, so those are nearest and likest unto us who do make the Bible the rule of their life, the end of all their studies, and the compendium of the universal world, from whom we require not that it should be continually in their mouth, but that they should appropriately apply its true interpretation to all ages of the world, for it is not our custom so to debase the divine oracle, that while there are innumerable expounders of the same, some adhere to the opinions of their party, some make sport of Scripture as if it were a tablet of wax to be indifferently made use of by theologians, philosophers, doctors, and mathematicians. Be it ours rather to bear witness, that from the beginning of the world there hath not been given to man a more excellent, admirable, and wholesome book then the Holy Bible; Blessed is he who possesses it, more blessed is he who reads it, most blessed of all is he who truly understandeth it, while he is most like to God who both understands and obeys it.

CHAPTER XI.

Now, whatsoever hath been said in the Fama, through hatred of impostors, against the transmutation of metals and the supreme medicine of the world, we desire to be so understood, that this so great gift of God we do in no manner set at naught, but as it bringeth not always with it the knowledge of Nature, while this knowledge bringeth forth both that and an infinite number of other natural miracles, it is right that we be rather earnest to attain to the knowledge of philosophy, nor tempt excellent wits to the tincture of metals sooner then to the observation of Nature. He must needs be insatiable to whom neither poverty, diseases, nor danger can any longer reach, who, as one raised above all men, hath rule over that which loth anguish, afflict, and pain others, yet will give himself again to idle things, will build, make wars, and domineer, because he hath of gold sufficient, and of silver an inexhaustible fountain. God judgeth far otherwise, who exalteth the lowly, and casteth the proud into obscurity; to the silent he sendeth his angels to hold speech with them, but the babblers he driveth into the wilderness, which is the judgment due to the Roman impostor who now poureth his blasphemies with open mouth against Christ, nor yet in the full light, by which Germany hath detected his caves and subterranean passages, will abstain from lying, that thereby he may fulfil the measure of his sin, and be found worthy of the axe. Therefore, one day it will come to pass, that the mouth of this viper shall be stopped, and his triple crown shall be brought to nought, of which things more fully when we shall have met together.

CHAPTER XII.

For conclusion of our Confession we must earnestly admonish you, that you cast away, if not all, yet most of the worthless books of pseudo chymists, to whom it is a jest to apply the Most Holy Trinity to vain things, or to deceive men with monstrous symbols and enigmas, or to profit by the curiosity of the credulous; our age doth produce many such, one of the greatest being a stage-player, a man with sufficient ingenuity for imposition; such doth the enemy of human welfare mingle among the good seed, thereby to make the truth more difficult to be believed, which in herself is simple and naked, while falshood is proud, haughty, and coloured with a lustre of seeming godly and humane wisdom. Ye that are wise eschew such books, and have recourse to us, who seek not your moneys, but offer unto you most willingly our great treasures. We hunt not after your goods with invented lying tinctures, but desire to make you partakers of our goods. We do not reject parables, but invite you to the clear and simple explanation of all secrets; we seek not to be received of you, but call you unto our more then kingly houses and palaces, by no motion of our own, but (lest you be ignorant of it) as forced thereto by the Spirit of God, commanded by the testament of our most excellent Father, and impelled by the occasion of this present time.

CHAPTER XIII.

What think you, therefore, O Mortals, seeing that we sincerely confess Christ, execrate the pope, addict ourselves to the true philosophy, lead a worthy life, and dayly call, intreat, and invite many more unto our Fraternity, unto whom the same Light of God likewise appeareth? Consider you not that, having pondered the gifts which are in you, having measured your understanding in the Word of God, and having weighed the imperfection and inconsistencies of all the arts, you may at length in the future deliberate with us upon their remedy, co-operate in the work of God, and be serviceable to the constitution of your time? On which work these profits will follow, that all those goods which Nature hath dispersed in every part of the earth shall at one time and altogether be given to you, *tanquam in centro solis et lunæ.* Then shall you be able to expel from the world all those things which darken human knowledge and hinder action, such as the vain (astronomical) epicycles and eccentric circles.

CHAPTER XIV.

You, however, for whom it is enough to be serviceable out of curiosity to any ordinance, or who are dazzled by the glistering of gold, or who, though now upright, might be led away by such unexpected great riches into an effeminate, idle, luxurious, and pompous life, do not disturb our sacred silence by your clamour, but think, that although there be a medicine which might fully cure all diseases, yet those whom God wishes to try or to chastise shall not be abetted by such an opportunity, so that if we were able to enrich and instruct the whole world, and liberate it from innumerable hardships, yet shall we never be manifested unto any man unless God should favour it, yea, it shall be so far from him who thinks to be partaker of our riches against the will of God that he shall sooner lose his life in seeking us, then attain happiness by finding us.

FRATERNITAS R. C.

CHAPTER V. THE CHYMICAL
MARRIAGE OF CHRISTIAN ROSENCREUTZ.

THE whole Rosicrucian controversy centres in this publication, which Buhle describes as "a comic romance of extraordinary talent." It was first published at Strasbourg in the year 1616, but, as will be seen in the seventh chapter, it is supposed to have existed in manuscript as early as 1601-2, thus antedating by a long period the other Rosicrucian books. Two editions of the German original are preserved in the Library of the British Museum, both bearing the date 1616. It was translated into English for the first time in 1690, under the title of "The Hermetic Romance: or The Chymical Wedding. Written in High Dutch by Christian Rosencreutz. Translated by E. Foxcroft, late Fellow of King's Colledge in Cambridge. Licensed and entered according to Order. Printed by A. Sowie, at the Crooked Billet in Holloway-Lane, Shoreditch; and Sold at the Three-Keys in Nags-Head-Court, Grace-church-street." It is this translation in substance, that is, compressed by the omission of all irrelevant matter and dispensable prolixities, which I now offer to the reader.

The Chymical Marriage of Christian Rosencreutz. Anno 1459.

Arcana publicata vilescunt, et gratiam prophanata amittunt. Ergo: ne Margaritas objice porcis, seu Asino substernere rosas.

THE FIRST BOOK.

The First Day.

On an evening before Easter-day, I sate at a table, and having in my humble prayer conversed with my Creator and considered many great mysteries (whereof the Father of Lights had shewn me not a few), and being now ready to prepare in my heart, together with my dear Paschal Lamb, a small, unleavened, undefiled cake, all on a sudden ariseth so horrible a tempest, that I imagined no other but that, through its mighty force, the hill whereon my little house was founded would fly all in pieces. But inasmuch as this, and the like, from the devil (who had done me many a spight) was no new thing to me, I took courage, and persisted in my meditation till somebody touched me on the back, whereupon I was so hugely terrified that I durst hardly look about me, yet I shewed myself as cheerful as humane frailty would permit. Now the same thing still twitching me several times by the coat, I glanced back and behold it was a fair and glorious lady, whose garments were all skye-colour, and curiously bespangled with golden stars. In her right hand she bare a trumpet of beaten gold, whereon a Name was ingraven which I could well read but am forbidden as yet to reveal. In her left hand she had a great bundle of letters in all languages, which she (as I afterwards understood) was to carry into all countries. She had also large and beautiful wings, full of eyes throughout, wherewith she could mount aloft, and flye swifter than any eagle. As soon as I turned about, she looked through her letters, and at length drew out a small one, which, with great reverence, she laid upon the table, and, without one word, departed from me. But in her mounting upward, she gave so mighty a blast on her gallant trumpet that the whole hill echoed thereof, and for a full quarter of an hour afterward I could hardly hear my own words.

In so unlooked for an adventure I was at a, loss how to advise myself, and, therefore, fell upon my knees, and besought my Creator to permit nothing contrary to my eternal happiness to befall me, whereupon, with fear and trembling, I went to the letter, which was now so heavy as almost to outweigh gold. As I was diligently viewing it, I found a little Seal, whereupon was ingraven a curious Cross, with this inscription IN HOC

SIGNO ♃ VINCES.

As soon as I espied this sign I was comforted, not being ignorant that it was little acceptable, and much less useful, to the devil. Whereupon I tenderly opened the letter, and within it, in an azure field, in golden letters, found the following verses written:--

"This day, this day, this, this
The Royal Wedding is.
Art thou thereto by birth inclined,
And unto joy of God design'd?
Then may'st thou to the mountain tend
Whereon three stately Temples stand,
And there see all from end to end.
Keep watch and ward,
Thyself regard;
Unless with diligence thou bathe,
The Wedding can't thee harmless save:
He'll damage have that here delays;
Let him beware too light that weighs." Underneath stood *Sponsus* and
Sponsa.

As soon as I read this letter, I was like to have fainted away, all my hair stood on end, and cold sweat trickled down my whole body. For although I well perceived that this was the appointed wedding whereof seven years before I was acquainted in a bodily vision, and which I had with great earnestness attended, and which, lastly, by the account and calculation of the plannets, I found so to be, yet could I never fore-see that it must happen under so grievous and perilous conditions. For whereas I before imagined that to be a well-come guest, I needed onely to appear at the wedding, I was now directed to Divine Providence, of which until this time I was never certain. I also found, the more I examined myself, that in my head there was onely gross misunderstanding, and blindness in mysterious things, so that I was not able to comprehend even those things which lay under my feet, and which I daily conversed with, much less that I should be born to the searching out and understanding of the secrets of Nature, since, in my opinion, Nature might everywhere find a more vertuous disciple, to whom to intrust her precious, though temporary and changeable treasures. I found also that my bodily behaviour, outward conversation, and brotherly love toward my neighbour was not duly purged and cleansed. Moreover, the tickling of the flesh manifested itself, whose affection was bent only to pomp, bravery, and worldly pride, not to the good of mankind; and I was always contriving how by this art I might in a short time abundantly increase my advantage, rear stately palaces, make myself an everlasting name, and other the like carnal designs. But the obscure words concerning the three Temples did particularly afflict me, which I was not able to make out by any after-speculation. Thus sticking between hope and fear, examining myself again and again, and finding only my own frailty and impotency, and exceedingly amazed at the fore-mentioned threatening, at length I betook myself to my usual course. After I had finished my most fervent prayer, I laid me down in my bed, that so perchance my good angel by the Divine permission might appear, and (as it had formerly happened) instruct me in this affair, which, to the praise of God, did now likewise fall out. For I was yet scarce asleep when me-thought I, together with a numberless multitude of men, lay fettered with great chains in a dark dungeon, wherein we swarmed like bees one over another, and thus rendered each other's affliction more grievous. But although neither I, nor any of the rest, could see one jot, yet I continually heard one heaving himself above the other, when his chains or fetters were become ever so little lighter. Now as I with the rest had continued a good while in this affliction, and each was still reproaching the other with his blindness and captivity, at length we heard many trumpets sounding together, and kettle-drums beating so artificially thereto, that it rejoyced us even in our calamity.

During this noise the cover of the dungeon was lifted up, and a little light let down unto us. Then first might truly have been discerned the bustle we kept, for all went pesle-mesle, and he who perchance had too much heaved up himself was forced down. again under the others' feet. In brief, each one strove to be uppermost, neither did I linger, but, with my weighty fetters, slipt from under the rest, and then heaved myself upon a Stone; howbeit, I was several times caught at by others, from whom, as well as I might, I guarded myself with hands and feet. We imagined that we should all be set at liberty, which yet fell out quite otherwise, for after the nobles who looked upon us through the hole had recreated themselves with our struggling, a certain hoary-headed man called to us to be quiet, and, having obtained it, began thus to say on:

If wretched mortals would forbear
Themselves to so uphold,
Then sure on them much good confer
My righteous Mother would:
But since the same will not insue,
They must in care and sorrow rue,
And still in prison lie.
Howbeit, my dear Mother will
Their follies over-see,
Her choicest goods permitting still
Too much in Light to be.
Wherefore, in honour of the feast
We this day solemnize,
That so her grace may be increast,
A good deed she'll devise;
For now a cord shall be let down,
And whosoe'er can hang thereon
Shall freely be release.

He had scarce done speaking when an Antient Matron commanded her servants to let down the cord seven times into the dungeon, and draw up whomsoever could hang upon it. Good God! that I could sufficiently describe the hurry that arose amongst us; every one strove to reach the cord, and only hindred each other. After seven minutes a little bell rang, whereupon at the first pull the servants drew up four. At that time I could not come near the cord, having to my huge misfortune betaken myself to the stone at the wall, whereas the cord descended in the middle. The cord was let down the second time, but divers, because their chains were too heavy, and their hands too tender, could not keep hold on it, and brought down others who else might have held on fast enough. Nay, many were forcibly pulled off by those who could not themselves get at it, so envious were we even in this misery. But they of all most moved my compassion whose weight was so heavy that they tore their hands from their bodies and yet could not get up. Thus it came to pass that at these five times very few were drawn up, for, as soon as the sign was given, the servants were so nimble at the draught that the most part tumbled one upon another. Whereupon, the greatest part, and even myself, despaired of redemption, and called upon God to have pitty on us, and deliver us out of this obscurity, who also heard some of us, for when the cord came down the sixth time, some hung themselves fast upon it, and whilst it swung from one side to the other, it came to me, which I suddenly catching, got uppermost, and so beyond all hope calve out; whereat I exceedingly rejoyced, perceiving not the wound which in the drawing up I received on my head by a sharp stone, till I, with the rest of the released (as was always before done) was fain to help at the seventh and last pull, at which, through straining, the blood ran down my cloathes. This, nevertheless, through joy I regarded not.

When the last draught, whereon the most of all hung, was finished, the Matron caused the cord to be laid away, and willed her aged son to declare her resolution to the rest of the prisoners, who thus spoke unto them.

Ye children dear
All present here,
What is but now compleat and done
Was long before resolved on;
Whate'er my mother of great grace
To each on both sides here hath shown;
May never discontent misplace!
The joyful time is drawing on
When every one shall equal be--
None wealthy, none in penury.
Whoe'er received great commands
Hath work enough to fill his hands
Whoe'er with much hath trusted been,
'Tis well if he may save his skin;
Wherefore, your lamentations cease,
What is't to waite for some few dayes?

The cover was now again put to and locked, the trumpets and kettle-drums began afresh, yet the bitter lamentation of the prisoners was heard above all, and soon caused my eyes to run over. Presently the Antient Matron, together with her son, sate down, and commanded the Redeemed should be told. As soon as she had written down their number in a gold-yellow tablet, she demanded everyone's name; this was also written down by a little page. Having viewed us all, she sighed, and said to her son--"Ah, how hardly am I grieved for the poor men in the dungeon! I would to God I durst release them all." Whereunto her son replied--"Mother, it is thus ordained by God, against Whom we may not contend. In case we all of us were lords, and were seated at table, who would there be to bring up the service!" At this his mother held her peace, but soon after she said--"Well, let these be freed from their fetters," which was presently done, and I, though among the last, could not refrain, hut bowed myself before the Antient Matron, thanking God that through her had graciously vouchsafed to bring me out of darkness into light. The rest did likewise to the satisfaction of the matron. Lastly, to every one was given a piece of gold for a remembrance, and to spend by the way. On the one side thereof was

stamped the rising sun; on the other these three letters D L S; therewith all had license to depart to his own business, with this intimation, *that we to the glory of God should benefit our neighbours, and reserve in silence what we had been intrusted with*, which we promised to do, and departed one from another. Because of the wounds the fetters had caused me, I could not well go forward, which the matron presently espying, calling me again to her side, said to me--"My son, let not this defect afflict thee, but call to mind thy infirmities, and thank God who hath permitted thee, even in this world, to come into so high a light. Keep these wounds for my sake."

Whereupon the trumpets began again to sound, which so affrighted me that I awoke, and perceived that it was onely a dream, which yet was so impressed on my imagination that I was perpetually troubled about it, and methought I was still sensible of the wounds on my feet. By all these things I well understood that God had vouchsafed me to be present at this mysterious and hidden Wedding, wherefore with childlike confidence I returned thanks to His Divine Majesty, and besought Him that He would preserve me in His fear, daily fill my heart with wisdom and understanding, and graciously conduct me to the desired end. Thereupon I prepared myself for the way, put on my white linnen coat, girded my loyns, with a blood-red ribbon bound cross-ways over my shoulder. In my hat I stuck four red roses, that I might the sooner by this token be taken notice of amongst the throng. For food I took bread, salt, and water, which by the counsel of an understanding person I had at certain times used, not without profit, in the like occurrences. Before I parted from my cottage, I first, in this my wedding garment, fell down upon my knees, and besought God to vouchsafe me a good issue. I made a vow that if anything should by His Grace be revealed to me, I would imploy it neither to my own honour nor authority in the world, but to the spreading of His name, and the service of my neighbour. With this vow I departed out of my cell with joy.

The Second Day.

I was hardly got out of my cell into a forrest when methought the whole heaven and all the elements had trimmed themselves against this wedding. Even the birds chanted more pleasantly then before, and the young fawns skipped so merrily that they rejoiced my old heart, and moved me also to sing with such a loud voice throughout the whole forrest, that it resounded from all parts, the hills repeating my last words, until at length I espyed a curious green heath, whither I betook myself out of the forrest. Upon this heath stood three tall cedars, which afforded an excellent shade, whereat I greatly rejoyced, for, although I had not gone far, my earnest longing made me faint. As soon as I came somewhat nigh, I espyed a tablet fastened to one of them, on which the following words were written in curious letters:--

God save thee, Stranger! If thou hast heard anything concerning the nuptials of the King, consider these words. By us doth the Bridegroom offer thee a choice between foure ways, all of which, if thou dost not sink down in the way, can bring thee to his royal court. The first is short but dangerous, and one which will lead thee into rocky places, through which it will be scarcely possible to pass. The second is longer, and takes thee circuitously; it is plain and easy, if by the help of the Magnet, thou turnest neither to left nor right. The third is that truly royal way which through various pleasures and pageants of our King, affords thee a joyful journey; but this so far has scarcely been allotted to one in a thousand. By the fourth shall no man reach the place, because it is a consuming way, practicable onely for incorruptible bodys. Choose now which thou wilt of the three, and persevere constantly therein, for know whichsoever thou shalt enter, that is the one destined for thee by immutable Fate, nor canst thou go back therein save at great peril to life. These are the things which we would have thee know, but, ho, beware! thou knowest not with how much danger thou dost commit thyself to this way, for if thou knowest thyself by the smallest fault to be obnoxious to the laws of our King, I beseech thee, while it is still possible, to return swiftly to thy house by the way which thou earnest.

As soon as I had read this writing all my joy vanished, and I, who before sang merrily, began inwardly to lament. For although I saw all three ways before me, and it was vouchsafed me to make choice of one, yet it troubled me that in case I went the stony and rocky way, I might get a deadly fall; or, taking the long one, I might wander through bye-ways and be detained in the great journey. Neither durst I hope that I, amongst thousands, should be the one who should choose the Royal way. I saw likewise the fourth before me, but so invironed with fire and exhalation that I durst not draw near it, and, therefore, again and again considered whether I should turn back or take one of the ways before me. I well weighed my own unworthiness, and though the dream, that I was delivered out of the tower, still comforted me, yet I durst not confidently rely upon it. I was so perplexed that, for great weariness, hunger and thirst seized me, whereupon I drew out my bread, cut a slice of it, which a snow-white dove, of whom I was not aware, sitting upon the tree, espyed and therewith came down, betaking herself very familiarly to me, to whom I willingly imparted my food, which she received, and with her prettiness did again a little refresh me. But as soon as her enemy, a most black Raven, perceived it, he straight darted down upon the dove, and taking no notice of me, would needs force away her meat, who could not otherwise guard herself but by flight. Whereupon, both together flew toward the South, at which I was so hugely incensed and grieved, that without thinking, I made haste after the filthy Raven, and so, against my will, ran into one of the fore-mentioned ways a whole field's length. The Raven being thus chased away, and the Dove delivered, I first observed what I had inconsiderately done, and that I was already entered into a way, from which, under peril of punishment, I durst not retire, and though I had still wherewith to comfort myself, yet that which was worst of all was, that I had left my bag and bread at the Tree, and could never retrieve them, for as soon as I turned myself about, a contrary wind was so strong against me that it was ready to fell me, but if I went forward, I perceived no hindrance, wherefore I patiently took up my cross, got upon my feet, and resolved I would use my utmost endeavour to get to my journey's end before night. Now, although many apparent byways showed themselves, I still proceeded with my compass, and would not budge one step from the meridian line. Howbeit, the way was oftentimes so rugged that I was in no little doubt of it. I constantly thought upon the Dove and Raven, and yet could not search out the meaning, until upon a high hill afar off I espyed a stately Portal, to which, not regarding that it was distant from the way I was in, I

hasted, because the sun had already hid himself under the hills, and I could elsewhere see no abiding place, which I verily ascribe only to God, Who might have permitted me to go forward, and withheld my eyes that so I might have gazed beside this gate, to which I now made mighty haste, and reached it by so much daylight as to take a competent view of it. It was an exceeding Royal, beautiful Portal, whereon were carved a multitude of most noble figures and devices, every one of which (as I afterwards learned) had its peculiar signification. Above was fixed a pretty large Tablet, with these words, "*Procul hinc procul ite profani,*" and more that I was forbidden to relate. As soon as I was come unto the portal, there streight stepped forth one in a sky-coloured habit, whom I saluted in friendly manner. Though he thankfully returned my greeting, he instantly demanded my Letter of Invitation. O how glad was I that I had brought it with me! How easily might I have forgotten it as chanced to others, as he himself told me. I quickly presented it, wherewith he was not only satisfied, but showed me abundance of respect, saying, "Come in, my Brother, an acceptable guest you are to me," withal entreating me not to withhold my name from him.

Having replied that I was a Brother of the RED ROSIE CROSS, he both wondred and seemed to rejoyce at it, and then proceeded thus:--"My brother, have you nothing about you wherewith to purchase a token?" I answered my ability was small, but if he saw anything about me he had a mind to, it was at his service. Having requested of me my bottle of water, and I granting it, he gave me a golden token, whereon stood these letters, S.C., entreating me that when it stood me in good stead, I would remember him. After which I asked him how many were got in before me, which he also told me; and lastly, out of meer friendship, gave me a sealed letter to the second Porter. Having lingered some time with him, the night grew on, whereupon a great beacon upon the gate was immediately fired, that if any were still upon the way, he might make haste thither. The road where it finished at the castle was enclosed with walls, and planted with all sorts of excellent fruit trees. On every third tree on each side lanterns were hung up, wherein all the candles were lighted with a glorious torch by a beautiful Virgin, habited in skye-colour, which was so noble and majestic a spectacle that I delayed longer then was requisite. At length, after an advantageous instruction, I departed from the first porter, and so went on the way, until I came to the second gate, which was adorned with images and mystick significations. In the affixed Tablet stood--*Date et dabitur volis*. Under this gate lay a terrible Lyon, chained, who, as soon as he espied me, arose and made at me with great roaring, whereupon the second porter, who lay upon a stone of marble, awaked, and wishing me not to be troubled nor affrighted, drove back the lyon, and having received the letter, which I reached him with trembling hand, he read it, and with great respect spake thus to me:--"Now well-come in God's name unto me the man whom of long time I would gladly have seen!" Meanwhile, he also drew out a token, and asked me whether I could purchase it. But I, having nothing else left but my salt, presented it to him, which he thankfully accepted. Upon this token again stood two letters, namely, S.M. Being just about to discourse with him, it began to ring in the castle, whereupon the porter counselled me to run apace, or all the paines I had taken would serve to no purpose, for the lights above began already to be extinguished, whereupon I dispatched with much haste that I heeded not the porter; the virgin, after whom all the lights were put out, was at my heels, and I should never have found the way, had not she with her torch afforded me some light. I was more-over constrained to enter the very next to her, and the gates were so suddenly clapt to that a part of my coate was locked out, which I was forced to leave behind me, for neither I nor they who stood ready without and called at the gate could prevail with the porter to open it again. He delivered the keys to the virgin, who took them with her into the court. I again surveyed the gate, which now appeared so rich that the world could not equal it. Just by the door were two columns, on one of which stood a pleasant figure with this inscription, *Congratulor*. On the other side was a statue with countenance veiled, and beneath was written, *Condoleo*. In brief, the inscriptions and figures thereon were so dark and mysterious that the most dexterous man could not have expounded them, yet all these I shall e'er long publish and explain. Under this gate I was again to give my name, which was written down in a little vellum-book, and immediately with the rest dispatched to the Lord Bridegroom. Here I first received the true guest-token, which was somewhat less than the former, but much heavier; upon this stood the letters S. P. N. Besides this, a new pair of shoes were given. me, for the floor of the castle was pure shining marble. My old ones I was to give to one of the poor who sate in throngs under the gate. I bestowed them on an old man, after which two pages with as many torches conducted me into a little room, where they willed me to sit down upon a form, and, sticking their torches in two holes made in the pavement, they departed, and left me sitting alone. Soon after I heard a noise but saw nothing; it proved to be certain men who stumbled in upon me, but since I could see nothing I was fain to suffer and attend what they would do with me. Presently finding that they were barbers I intreated them not to jostle me, for I was content to do what they desired, whereupon one of them, whom I yet could not see, gently cut away the hair from the crown of my head, but on my forehead, ears, and eyes he permitted my ice-grey locks to hang. In this first encounter I was ready to despair, for, inasmuch as some of them shoved me so forceably, and were still invisible, I could onely think that God for my curiosity had suffered me to miscarry. The unseen barbers carefully gathered up the hair which was cut off, and carried it away. Then the two pages reentered and heartily laughed at me for being so terrified. They had scarce spoken a few words with me when again a little bell began to ring, which (as the pages informed me) was to give notice for assembling, whereupon they willed me to rise, and through many walks, doors, and winding stairs lighted me into a spacious hall, where there was a great multitude of guests--emperors, kings, princes, and lords, noble and ignoble, rich and poor, and all sorts of people, at which I hugely marvelled, and thought to myself, "Ah! how gross a fool hast thou been to ingage upon this journey with so much bitterness and toil, when here are fellows whom thou well knowest, and yet hadst never any reason to esteem, while thou, with all thy prayers and supplications, art hardly got in at last."

This and more the devil at that time injected. Meantime one or other of my acquaintance spake to me:--"Oh! Brother Rosencreutz, art thou here too?" "Yea, my brethren," I replied, "The grace of God hath helped me in also," at which they raised a mighty laughter, looking upon it as ridiculous that there should be need of God in so slight an occasion. Having demanded each of them concerning his way, and finding most of them were forced to clamber over the rocks, certain invisible trumpets began to sound to the table, whereupon all seated themselves, every one as he judged himself above the rest, so that for me and some other sorry fellows there was hardly a little nook left at the lowermost table. Presently the two pages entred, and one of them said grace in so handsom and excellent a manner as rejoyced the very heart in my body. Howbeit, some made but little reckoning of them, but fleired and winked one at another, biting their lips within their hats, and using like unseemly gestures. After this, meat was brought in, and, albeit none could be seen, everything was so orderly managed that it seemed as if every guest had his proper attendant. Now my Artists having somewhat recruted themselves, and the wine having a little removed shame from their hearts, they presently began to vaunt of their abilities. One would prove this, another that, and commonly the most sorry idiots made the loudest noise. When I call to mind what preternatural and impossible enterprises I then heard, I am still ready to vomit at it. In fine, they never kept in their order, but whenever possible a rascal would insinuate himself among the nobles. Every man had his own prate, and yet the great lords were so simple that they believed their pretences, and the rogues became so audacious, that although some of them were rapped .over the fingers with a knife, yet they flinched not at it, but when any one perchance had filched a gold-chain, then would all hazard for the like. I saw one who heard the movements of the Heavens, the second could see Plato's Ideas, a third could number the atoms of Democritus. There were not a few pretenders to perpetual motion. Many an one (in my opinion) had good understanding, but assumed too much to himself to his own destruction. Lastly, there was one who would needs persuade us that he saw the servitors who attended, and would have pursued his contention, had not one of those invisible waiters reached him so handsom a cuff upon his lying muzzle, that not only he, but many who were by him, became mute as mice. It best of all pleased me that those of whom I had any esteem were very quiet in their business, acknowledging themselves to be misunderstanding men for whom the mysteries of nature were too high. In this tumult I had almost cursed the day wherein I came hither, for I could not but with anguish behold that those lewd people were above at the board, but I in my sorry place could not even rest in quiet, one of these rascals scornfully reproaching me for a motley fool. I dreamed not that there was one gate behind through which we must pass, but imagined during the whole wedding I was to continue in this scorn and indignity which I had at no time deserved, either of the Lord Bride-groom or the Bride. And, therefore, I opined he would have done well to seek some other fool than me for his wedding. To such impatience doth the iniquity of this world reduce simple hearts. But this was really one part of the lameness whereof I had dreamed.

The longer all this clamour lasted, the more it increased. Howbeit, there sate by me a very fine, quiet man, who discoursed of excellent matters, and at length said:--"My Brother, if any one should come now who were willing to instruct these blockish people in the right way, would he be heard?" "No, verily," I replyed. "The world," said he, "is now resolved to be cheated, and will give no ear to those who intend its good. Seest thou that Cock's-comb, with what whimsical figures and foolish conceits he allures others. There one makes mouths at the people with unheard-of mysterious words. Yet the time is now coming when those shameful vizards shall be plucked off, and the world shall know what vagabond imposters were concealed behind them. Then perhaps that will be valued which at present is not esteemed."

While he was thus speaking, and the clamour was still increasing, all on a sudden there began in the hall such excellent and stately musick of which, all the days of my life, I never heard the like. Every one held his peace, and attended what would come of it. There were all stringed instruments imaginable, sounding together in such harmony that I forgot myself, and sate so unmovably that those by me were amazed. This lasted nearly half an hour, wherein none of us spake one word, for as soon as anyone was about to open his mouth, he got an unexpected blow. After that space this musick ceased suddenly, and presently before the door of the hall began a great sounding and beating of trumpets, shalms, and kettle-drums, all so master-like as if the Emperor of Rome had been entring. The door opened of itself, and then the noise of the trumpets was so loud that we were hardly able to indure it. Meanwhile, many thousand small tapers came into the hall, marching of themselves in so exact an order as amazed us, till at last the two fore-mentioned pages with bright torches entred lighting in a most beautiful Virgin, drawn on a gloriously gilded, triumphant self-moving throne. She seemed to me the same who on the way kindled and put out the lights, and that these her attendants were the very ones whom she formerly placed at the trees. She was not now in skye-colour, but in a snow-white, glittering robe, which sparkled of pure gold, and cast such a lustre that we durst not steadily behold it. Both the pages were after the same manner habited, albeit somewhat more slightly. As soon as they were come into the middle of the hall, and were descended from the throne, all the small tapers made obeisance, before her, whereupon we all stood up, and she having to us, as we again to her, shewed all respect and reverence, in a most pleasant tone she began thus to speak:--

> "The King my Lord most gracious,
> Who now 's not very far from us,
> As also his most lovely Bride,
> To him in troth and honour tied,
> Already, with great joy indued,
> Have your arrival hither view'd;
> And do to every one and all
> Promise their grace in special;

And from their very heart's desire
You may the same in time acquire,
That so their future nuptial joy
May mixed he with none's annoy."
Hereupon, with all her small tapers, she again courteously bowed, and
presently began thus:--
"In th' Invitation writ you know
That no man called was hereto
Who of God's rarest gifts good store
Had not received long before.
Although we cannot well conceit
That any man's so desperate,
Under conditions so hard,
Here to intrude without regard,
Unless he have been first of all
Prepared for this Nuptial,
And, therefore, in good hopes do dwell
That with all you it will be well;
Yet men are grown so bold and rude,
Not weighing their ineptitude,
As still to thrust themselves in place
Whereto none of them called was.
No cock's-comb here himself may sell,
No rascal in with others steal,
For we resolve without all let
A Wedding pure to celebrate.
So, then, the artists for to weigh,
Scales shall be fixt th' ensuing day;
Whereby each one may lightly find
What he hath left at home behind.
If here be any of that rout,
Who have good cause themselves to doubt,
Let him pack quickly hence aside,
Because in case he longer bide,
Of grace forelorn, and quite undone,
Betimes he must the gantlet run.
If any now his conscience gall,
He shall to-night be left in th' hall,
And be again release by morn,
Yet so he hither ne'er return.
If any man have confidence,
He with his waiter may go hence,

Who shall him to his chamber light,
Where he may rest in peace to-night."

As soon as she had done speaking, she again made reverence, and sprung chearfully into her throne, after which the trumpets began again to sound, and conducted her invisibly away, but the most part of the small tapers remained, and still one of them accompanied each of us. In our perturbation, 'tis scarcely possible to express what pensive thoughts and gestures were amongst us, yet most part resolved to await the scale, and in case things sorted not well to depart (as they hoped) in peace. I had soon cast up my reckoning, and seeing my conscience convinced me of all ignorance and unworthiness, I purposed to stay with the rest in the hall, and chose rather to content myself with the meal I had taken than to run the risk of a future repulse. After every one by his small taper had been severally conducted to a chamber (each, as I since understood, into a peculiar one), there staid nine of us, including he who discoursed with me at the table. Although our small tapers left us not, yet within an hour's time one of the pages came in, and, bringing a great bundle of cords with him, first demanded whether we had concluded to stay there, which when we had with sighs affirmed, he bound each of us in a several place, and so went away with our tapers, leaving us poor wretches in darkness. Then first began some to perceive the imminent danger, and myself could not refrain tears, for, although we were not forbidden to speak, anguish and affliction suffered none of us to utter one word. The cords were so wonderfully made that none could cut them, much less get them off his feet, yet this comforted me, that the future gain of many an one who had now betaken himself to rest would prove little to his satisfaction, but we by one night's pennance might expiate all our presumption. At length in my sorrowful thoughts I fell asleep, during which I had a dream which I esteem not impertinent to recount. Methought I was upon an high mountain, and saw before me a great valley, wherein were gathered an unspeakable multitude, each of whom had at his head a string by which he was hanging. Now one hung high, another low, some stood even quite upon the earth. In the air there flew up and down an ancient man, who had in his hand a pair of sheers, wherewith here he cut one's and there another's thread. Now he that was nigh the earth fell without noise, but when this happened to the high ones the earth quaked at their fall. To some it came to pass that their thread was so stretched they came to the earth before it was cut I took pleasure at this tumbling, and it joyed me at the heart when he who had over-exalted himself in the air, of his wedding, got so shameful a fall that it carried even some of his neighbours along with him. In like manner it rejoyced me that he who had kept so near the earth could come down so gently that even his next men perceived it not. But in my highest fit of jollity, I was unawares

69

jogged by one of my fellow-captives, upon which I waked and was much discontented with hint. Howbeit, I considered my dream and recounted it to my brother, who lay by me on the other side, and who hoped some comfort might thereby be intended. In such discourse we spent the remaining part of the night, and with longing expected the day.

The Third Day.

As soon as the lovely day was broken, and the bright sun, having raised himself above the hills, had betaken himself to his appointed office, my good champions began to rise and leisurely make themselves ready unto the inquisition. Whereupon, one after another they came again into the hall, and giving us a good morrow, demanded how we had slept; and having espied our bonds, some reproved us for being so cowardly, that we had not, as they, hazarded upon all adventures. Howbeit, some, whose hearts still smote them, made no loud cry of the business. We excused ourselves with our ignorance, hoping we should soon be set at liberty and learn wit by this disgrace, that they also had not altogether escaped, and perhaps their greatest danger was still to be expected. At length all being assembled, the trumpets began again to sound and the kettle-drums to beat, and we imagined that the Bride-groom was ready to present himself, which, nevertheless, was a huge mistake, for again it was the Virgin, who had arrayed herself all in red velvet, and girded herself with a white scarfe. Upon her head she had a green wreath of laurel, which much became her. Her train was no more of small tapers, but consisted of two hundred men in harness, all cloathed, like herself, in red and white. As soon as they were alighted from the throne, she comes streight to us prisoners, and, after she had saluted us, said in few words:--"That some of you have been sensible of your wretched condition is pleasing to my most mighty Lord, and he is also resolved you shall fare the better for it." Having espied me in my habit, she laughed and spake:--"Good lack! Hast thou also submitted thyself to the yoke! I imagined thou wouldst have made thyself very snug," which words caused my eyes to run over. After this she commanded we should be unbound, cuppled together, and placed in a station where we might well behold the scales." For," said she, "it may fare better with them than with the presumptuous who yet stand at liberty."

Meantime the scales, which were intirely of gold, were hung up in the midst of the hall. There was also a little table covered with red velvet, and seven weights thereon--first of all stood a pretty great one, then four little ones, lastly, two great ones severally, and these weights in proportion to their bulk were so heavy that no man can believe or comprehend it. Each of the harnised men carried a naked sword and a strong rope. They were distributed according to the number of weights into seven bands, and out of every band was one chosen for their proper weight, after which the Virgin again sprung up into her high throne, and one of the pages commanded each to place himself according to his order, and successively step into the scale. One of the Emperors, making no scruple, first bowed himself a little towards the Virgin, and in all his stately attire went up, whereupon each captain laid in his weight, which (to the wonder of all) he stood out. But the last was too heavy for him, so that forth he must, and that with such anguish that the Virgin herself seemed to pitty him, yet was the good Emperor bound and delivered to the sixth band. Next him came forth another Emperor, who stept hautily into the scale, and, having a thick book under his gown, he imagined not to fail; but, being scarce able to abide the third weight, he was unmercifully slung down, and his book in that affrightment slipping from him, all the soldiers began to laugh, and he was delivered up bound to the third band. Thus it went also with some others of the Emperors, who were all shamefully laughed at and made captive. After these comes forth a little short man, with a curled brown beard, an Emperor too, who, after the usual reverence, got up and held out so stedfastly that methought had there been more weights he would have outstood them. To him the Virgin immediately arose and bowed before him, causing him to put on a gown of red velvet, then reaching him a branch of laurel, whereof she had good store upon her throne, on the steps of which she willed him to sit down. How after him it fared with the rest of the Emperors, Kings, and Lords, would be too long to recount; few of those great personages held out, though sundry eminent vertues were found in many. Everyone who failed was miserably laughed at by the bands. After the inquisition had passed over the gentry, the learned, and unlearned, in each condition one, it may be, two, but mostly none, being found perfect, it came to those vagabond cheaters and rascally *Lapidem Spilalanficum* makers, who were set upon the scale with such scorn, that for all my grief I was ready to burst my belly with laughing, neither could the prisoners themselves refrain, for the most part could not abide that severe trial, but with whips and scourges were jerked out of the scale. Thus of so pert a throng so few remained that I am ashamed to discover their number. Howbeit, there were persons of quality also amongst them who, notwithstanding, were also honoured with velvet robes and wreaths of lawrel.

The inquisition being finished, and none but we poor coupled hounds standing aside, one of the captains stept forth, and said:--"Gratious madam, if it please your ladyship, let these poor men, who acknowledged their misunderstanding, be set upon the scale also without danger of penalty, and only for recreation's sake, if perchance anything right be found among them." At this I was in great perplexity, for in my anguish this was my only comfort, that I was not to stand in such ignominy, or be lashed out of the scale. Yet since the Virgin consented, so it must be, and we being untied were one after another set up. Now, although the most part miscarried, they were neither laughed at nor scourged, but peaceably placed on one side. My companion was the fifth, who held out bravely, whereupon all, but especially the captain who made the request for us, applauded him, and the Virgin showed him the usual respect. After him two more were despatched in an instant. But I was the eighth, and as soon as (with trembling) I stepped up, my companion, who already sat by in his velvet, looked friendly upon me, and the Virgin herself smiled a little. But, for as much as I outstayed all the weights, the Virgin commanded them to draw me up by force, wherefore three men moreover hung on the other-side of the beam, and yet could nothing prevail. Whereupon one of the pages immediately stood up, and cryed out exceeding loud, "THAT IS HE," upon which the other replyed: "Then let him gain his liberty!" which the Virgin accorded, and being received with due ceremonies, the choice was given me to release one of the captives, whomsoever I pleased, whereupon I made no long deliberations, but elected the first Emperor, whom I had long pittied, who was immediately set free, and with all respect seated among us. Now, the last being set up the weights proved too heavy for him; meanwhile the Virgin espied my roses, which I had taken out of my hat into my hands, and thereupon by her page graciously requested them of me, which I readily sent her. And so this first act was finished about ten in the forenoon.

The trumpets again began to sound, which, nevertheless, we could not as yet see. Meantime the bands were to step aside with their prisoners and expect the judgment, after which a council of the seven captains and ourselves was set, with the Virgin as president, whereat it was concluded that all the principal lords should with befitting respect be led out of the castle, that others should be stripped and caused to run out naked, while others yet with rods, whips, or dogs, should be hunted out. Those who the day before willingly surrendered themselves might be suffered to depart without any blame, but those presumptuous ones, and they who had behaved themselves so unseemly at dinner, should be punished in body and life according to each man's demerit. This opinion pleased the Virgin well, and obtained the upper hand. There was moreover another dinner vouchsafed them, the execution itself being deferred till noon. Herewith the senate arose, and the Virgin, together with her attendants, returned to her usual quarter. The uppermost table in the room was allotted to us till the business was fully dispatched, when we should be conducted to the Lord Bride-groom and Bride, with which we were well content. The prisoners were again brought into the hall, and each man seated according to his quality. They were enjoyned to behave somewhat more civilly than they had done the day before, which admonishment they needed not, for they had already put up their pipes, and this I can boldly say, that commonly those who were of highest rank best understood how to comport themselves in so unexpected a misfortune. Their treatment was but indifferent, yet with respect, neither could they see their attendants, who were visible to us, whereat I was exceeding joyful. Although fortune had exalted us, we took not upon us more than the rest, advising them to be of good cheer, and comforting them as well as we could, drinking with them to try if the wine might make them cheerful. Our table was covered with red velvet, beset with drinking cups of pure silver and gold, which the rest could not behold without amazement and anguish. Ere we had seated ourselves in came the two pages, presenting every one, in the Bride-groom's behalf, the Golden Fleece with a flying Lyon, requesting us to wear them at the table, and to observe the reputation and dignity of the order which his Majesty had vouchsafed us and would ratify with sutable ceremonies. This we received with profoundest submission, promising to perform whatever his Majesty should please. Beside these, the noble page had a schedule wherein we were set down in order. Now because our entertainment was exceeding stately, we demanded one of the pages whether we might have leave to send some choice bit to our friends and acquaintance, who making no difficulty, every one sent by the waiters; howbeit the receivers saw none of them; and forasmuch as they knew not whence it came, I was myself desirous to carry somewhat to one of them, but, as soon as I was risen, one of the waiters was at my elbow, desiring me to take friendly warning, for in case one of the pages had seen it, it would have come to the King's ear, who would certainly take it amiss of me; but since none had observed it save himself, he purposed not to betray me, and that I must for the time to come have better regard to the dignity of the order. With these words, the servant did really so astonish me that for long I scarce moved upon my seat, yet I returned him thanks for his faithful warning as well as I was able. Soon after the drums began to beat, wherefore we prepared ourselves to receive the Virgin, who now came in with her train, upon her high seat, one of the pages bearing before her a very tall goblet of gold, and the other a patent in parchment. Being now after a marvellous artificial manner alighted from her seat, she takes the goblet from the page and presents it in the King's behalf, saying that it was brought from his Majesty, and that in honour of him we should cause it to go round. Upon the cover of this goblet stood Fortune curiously cast in gold, who had in her hand a red flying ensign, for which cause I drunk somewhat the more sadly, as having been too well acquainted with For tune's waywardness. But the Virgin who also was adorned with the Golden Fleece and Lyon, hereupon began to distinguish the patent which the other page held into two different parts, out of which thus much was read before the first company:--

That they should confess that they had too lightly given credit to false, fictitious books, had assumed too much to themselves, and so come into this castle uninvited, and perhaps designing to make their markets here and afterwards to live in the greater pride and lordliness. Thus one had seduced another, and plunged him into disgrace and ignominy, wherefore they were deservedly to be soundly punished--all which they, with great humility, readily acknowledged, and gave their hands upon it, after which a severe check was given to the rest, much to this purpose:--

That they were convinced in their consciences of forging false, fictitious books, had befooled and cheated others, thereby diminishing regal dignity amongst all. They knew what ungodly, deceitful figures they had made use of; not even sparing the Divine Trinity. It was also clear as day with what practices they had endeavoured to ensnare the guests; in like manner, it was manifest to all the world that they wallowed in open whoredom, adultery, gluttony, and other uncleannesses. In brief, they had disparaged Kingly Majesty, even amongst the common sort, and therefore should confess themselves to be convicted vagabond-cheats, and rascals, for which they deserved to be cashiered from the company of civil people, and severely to be punished.

The. good Artists were loath to come to this confession, but inasmuch as the Virgin not only herself threatned, and sware their death, but the other party also vehemently raged at them, crying that they had most wickedly seduced them out of the Light, they at length, to prevent a huge misfortune, confessed the same with dolour, yet alledged their actions should not be animadverted upon in the worst sense, for the Lords were resolved to get into the castle, and had promised great sums of money to that effect, each one had used all craft to seize upon something, and so things were brought to the present pass. Thus they had disserved no more than the Lords themselves. Their books also sold so mightily that whoever had no other means to maintain himself was fain to ingage in this consonage. They hoped, moreover, they should be found no way to have miscarried, as having behaved towards the Lords, as became servants, upon their earnest entreaty. But answer was made that his Royal Majesty had determined to punish all, albeit one more severely than another. For although what they had alledged was partly true, and therefore the Lords should not wholly be indulged, yet they had good reason to prepare themselves for death, who had so presumptuously obtruded themselves, and perhaps seduced the ignorant against their will. Thereupon many began most pitteously to lament and prostrate themselves, all which could avail them nothing, and I much marvelled how the Virgin could be so resolute, when their misery caused our eyes to run over. She presently dispatched her page, who brought with him all the cuirassiers which had been appointed at the scales, who were each commanded to take his own man, and, in an orderly procession, conduct him into her great garden. Leave was given to my yesterday companions to go out into the garden unbound, and be present at the execution of the sentence. When every man was come forth, the Virgin mounted up into her high throne, requesting us to sit down upon the steps,

74

and appear at the judgment. The goblet was committed to the pages' keeping, and we went forth in our robes upon the throne, which of itself moved so gently as if we had passed in the air, till we carne into the garden, where we arose altogether. This garden was not extraordinarily curious, only it pleased me that the trees were planted in so good order. Besides there ran in it a most costly fountain, adorned with wonderful figures and inscriptions and strange characters (which, God willing, I shall mention in a future book). In this garden was raised a wooden scaffold, hung with curiously painted figured coverlets. There were four galleries made one over another; the first was more glorious than the rest and covered with a white Taffata curtain, so that we could not perceive who was behind it. The second was empty and uncovered, while the two last were draped with red and blew Taffata. As soon as we were come to the scaffold the Virgin bowed herself down to the ground, at which we were mightily terrified, for we could easily guess that the King and Queen must not be far off. We also having duely performed our reverence, the Virgin led us by the winding stairs into the second gallery, where she placed herself uppermost, and us in our former order. But how the emperor whom I had released behaved towards me, I cannot relate for fear of slander, for he might well imagine in what anguish he now should have been, and that only through me he had attained such dignity and worthiness. Meantime, the virgin who first brought me the invitation, and whom I had hitherto never since seen, stepped in, and giving one blast upon her trumpet declared the sentence with a very loud voice:--

"The King's Majesty, my most gracious Lord, could from his heart wish that all here assembled had, upon his Majestie's invitation, presented themselves so qualified that they might have adorned his nuptial and joyous Feast. But since it hath otherwise pleased Almighty God, he hath not wherewith to murmur, but is forced, contrary to his inclination, to abide by the antient and laudable constitutions of this Kingdom, albeit, that his Majesty's clemency may be celebrated, the usual sentence shall be considerably lenified. He vouchsafes to the Lords and Potentates not only their lives intirely, but also freely dismisses them, courteously intreating your Lordships not to take it in evil part that you cannot be present at his Feast of Honour. Neither is your reputation hereby prejudiced, although you be rejected by this our Order, since we cannot at once do all things, and forasmuch as your Lordships have been seduced by base rascals, it shall not pass unrevenged. Furthermore, his Majesty resolveth shortly to communicate with you a Catalogue of Hereticks, or Index Expurgatorius, that you may with better judgment discern between good and evil. And because his Majesty also purposeth to rummage his library, and offer the seductive writings to Vulcan, he courteously entreats every one of you to put the same in execution with your own, whereby it is to be hoped that all evil and mischief may be remedied. And you are admonished never henceforth so inconsiderately to covet entrance hither, least the former excuse of seducers be taken from you. In fine, as the estates of the Land have still somewhat to demand of your Lordships, his Majesty hopes that no man will think it much to redeem himself with a chain, or what else he hath about him, and so, in friendly manner, depart from us.

"The others who stood not at the first, third, and fourth weight, his Majesty will not so lightly dismiss, but that they also may experience his gentleness, it is his command to strip them naked, and so send them forth. Those who in the second and fifth weight were found too light shall, besides stripping, be noted with one or more brands, according as each was lighter or heavier. They who were drawn up by the sixth or seventh shall be somewhat more gratiously dealt with, and so forward, for unto every combination there is a certain punishment ordained. They who yesterday separated themselves of their own accord shall go at liberty without blame. Finally, the convicted vagabond-cheats, who could move up none of the weights, shall be punished, in body and life, with sword, halter, water, and rods, and such execution of judgment shall be inviolably observed for an example unto others."

Herewith one virgin broke her wand; the other, who read the sentence, blew her trumpet, and stepped with profound reverence towards the curtain. Now this judgment being read over, the Lords were well satisfied, for which cause they gave more than they were desired, each one redeeming himself with chains, jewels, gold, monies, and other things, and with reverence they took leave. Although the King's servants were forbidden to jear any at his departure, some unlucky birds could not hold laughing, and certainly it was sufficiently ridiculous to see them pack away with such speed, without once looking behind them. At the door was given to each of them a draught of FORGETFULNESS, that he might have no further memory of misfortune. After these the volunteers departed, who, because of their ingenuity, were suffered to pass, but so as never to return in the same fashion, albeit if to them (as likewise to the others) anything further were revealed, they should be well-come guests.

Meanwhile, others were stripping, in which also an inequality, according to demerit, was observed. Some were sent away naked, without other hurt; others were driven out with small bells; some again were scourged forth. In brief, the punishments were so various, that I am not able to recount them all. With the last a somewhat longer time was spent, for whilst some were hanging, some beheading, some forced to leap into the water, much time was consumed. Verily, at this execution my eyes ran over, not indeed in regard of the punishment which impudency well deserved, but in contemplation of human blindness, in that we are continually busying ourselves over that which since the first fall hath been sealed to us. Thus the garden which lately was quite full was soon emptied. As soon as this was done, and silence had been kept for the space of five minutes, there came forward a beautiful snow-white Unicorn, with a golden collar, ingraved with certain letters, about his neck. He bound himself down upon his fore-feet, as if hereby he had shown honour to the Lyon, who stood so immoveably upon the fountain that I took him to be stone or brass, but who immediately took the naked sword which he bare in his paw, brake it into two in the middle, the two pieces whereof sunk into the fountain, after which he so long reared until a white Dove brought a branch of olive in her bill, which the Lyon devoured in an instant, and so was quieted. The Unicorn returned to his place with joy, while our Virgin led us down by the winding staires from the scaffold, and so we again made our reverence towards the curtain. We washed our hands and heads in the fountain, and thereby waited in order till the King through a secret gallery returned into his hall, and then we also, with choice musick, pomp, state, and pleasant discourse, were conducted into our former lodging. Here, that the time might not seem too long to us, the Virgin bestowed on each of us a noble Page, not only richly habited but also exceeding learned, and able aptly to discourse on all subjects, so that we had reason to be ashamed of ourselves. These were commanded to lead us up and down the castle, yet only in certain places, and, if possible, to shorten the time according to our desire. Meantime, the Virgin took leave, promising to be with us again at supper, and after that to celebrate the ceremonies of hanging up the weights, while on the morrow we should be presented to the King. Each of us now did what best pleased him, one part viewing the excellent paintings, which they copied for themselves, and considered what the wonderful characters might signify, others recruiting themselves with meat and drink. I caused my Page to conduct me, with my Companion, up and down the castle, of which walk it will never repent me so long as I live. Besides many other glorious antiquities, the Royal Sepulcher was shewed me, by which I learned more than is extant in all books. There in the same place stands the glorious Phœnix, of which two years since I published a small discourse, and am resolved, in case this narrative prove useful, to set forth several treatises concerning the Lyon, Eagle, Griffon, Falcon, &c., together with their draughts and inscriptions. It grieves me also for my other consorts that they neglected such pretious treasures. I indeed reaped the most benefit by my Page, for according as each one's genius lay, so he led his intrusted one into the quarters pleasing to him. Now the kyes hereunto belonging were committed to my Page, and, therefore, this good fortune happened to me before the rest, for though he invited others to come in, yet they imagining such tombs to be only in the churchyard, thought they should well enough get thither when ever anything was to be seen there. Neither shall these monuments be with-held from my thankful schollars. The other thing that was shewed us two was the noble Library as it was altogether before the

Reformation, of which I have so much the less to say, because the catalogue is shortly to be published. At the entry of this room stands a great Book the like whereof I never saw, in which all the figures, rooms, portals, writings, riddles, and the like, to be seen in the whole castle are delineated. In every book stands its author painted, whereof many were to be burnt, that even their memory might be blotted out from amongst the righteous. Having taken a full view, and being scarce gotten forth, there comes another Page, and having whispered somewhat in our Page's ear, he delivered up the kyes to him, who immediately carried them up the winding stairs; but our Page was very much out of countenance, and we, setting hard upon him with intreaties, he declared to us that the King's Majesty would by no means permit that either the library or sepulchers should be seen by man, and he besought us as we tendered his life to discover it not to anyone, he having already utterly denied it; whereupon both of us stood hovering between joy and fear, yet it continued in silence, and no man made further inquiry about it. Thus in both places we consumed three hours, and now, although it had struck seven, nothing was hitherto given us to eat, but our hunger was abated by constant revivings, and I could be content to fast all my life with such an entertainment. About this time the curious fountains, mines, and all kind of art shops were also shown us, of which there was none but surpassed all our arts even if melted into one mass. Every chamber was built in semi-circle, that so they might have before their eyes the costly clock-work which was erected upon a fair turret in the centre, and regulate themselves according to the course of the planets which were to be seen on it in a glorious manner. At length I came into a spacious room, in the middle whereof stood a terestrial globe, whose diameter contained thirty foot, albeit near half, except a little which was covered with the steps, was let into the earth. Two men might readily turn it about, so that more of it was never to be seen but so much as was above the horizon. I could not understand whereto those ringlets of gold (which were upon it in several places) served, at which my Page laughed, and advised me to view them more narrowly, when I found there my native country noted with gold also, whereupon my companion sought his and found that too. The same happened to others who stood by, and the Page told us that it was yesterday declared to the King's Majesty by their old astronomer Atlas, that all the gilded points did exactly answer to their native countries, and, therefore, he, as soon as he perceived that I undervalued myself, but that nevertheless there stood a point upon my native country, moved one of the captains to intreat for us to be set upon the scale at all adventures, especially seeing one of our native countries had a notable good mark. And truly it was not without cause that he, the Page of greatest power, was bestowed on me. For this I returned him thanks, and looking more diligently upon my native country, I found that, besides the ringlets, there were also certain delicate streaks upon it. I saw much more even upon this globe than I am willing to discover. Let each man take into consideration why every city produceth not a philosopher. After this he led us within the globe, for on the sea there was a tablet (whereon stood three dedications and the author's name) which a man might gently lift up, and by a little board go into the center, which was capable of four persons, being nothing but a round board whereon we could sit and at ease by broad daylight (it was now already dark) contemplate the stars, which seemed like mere carbuncles glittering in an agreeable order, and moving so gallantly that I had scarce any mind ever to go out again, as the Page afterwards told the Virgin, and with which she often twitted me, for it was already supper time and I was almost the last at table. The waiters treated me with so much reverence and honour that for shame I durst not look up. To speak concerning the musick, or the rest of that magnificent entertainment, I hold needless, because it is not possible sufficiently to express it. In brief there was nothing there but art and amenity. After we had each to other related our employment since noon (howbeit, not a word was spoken of the library and monuments), being already merry with wine, the Virgin began thus:--"My Lords, I have a great contention with one of my sisters. In our chamber we have an eagle, whom we cherish with such diligence that each of us is desirous to be the best beloved, and upon that score have many a squabble. On a day we concluded to go both together to him, and toward whom he should show himself most friendly, hers should he properly be. This we did, and I, as commonly, bare in my hand a branch of lawrel, but my sister had none. As soon as he espyed us both, he gave my sister another branch which he had in his beak, and offered at mine, which I gave him. Each of us hereupon imagined herself best beloved of him. Which way am I to resolve myself?"

This modest proposal pleased us mightily well, and each one would gladly have heard the solution, but inasmuch as all looked upon me, and desired to have the beginning from me, my mind was so extreamly confounded that I knew not what to do but propound another in its stead, and said, therefore:--"Gracious. Lady, your Ladyship's question were easily to be resolved if one thing did not perplex me. I had two companions who both loved me exceedingly; they being doubtful which was most dear to me, concluded to run to me unawares, and that he whom I should then embrace should be the right; this they did, yet one of them could not keep pace with the other, so he staid behind and wept; the other I embraced with amazement. When they had afterwards discovered the business to me, I knew not how to resolve, and have hitherto let it rest in this manner till I may find some good advice herein."

The Virgin wondered at it, and well observed where about I was, upon which she replied, that we should both be quit, and then desired the solution from the rest. But I had already made them wise, wherefore the next began thus--"In my city a Virgin was condemned to death, but the judge being pittiful towards her, proclaimed that if any man desired to be her champion, he should have free leave. Now she had two lovers; one made himself ready, and came into the lists to expect his adversary; afterwards the other presented himself, but coming too late, resolved nevertheless to fight, and suffer himself to be vanquished that the Virgin's life might be preserved, which succeeded accordingly. Thereupon each challenged her, and now, my lords, instruct me to which of them of right she belongeth." The Virgin could hold no longer, but said:--"I thought to have gained much information, and am my self gotten into the net; yet I would gladly hear whether there be any more behind." "Yes, that there is," answered the third, "a stranger adventure hath not been recounted then that which happened to myself. In my youth I loved a worthy maid, and that my love might attain its end I made use of an ancient matron, who easily brought me to her. Now it happened that the maid's brethren came in upon us as we three were together, and were in such a rage that they would have taken my life, but, on my vehement supplication, they at length forced me to swear to take each of them for a year to my wedded wife. Now, tell me, my Lords, should I take the old or the young one first?" We all laughed sufficiently at this riddle, yet none would undertake to unfold it, and the fourth began. "In a certain city there dwelt an honourable lady, beloved of all, but especially of a noble young man, who would needs be too importunate with her. At length she gave him this determination, that in case he would, in a cold winter, lead her into a fair green garden of Roses, then he should obtain, but if not he must resolve never to see her more. The noble man travelled into all countries to find one who might perform this, till at length he lite upon a little old man who promised to do it for him, in case he would assure him of half his estate, which he having consented to the other was as good as his word. Whereupon he invited the Lady home to his garden, where, contrary to her expectation, she found all things green, pleasant, and warm; and remembring her promise, she only requested that she might once more return to her lord, to whom with sighs and tears she bewailed her lamentable condition. Her lord, sufficiently perceiving her faithfulness, dispatched her back to her lover, who had so dearly purchased her, that she might give him satisfaction, when the husband's integrity so mightily affected the noble man that he thought it a sin to touch so honest a wife, and sent her home with honour to her lord. The little man, perceiving such faith in all these, would not, how poor soever he were, be the least, but restored the noble man all his goods, and went his way. Now, my lords, which of these persons showed the greatest ingenuity?" Here our tongues were quite cut off, neither would the Virgin make any reply but that another should go on; wherefore the fifth began:-- "I desire not to make long work. Who hath the greater joy, he that beholdeth what he loveth, or he that only thinketh on it?" "He that beholdeth it," said the Virgin. "Nay," answered I, and hereupon rose a contest till the sixth called out:--"My lords, I am to take a wife; I have before me a maid, a married wife, and a widdow; ease me of this doubt, and I will help to order the rest." "It goes well there," replied the seventh, "when a man hath his choice, but with me the case is otherwise. In my youth I loved a fair and virtuous virgin, and she me in like manner; howbeit, because of her friends' denyal, we could not come together in wedlock, whereupon she was married to another, who maintained her honourably and with affection, till she came into the pains of childbirth, which went so hard with her that all thought she was dead, so with much state and mourning she was interred. Now, I thought with myself, during her life thou couldst have no part in this woman, but dead as she is, thou mayst embrace her sufficiently, whereupon I took my servant with me, who dug her up by night. Having opened the coffin and locked her in my arms, I found some little motion in her heart, which increased from my warmth, till I perceived she was indeed alive. I quietly bore her home, and after I had warmed her chilled body with a costly bath of herbs, I committed her to my mother until she brought forth a fair son, whom I caused faithfully to be nursed. After two days (she being then in a mighty amazement) I discovered to her all the affair, requesting that for the time to come she would live with me as a wife, against which she excepted thus, in case it should be grievous to her husband, who had maintained her well and honourably, but if it could otherwise be, she was the present obliged in love to one as well as the other. After two months (being then to make a journey elsewhere) I invited her husband as a guest, and amongst other things demanded of him whether if his deceased wife should come home again he could be content to receive her, and he affirming it with tears and lamentations, I brought him his wife and son, recounting all the fore-passed business, and intreating him to ratifie with his consent my fore-purposed espousals. After a long dispute he could not beat me from my right, but was fain to leave me the wife. But still the contest was about the son." Here the Virgin interrupted him and said:--"It makes me wonder how you could double the afflicted man's grief." Upon this there arose a dispute amongst us, the most part affirming he had done but right. "Nay," said he, "I freely returned him both his wife and son. Now tell me, my lords, was my honesty or this man's joy the greater?" These words so mightily cheared the Virgin that she caused a health to go round, after which other proposals went on somewhat perplexedly, so that I could not retain them all; yet this comes to my mind, that one told how a few years before he had seen a physitian, who bought a parcel of wood against winter, with which he warmed himself all winter long; but as soon as spring returned he sold the very same wood again, and so had the use of it for nothing. "Here must needs be skill," said

81

the Virgin, "but the time is now past." "Yea," replyed my companion, "whoever understands how to resolve all the riddles may give notice of it by a proper messenger; I conceive he will not be denied." At this time they began to say grace, and we arose altogether from the table rather satisfied and merry than glutted; it were to be wished that all invitations and feastings were thus kept. Having taken some few turns up and down the hall, the Virgin asked us whether we desired to begin the wedding. "Yes," said one, "noble and vertuous lady;" whereupon she privately dispatched a Page, and, meantime, proceeded in discourse with us. In brief, she was become so familiar that I adventured and requested her Name. The Virgin smiled at my curiosity, and replyed:--"My name contains five and fifty, and yet hath only eight letters; the third is the third part of the fifth, which added to the sixth will produce a number, whose root shall exceed the third itself by just the first, and it is the half of the fourth. Now the fifth and seventh are equal, the last and first also equal, and make with the second as much as the sixth hath, which contains four more than the third tripled. Now tell me, my lord, how am I called?"

The answer was intricate enough, yet I left not off, but said:--"Noble and vertuous Lady, may I not obtain one only letter?" "Yea," said she, "that may well be done. "What, then," I proceeded, "may the seventh contain?" "It contains," said she, "as many as there are lords here." With this I easily found her Name, at which she was well pleased, saying that much more should yet be revealed to us. Meantime certain virgins had made themselves ready, and came in with great ceremony. Two youths carried lights before them, one of whom was of jocond countenance, sprightly eyes, and gentile proportion, while the other lookt something angerly, and whatever he would have must be, as I afterwards perceived. Four Virgins followed them; one looked shamefully towards the earth; the second also was a modest, bashful Virgin; the third, as she entered, seemed amazed at somewhat, and, as I understood, she cannot well abide where there is too much mirth. The fourth brought with her certain small wreaths, to manifest her kindness and liberality. After these four came two somewhat more gloriously apparelled; they saluted us courteously. One of them had a gown of skeye-colour, spangled with golden stars: the other's was green, beautified with red and white stripes. On their heads they had thin flying white tiffaties, which did most becomingly adorn them. At last came one alone, wearing a coronet, and rather looking up towards heaven than towards earth. We all took her for the Bride, but were much mistaken, although in honour, riches, and state she much surpassed the bride, and afterwards ruled the whole Wedding. On this occasion we all followed our Virgin, and fell on our knees; howbeit, she shewed herself extreamly humble, offering each her hand, and admonishing us not to be too much surprised at this, which was one of her smallest bounties, but to lift up our eyes to our Creator and acknowledge his Omnipotency, and so proceed in our enterprised course, employing this grace to the praise of God and the good of man. In sum her words were quite different from those of our Virgin, who was somewhat more worldly. They pierced even through my bones and marrow. "Thou," said she further to me, "hast received more than others; see that thou also make a larger return."

This to me was a very strange sermon, for as soon as we saw the Virgins with the musick, we imagined we should fall to dancing. Now the Weights stood still in the same place, wherefore the Queen (I yet know not who she was) commanded each Virgin to take up one, but to our Virgin she gave her own, which was the largest, and commanded us to follow behind. Our majesty was then somewhat abated, for I observed that our Virgin was but too good for us, and that we were not so highly reputed as we ourselves were almost willing to phantsie. We were brought into the first Chamber, where our Virgin hung up the Queen's weight, during which an excellent spiritual hymn was sung. There was nothing costly in this room save certain curious little Prayer-Books which should never be missing. In the midst was a pulpit, convenient for prayer, where in the Queen kneeled down, and about her we also were fain to kneel and pray after the Virgin, who read out of a book, that this Wedding might tend to the honour of God, and our own benefit. We then came into the second chamber, where the first Virgin hung up her weight also, and so forward till all the ceremonies were finished, upon which the Queen again presented her hand to every one, and departed with her Virgins. Our president staied awhile with us, but because it had been already two hours night she would then no longer detain us, and, though methought she was glad of our company, she bid us good night, wishing us quiet rest. Our Pages were well instructed, and shewed every man his chamber, staying with us in another pallet, in case we wanted any thing. My chamber was royally furnished with rare tapistries, and hung about with paintings; but above all things I was delighted in my Page, who was so excellently spoken, and experienced in the arts, that he yet spent me another hour, and it was half an hour after three when I fell asleep. This was the first night that I slept in quiet, and yet a scurvy dream would not suffer me to rest, for I was troubled with a Door which I could not get open, though at last I did so. With these phantasies I passed the time, till at length, towards day, I awaked.

The Fourth Day.

I still lay in my bed, and leisurely surveighed the noble images and figures about my chamber, during which, on a sudden, I heard the musick of coronets, as if already they had been in procession. My Page skipped out of the bed as if he had been at his wits' end, and looked more like one dead than living. "The rest are already presented to the King," said he. I knew not what else to do but weep outright, and curse my own sloathfulness. I dressed myself, but my Page was ready long before me, and ran out of the chamber to see how affairs might yet stand. He soon returned with the joyful news that the time was not past, only I had over-slept my breakfast, they being unwilling to waken me because of my age, but that now it was time for me to go with him to the Fountain, where most were assembled. With this consolation my spirit returned, wherefore I was soon ready with my habit, and went after the Page to the Fountain in the Garden, where I found that the Lyon, instead of his sword, had a pretty large tablet by him. Having well viewed it, I found that it was taken out of the ancient monuments, and placed here for some especial honour. The inscription was worn with age, and, therefore, I am minded to set it down here, as it is, and give every one leave to consider it.

HERMES PRINCEPS.
POST TOT ILLATA
GENERI HUMANO DAMNA,
DEI CONSILIO:
ARTISQUE ADMINICULO
MEDICINA SALUBRIS FACTUS
HEIC FLUO.
Bibat ex me qui potest: lavet, qui vult: turbet, qui audet:
BIBITE FRATRES, ET VIVITE.

This writing might well be read and understood, being easier than any of the rest. After we had washed ourselves out of the Fountain, and every man had taken a draught out of an intirely golden cup, we once more followed the Virgin into the hall, and there put on new apparel, all of cloth of gold gloriously set out with flowers. There was also given to everyone another Golden Fleece, set about with pretious stones, and various workmanship according to the utmost skill of each artificer. On it hung a weighty medal of gold, whereupon were figured the sun and moon in opposition, but on the other side stood this poesie:--"The light of the moon shall be as the light of the sun, and the light of the sun shall be seven times brighter than at present." Our former jewels were laid in a little casket, and committed to one of the waiters. After this the Virgin led us out in our order, where the musitians waited ready at the door, all apparelled in red velvet with white guards. After which a door, that I never before saw open, was unlocked; it opened on the Royal winding-stairs. There the Virgin led us, together with the musick, up three hundred sixty-five stairs; we saw nothing but what was of extream costly and artificial workmanship; the further we went, the more glorious still was the furniture, until at the top we came under a painted arch, where the sixty virgins attended us, all richly apparelled. As soon as they had bowed to us, and we as well as we could had returned our reverence, the musitians were dispatched away down the winding-stairs, the Door being shut after them. Then a little Bell was told, when in came a beautiful Virgin, who brought every one a wreath of lawrel, but our Virgins had branches given them. Meanwhile, a curtain was drawn up, where I saw the King and Queen as they sate in their majesty, and had not the yesterday queen warned me I should have equalled this unspeakable glory to Heaven; for besides that the room glittered of meer gold and pretious stones, the Queen's robes were so made that I was not able to behold them. In the meantime the Virgin stept in, and then each of the other virgins, taking one of us by the hand, with most profound reverence presented us to the King. Whereupon the Virgin began thus to speak:--"That to honour your most gratious, royal Majesties, these Lords have adventured hither with peril of body and life, your Majesties have reason to rejoyce, especially since the greatest part are qualified for inlarging your Majesties' dominions, as you will find by a most gratious particular examination of each. Herewith I was desirous thus to have them in humility presented to your Majesties, with most humble suit to discharge me of this my commission, and to take information from each of them concerning my actions and omissions." Hereupon she laid her branch on the ground. It would have been fitting for one of us to have spoken somewhat on this occasion, but, seeing we were all troubled with the falling of the uvula, old Atlas stept forward and spoke on the King's behalf--"Their Royal Majesties most gratiously rejoyce at your arrival, and will that their grace be assured to all. With thy administration, gentle Virgin, they are most gratiously satisfied, and a Royal Reward shall be provided for thee; yet it is their intention that thou shalt this day also continue with them, inasmuch as they have no reason to mistrust thee."

Here the Virgin humbly took up the branch, and we for this first time were to step aside with her. This room was square on the front, five times broader than it was long, but towards the West it had a great arch like a porch, where stood in circle three glorious thrones, the middlemost being somewhat higher than the rest. In each throne sate two persons--in the first sate a very antient King with a gray beard, yet his consort was extraordinarily fair and young. In the third throne sate a black King of middle age, and by him a dainty old matron, not crowned, but covered with a vail. But in the middle sate the two young persons, who though they had likewise wreaths of lawrel upon their heads, yet over them hung a large and costly crown. Now albeit they were not at this time so fair as I had before imagined to my self, yet so it was to be. Behind them on a round form sat for the most part antient men, yet none had any sword or other weapon about him. Neither saw I any life-guard but certain Virgins which were with us the day before, and who sate on the sides of the arch. I cannot pass in silence how the little Cupid flew to and again there, but for the most part he hovered about the great crown. Sometimes he seated himself in between the two lovers, somewhat smiling upon them with his bow. Sometimes he made as if he would shoot one of us; in brief, this knave was so full of his waggery, that he would not spare even the little birds, which in multitudes flew up and down the room, but tormented them all he could. The virgins also had their pastimes with him, and when they could catch him it was no easie matter for him to get from them again. Thus this little knave made all the sport and mirth. Before the Queen stood a small but inexpressibly curious altar, wherein lay a book covered with black velvet, only a little overlaid with gold. By this stood a taper in an ivory candlestick, which, although very small, burnt continually, and stood in that manner, that had not Cupid, in sport, now and then puffed upon it, we could not have conceived it to be fire. By this stood a sphere or celestial globe, which of itself turned about. Next this was a small striking-watch, by that a little christal pipe or syphon-fountain, out of which perpetually ran a clear blood-red liquor, and last of all there was a scull or death's head, in which was a white serpent, of such a length, that though she crept circle-wise about the rest of it, yet her taile still remained in one of the eye-holes until her head again entered at the other; so she never stirred from her scull, unless Cupid twitched a little at her, when she slipt in so suddenly that we could not choose but marvel at it. There were hung up and down the room wonderful images, which moved as if alive. Likewise, as we were passing out, there began such marvellous vocal musick that I could not tell whether it were performed by the virgins who yet stayed behind, or by the images themselves. We, being for this time satisfied, went thence with our virgins who, the musitians, being already present, led us down the winding stairs, the door being diligently locked and bolted. As soon as we were come again into the hall, one of the virgins began:--"I wonder, Sister, that you durst adventure yourself amongst so many persons." "My Sister," replyed our president, "I am fearful of none so much as of this man," pointing at me. This speech went to my heart, for I understood that she mocked at my age, and indeed I was the oldest of all; yet she comforted me by promising, that in case I behaved myself well towards her, she would easily rid me of this burden.

Meantime a collation was again brought in, and every one's Virgin seated by him, who well knew how to shorten the time with handsom discourses, but what these and their sports were I dare not blab out of school. Most of the questions were about the arts, whereby I could lightly gather that both young and old were conversant in the sciences. Still it run in my thoughts how I might become young again, whereupon I was somewhat the sadder. This the Virgin perceived, and, therefore, began:--"I dare lay anything, if I lye with him to-night, he shall be pleasanter in the morning." Hereupon they began to laugh, and albeit I blushed all over, I was fain to laugh too at my own ill-luck. Now there was one there that had a mind to return my disgrace upon the Virgin, whereupon he said:--"I hope not only we but the virgins themselves will bear witness, that our Lady President hath promised herself to be his bed-fellow to-night." "I should be well content with it," replyed the Virgin, "if I had not reason to be afraid of these my sisters; there would be no hold with them should I choose the best and handsomest for myself." "My Sister," presently began another, "we find hereby that thy high office makes thee not proud, wherefore if by thy permission we might by lot part the Lords here present, thou shouldst, with our goodwill, have such a prerogative." We let this pass for a jest, and began again to discourse together, but our Virgin could not leave tormenting us, and continued:--"My lords, how if we should permit fourtune to decide which of us must be together to-night?" "Well," said I, "if it may be no otherwise, we cannot refuse such a proffer." Now because it was concluded to make this trial after meat, we resolved to sit no longer at table, so we arose and each walked up and down with his Virgin. "Nay," said the president, "it shall not be so yet, but let us see how fortune will couple us," upon which we were separated. Now first arose a dispute how the business should be carried out, but this was only a premeditated device, for the Virgin instantly proposed that we should mix ourselves in a ring, and that she beginning to count from herself, the seventh was to be content with the following seventh, were it a virgin or man. We were not aware of any craft, and therefore permitted it so to be; but when we thought we had very well mingled ourselves, the Virgins were so subtil that each knew her station before-hand. The president began to reckon, the seventh next her was a Virgin, the third seventh a Virgin likewise, and this continued till, to our amazement, all the Virgins came forth and none of us was hit. Thus we poor wretches remained standing alone, and were forced to confess that we had been handsomely couzened, albeit, whoever had seen us in our order might sooner have expected the sky to fall then that it should never have come to our turn. Herewith our sport was abandoned. In the interim the little wanton Cupid came also in unto us, but because he presented himself on behalf of their Royal Majesties, and deliverd us a health from them out of a golden cup, and was to call our Virgin to the King, withal declaring he could not at this time tarry, we could not sport ourselves with him, so, with a due return of our most humble thanks we let him flye forth again. Now because the mirth began to fall into my consort's feet, and the Virgins were nothing sorry to see it, they lead up a civil dance which I rather beheld with pleasure then assisted, for my mercurialists were so ready with their postures, as if they had been long of the trade. After some few dances, our president came in again, and told us how the artists and students had offered themselves to their Royal Majesties before their departure to act a merry comedy; and if we thought good to be present thereat, and to waite upon their Royal Majesties to the House of the Sun, it would be acceptable to them. Hereupon we returned our humble thanks for the honour vouchsafed us, and most submissively tendered our small service, which the Virgin related, and presently brought word to attend their Royal Majesties in the gallery, whither we were soon led, and staid not long there, for the Royal Procession was just ready, yet without musick. The unknown Queen who was yesterday with us went foremost with a small and costly coronet, apparelled in white satin, and carrying nothing but a small crucifix made of a pearl, and this very day wrought between the young King and his Bride. After her went the six fore-mentioned Virgins in two ranks, carrying the King's jewels belonging to the little altar. Next to these came the three Kings. The Bridegroom was in the midst of them with a plain dress of black sattin, after the Italian mode. He had on a small round black hat, with a little black pointed feather, which he courteously put off to us, thereby to signify his favour towards us. To him we bowed, as we had been before instructed. After the Kings came the three Queens, two whereof were richly habited; she in the middle went likewise all in black, and Cupid held up her train. Intimation was given us to follow, and after us the Virgins, old Atlas bringing up the rear. Through many stately walks we came to the House of the Sun, there next to the King and Queen, upon a richly furnished scaffold, to behold the foreordained comedy. We, though separated, stood on the right hand of the Kings, but the Virgins on the left, except those to whom the Royal Ensignes were committed. To them was allotted a peculiar standing at top of all, but the rest of the attendants were content to stand below between the columns. Now because there are many remarkable passages in this Comedy, I will in brief run it over.

First of all came forth a very antient King with some servants; before his throne was brought a little chest, with mention that it was found upon the water. Being opened, there appeared in it a lovely babe, together with certain jewels, and a small parchment sealed, and superscribed to the King. This the King presently opened, and having read it, he wept and declared to his servants how injuriously the King of the **Moores** had deprived his aunt of her country, and had extinguished all the royal seed even to this infant, with the Daughter of which country he had purposed to match his Son. Hereupon he swore to maintain perpetual enmity with the Moore and his allies, and to revenge this on him. He commanded that the Child should be tenderly nursed, and to make preparations against the Moore. This provision, and the discipline of the young lady (who after she was a little grown up was committed to an ancient tutor), continued all the first act, with many laudable sports beside. In the interlude a Lyon and Griffon were set at one another, and the Lyon got the victory; this was also a pretty sight.

In the second act, the Moore, a black, treacherous fellow, came forth, who having with vexation understood that his murder was discovered, and that a little lady was craftily stollen from him, began to consult how by stratagem he might encounter so powerful an adversary, whereof he was at length advised by certain fugitives who fled to him through famine. So the young lady, contrary to all expectation, fell again into his hands, whom had he not been wonderfully deceived by his own servants, he had like to have slain. Thus this act was concluded with a mervelous triumph of the Moore.

In the third act a great army on the King's part was raised against the Moore, and put under the conduct of an ancient, valiant knight, who fell into the Moore's country, till he forceably rescued the young Lady from a tower, and apparelled her anew. After this they erected a glorious scaffold and placed her upon it; presently came twelve royal embassadors, amongst whom the Knight made a speech, alledging that the King, his most gracious Lord, had not only heretofore delivered her from death, and caused her to be royally brought up, though she had not behaved herself altogether as became her, but, moreover, had, before others, elected her as a spouse for the young Lord, his Son, most gratiously desiring that the espousals might be really executed in case they would be sworn to his Majesty upon the following articles. Hereupon out of a patent he caused certain glorious conditions to be read; the young Lady took an oath inviolably to observe the same, returning thanks in most seemly sort for so high a grace. Whereupon they began to sing to the praise of God, of the King, and the young Lady, and for this time so departed. In sport, meanwhile, the four beasts of 𝕯𝖆𝖓𝖎𝖊𝖑, as he saw them in the vision, were brought ilk, all which had its certain signification.

In the fourth act the young Lady was restored to her lost kingdom and crowned, being in this array conducted about the place with extraordinary joy. After various embassadors presented themselves not only to wish her prosperity but also to behold her glory. Yet it was not long that she preserved her integrity, but began to look wantonly about her, and to wink at the embassadors and lords. These her manners were soon known to the Moore, who would by no means neglect such an opportunity; and because her steward had not sufficient regard to her, she was easily blinded with great promises, so that she had no good confidence in her King, but privily submitted herself to the intire disposal of the Moore, who having by her consent gotten her into his hands, he gave her words so long till all her kingdom had subjected itself to him; after which, in the third scene of this act, he caused her to be led forth, stript naked, and then upon a scurvy wooden scaffold bound to a post, well scourged, and at last sentenced to death. This woful spectacle made the eyes of many to run over. Naked as she was, she was cast into prison, there to expect death by poyson, which, however, killed her not, but made her leprous all over. Thus this act was for the most part lamentable. Between they brought forth 𝕹𝖊𝖇𝖚𝖈𝖍𝖆𝖉𝖓𝖊𝖟𝖟𝖆𝖗'𝖘 image, which was adorned with all manner of arms on the head, breast, legs, and feet, of which more shall be spoken in the future explication. In the fifth act the young King was acquainted with all that had passed between the Moore and his future spouse, who interceded with his father for her, intreating that she might not be left in that condition, and embassadors were dispatched to comfort her, but withal to give her notice of her inconsiderateness. She, nevertheless, would not receive them, but consented to be the Moore's concubine, and the young King was acquainted with it. After this comes a band of fools, each of which brought a cudgel, wherewith they made a great globe of the world, and undid it again, the which was a fine sportive phantsie.

In the sixth act, the young King resolved to bid battle to the Moore, which was done, and albeit the Moore was discomfited, yet all held the young King for dead, but he came again to himself, released his spouse, and committed her to his steward and chaplain, the first whereof tormented her mightily, while the priest was so insolently wicked that he would needs be above all, till the same was reported to the young King, who dispatched one to break the neck of the priest's mightiness, and adorn the bride in some measure for the nuptials. After this act a vast artificial elephant was brought in, carrying a great tower with musitians, which was well pleasing to all.

In the last act the bride-groom appeared in such pomp as is not well to be believed. The bride met him in the like solemnity, whereupon all the people cried out--VIVAT SPONSUM, VIVAT SPONSA, so that by this comedy they did withal congratulate our King and Queen in the most stately manner, which pleased them most extraordinary well. At length they made some pastes about the stage, till at last they altogether began thus to sing.

I
This time full of love
Does our joy much approve
Because of the King's Nuptial;
And, therefore, let's sing,
Till from all parts it ring,
Blest be he that granted us all!
II.
The Bride most exquisitely faire,
Whom we attended long with care,
To him in troth is plighted;
We fully have at length obtain'd
The same for which we did contend
He's happy that's fore-sighted.

III.

Now the parents kind and good
By intreaties are subdued;
Long enough in hold was she mew'd;
So in honour increase
Till 𝕿𝖍𝖔𝖚𝖘𝖆𝖓𝖉𝖘 arise
And spring from your own proper blood.

After this thanks were returned, and the comedy was finished with joy to the particular liking of the Royal Persons, who, the evening being already hard by, departed in their fore-mentioned order, we attending them up the winding stairs into the previous hall, where the tables were already richly furnished. This was the first time that we were invited to the King's table. The little altar was placed in the midst of the hall, and the six royal ensignes were laid upon it. The young King behaved himself very gratiously towards us, yet he could not be heartily merry; he discoursed a little with us, yet often sighed, at which the little Cupid only mocked, and played his waggish tricks. The old King and Queen were very serious, but the wife of one of the ancient Kings was gay enough, the cause whereof I understood not. The Royal Persons took up the first table, at the second we only sate; at the third some of the principal Virgins placed themselves. The rest were fain to wait. This was performed with such state and solemn stillness that I am afraid to make many words of it. All the Royal Persons, before meat, attired themselves in snow-white glittering garments. Over the table hung the great golden crown, the pretious stones whereof, without other light, would have sufficiently illuminated the hall. All the lights were kindled at the small taper upon the altar. The young king frequently sent meat to the white serpent, which caused me to muse. Almost all the prattle at this banquet was made by Cupid, who could not leave us, and me especially, untormented, and was perpetually producing some strange matter. However, there was no considerable mirth, from whence I could imagine some great imminent peril. There was no musick heard, and if we were demanded anything, we were fain to give short answers, and so let it rest. In short, all things had so strange a face that the sweat began to trickle down over my body, and I believe that the stoutest-hearted man would have lost courage. Supper being almost ended, the young King commanded the book to be reached him from the altar. This he opened and caused it again to be propounded to us by an old man whether we resolved to abide with him in prosperity and adversity, which we having with trembling consented to, he further caused us sadly to be demanded whether we would give him our hands on it, which, when we could fain no reason, was fain so to be. One after another rose and with his own hand writ himself down in this book, after which the little christal fountain was brought near, together with a very small christal

91

glass, out of which all the Royal Persons drank; afterwards it was reached to us, and so forward to all, and this was called the Draught of Silence. Hereupon all the Royal Persons presented us their hands, declaring that in case we did not now stick to them we should never hereafter see them, which verily made our eyes run over. But our president engaged herself and promised largely on our behalf, which gave them satisfaction. Mean time a little bell was tolled, at which all the Royal Persons waxed so mighty bleak that we were ready utterly to despair. They quickly put off their white garments and assumed intirely black ones; the whole hall was hung with black velvet, the floor covered with the same, with which also the ceiling was overspread. The tables were also removed, all seated themselves upon the form, and we also had put on black habits. Our president, who was before gone out, comes in again, bearing six black taffeta scarffs, with which she bound the six Royal Persons' eyes, and there were immediately brought in by the servants six covered coffins, which were set down, a low black seat being placed in their midst. Finally, there stept in a cole-black, tall man, who bare in his hand a sharp ax. Now after that the old King had been brought to the seat, his head was instantly whipt off and wrapped in a black cloth, the blood being received in a great golden goblet, and placed with him in the coffin that stood by, which, being covered, was set aside. Thus it went with the rest, so that I thought it would have come to me too, but as soon as the six Royal Persons were beheaded, the black man retired, another following who just before the door beheaded him also, and brought back his head, which, with the ax, was laid in a little chest. This indeed seemed to me a bloody Wedding, but, because I could not tell what the event would be, I was fain to captivate my understanding until I were further resolved. The Virgin, seeing that some of us were faint-hearted and wept, bid us be content, saying:--"The life of these standeth now in your hands, and in case you follow me, this death shall make many alive."

Herewith she intimated we should go sleep and trouble ourselves no further, for they should have their due right. She bade us all good night, saying that she must watch the dead corps. We then were conducted by our Pages into our lodgings. My Page talked with me of sundry matters, and gave me cause enough to admire his understanding, but his intention was to lull me asleep, which at last I observed, whereupon I made as though I was fast asleep, but no sleep came to my eyes, and I could not put the beheaded out of my mind. Now my lodging was directly over against the great lake, so that I could look upon it, the windows being nigh the bed. About midnight I espied on the lake a great fire, wherefore I quickly opened the window to see what would become of it. Then from far I saw seven ships making forward all full of lights. Above each of them hovered a flame that passed to and fro, and sometimes descended, so that I could lightly judge that it must needs be the spirits of the beheaded. The ships gently approached to land, and each had no more than one mariner. When they were gotten to shore, I espied our Virgin with a torch going towards them, after whom the six covered coffins, together with the little m. chest, were carried, and each was privily laid in a ship. Wherefore I awaked my Page, who hugely thanked me, for having run much up and down all day, he might quite have overslept this, though he well knew it. As soon as the coffins were laid in the ships, all the lights were extinguished, and the six flames passed back together over the lake, so that there was but one light for a watch in each ship. There were also some hundreds of watchmen encamped on the shore, who sent the Virgin back again into the Castle, she carefully bolting all up again; so that I could judge that there was nothing more to be done this night. We again betook ourselves to rest. I only of all my company had a chamber towards the lake and saw this. Then being extream weary I fell asleep in my manifold speculations.

The Fifth Day.

The night was over, and the dear wished-for day broken, when hastily I got me out of bed, more desirous to learn what might insue than that I had sufficiently slept. After I had put on my cloathes, and according to my custom was gone down stairs, it was still too early, and I found nobody else in the hall, wherefore I entreated my Page to lead me a little about the castle, and shew me somewhat that was rare, who now (as always) willing, presently lead me down certain steps underground to a great iron door, on which the following words were fixed in large copper letters:--

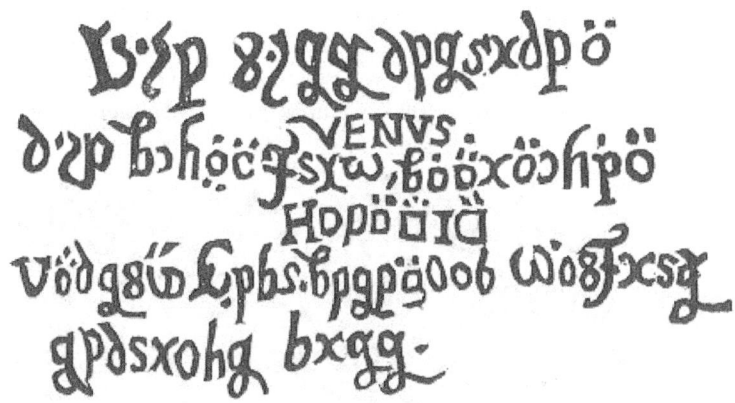

These I copied and set down in my table-book. After this door was opened, the Page lead me by the hand through a very dark passage till we came to a little door now only put too, for, as the Page informed me, it was first opened yesterday when the coffins were taken out, and had not since been shut. As soon as we stepped in I espied the most pretious thing that

Nature ever created, for this vault had no other light but from certain huge carbuncles. This was the King's Treasury, but the most glorious and principal thing was a sepulchre in the middle, so rich that I wondered it was no better guarded, whereunto the Page answered me, that I had good reason to be thankful to my planet, by whose influence I had now seen certain pieces which no humane eye (except those of the King's family) had ever viewed. This sepulcher was triangular, and had in the middle of it a kettle of polished copper, the rest was of pure gold and pretious stones. In the kettle stood an angel, who held in his arms an unknown tree, whose fruit continually falling into the kettle, turned into water therein, and ran out into three small golden kettles standing by. This little altar was supported by an eagle, an ox, and a lion, which stood on an exceeding costly base. I asked my Page what this might signifie. "Here," said he, "lies buried Lady Venus, that beauty which hath undone many a great man, both in fourtune, honour, blessing, and prosperity"; after which he showed me a copper door in the pavement, saying, "Here, if you please, we may go further down." We descended the steps, where it was exceeding dark, but the Page immediately opened a little chest in which stood a small ever-burning taper, wherefrom he kindled one of the many torches that lay by. I was mightily terrified and asked how he durst do this. He gave me for answer, "as long as the Royal Persons are still at rest I have nothing to fear." Herewith I espied a rich bed ready made, hung about with curious curtains, one of which he drew, and I saw the Lady Venus stark naked (for he heaved up the coverlets too), lying there in such beauty, and a fashion so surprising, that I was almost besides myself, neither do I yet know whether it was a piece thus carved, or an humane corps that lay dead there, for she was altogether immoveable, and yet I durst not touch her. So she was again covered, yet she was still, as it were, in my eye. But I soon espyed behind the bed a tablet on which it was thus written.

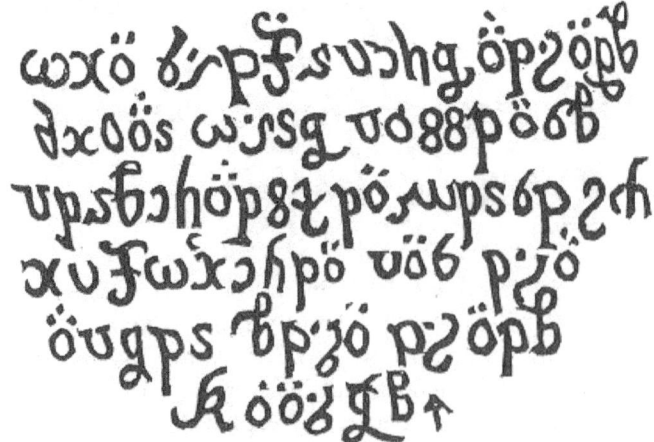

I asked my Page concerning this writing, but he laughed, with promise that I should know it too, and, he putting out the torch, we again ascended. Then I better viewed all the little doors, and found that on every corner there burned a small taper of pyrites of which I had before taken no notice, for the fire was so clear that it looked much liker a stone than a taper. From this heat the tree was forced continually to melt, yet it still produced new fruit. "Now, behold," said the Page, "when the tree shall be quite melted down, then shall Lady Venus awake and be the mother of a King." Whilst he was thus speaking, in flew the little Cupid, who at first was somewhat abashed at our presence, but seeing us both look more like the dead then the living, he could not refrain from laughing, and demanded what spirit had brought me thither, whom I with trembling answered, that I had lost my way in the castle, and was by chance come hither, that the Page had likewise been looking up and down for me, and at last lited upon me here, and that I hoped he would not take it amiss. "Nay, then, 'tis well enough yet," said Cupid, "my old busie gransir, but you might lightly have served me a scurvy trick, had you been aware of this door. I must look better to it," and so he put a strong lock on the copper door where we before descended. I thanked God that he lited upon us no sooner; my Page, too, was the more jocond because I had so well helped him at this pinch. "Yet can I not," said Cupid, "let it pass unrevenged that you were so near stumbling upon my dear mother." With that he put the point of his dart into one of the little tapers, and heating it somewhat, pricked me with it on the hand, which at that time I little regarded, but was glad that it went so well with us. Meantime my companions were gotten out of bed and were come into the hall, to whom I joyned myself, making as if I were then first risen. After Cupid had carefully made all fast again, he came likewise to us, and would needs have me shew him my hand, where he still found a little drop of blood, at which he heartily laughed, and had the rest have a care of me, as I would shortly end my days. We all wondered how he could be so merry and have no sence of yesterday's sad passages. Our President had meantime made herself ready for a journey, coming in all in black velvet, yet she and her Virgins still bare their branches of lawrel. All things being in readiness, she bid us first drink somewhat, and then presently prepare for the procession, wherefore we made no long tarrying, but followed her out of the hall into the court, where stood six coffins, and my companions thought no other but that the six Royal Persons lay in them, but I well observed the device, though I knew not what was to be done with these other. By each coffin were eight muffled men. As soon as the musick went, it was so doleful a tune that I was astonished at it, they took up the coffins, and we followed them into the Garden, in the midst of which was erected a wooden edifice, have round about the roof a glorious crown, and standing upon seven columns. Within it were formed six sepulchers; by each of them was a stone, but in the middle it had a round hollow rising stone. In these graves the coffins were quietly, and with many ceremonies, laid; the stones were shoved over them, and they shut fast, but the little chest was to lie in the middle. Herewith were my companions deceived, for they imagined that the dead corps were there. On the top of all was a great flag, having a Phœnix painted on it, perhaps the more to delude us. After the funerals were done, the Virgin, having placed herself upon the midmost stone, made a short oration, exhorting us to be constant to our ingagements, not to repine at the pains we must undergo, but be helpful in restoring the buried Royal Persons to life, and therefore, without delay, to rise and make a journey with her to the Tower of Olympus, to fetch thence the medicines necessary for this purpose.

This we soon agreed to, and followed her through another little door to the shore, where the seven ships stood empty, and on them all the Virgins stuck up their Laurel branches, and, having distributed us in the six ships, they caused us in God's name to begin our voyage, and looked upon us as long as we were in sight, after which they, with all the watchmen, returned into the Castle. Our ships had each of them a peculiar device; five of them, indeed, had the five regular bodies, each a several one, but mine, in which the Virgin too sate, carried a globe. Thus we sailed on in a singular order, and each had only two mariners. Foremost went the ship *a* in which, as I conceive, the Moor lay. In this were twelve musitians who played excellently well, and its device was a pyramid. Next followed three abreast, *b*, *c*, and *d*, in which we were disposed; I sate in *c*. Behind these came the two fairest and stateliest ships, *e* and *f*, stuck about with many branches of lawrel, and having no passengers in them; their flags were the sun and moon. But in the rear was only one ship, *g*, and in this were forty Virgins. Having passed over this lake, we came through a narrow arm into the right sea, where all the sirens, nymphs, and sea-goddesses attended us, and immediately dispatched a sea-nymph unto us to deliver their present of honour to the Wedding. It was a costly, great, set, round, and orient pearl, the like to which hath not at any time been seen,

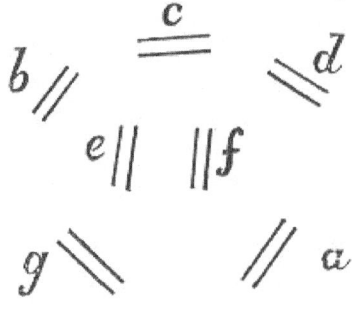

either in ours or in the new world, The Virgins having friendly received it, the nymph intreated that audience might be given to their divertisements, which the Virgin was content to give, and commanded the two great ships to stand into the middle, and to the rest to incompass them in pentagon, after which the nymphs fell into a ring about them, and with a most delicate sweet voice began thus to sing

I.

There's nothing better here below
Than beauteous, noble Love,
Whereby we like to God do grow,
And none to grief do move;
Wherefore let's chant it to the King,
That all the sea therewith may ring.
We question, answer you!

II.

What was it that at first us made?
'Twas Love.
And what hath grace afresh conveigh'd?
'Twas Love.
And whence (pray tell us!) were we born?
Of Love.
How came we then again forlorn?
Sans Love.

III.

Who was it, say, that us conceived?
'Twas Love.
Who suckled, nursed, and relieved?
'Twas Love.
What do we to our parents owe?
'Tis Love.
Why do they us such kindness show?
Of Love.

IV.

Who gets herein the victory?
'Tis Love.
Can Love by search obtained be?
By Love.
How may a man good works perform?
Through Love.
Who into one can two transform?
'Tis Love. V.

Then let our song sound,
Till its eccho rebound,
To Love's honour and praise;
May it ever increase
With our noble Princes, the King and the Queen,
The soul is departed, their body's within.

VI.

And as long as we live
God graciously give,
That as great love and amity
They bear each other mightily,
So we, likewise, by love's own flame
May reconjoyn them once again.
VII.
Then this annoy Into great joy
(If many thousand younglings deign)
Shall change, and ever so remain.

These having, with most admirable concent and melody, finished this song, I no more wondred at Ulisses for stopping the ears of his companions; I seemed to myself the most unhappy man alive that Nature had not made me too so trim a creature. But the Virgin soon dispatched them, and commanded to set sail; wherefore the nymphs, having been presented with a long red scarf for a gratuity, dispersed themselves in the sea. I was at this time sensible that Cupid began to work with me too, which tended little to my credit; but as my giddiness is likely to be nothing beneficial to the reader, I am resolved to let it rest. This was the wound that in the first book I received on my head in a dream. Let every one take warning by me of loitering about Venus' bed, for Cupid can by no means brook it. After some hours, we came within ken of the Tower of Olympus; wherefore the Virgin commanded by the discharge of some pieces to give signal of our approach, and immediately we espyed a great white flag thrust out, and a small gilded pinnace sent forth to meet us, wherein was a very antient man, the Warder of the Tower, with certain guards in white, by whom we were friendly received, and conducted to the Tower, which was situated upon an island exactly square, and invironed with a wall so firm and thick that I counted two hundred and sixty paces over. On the other side was a fine meadow with certain little gardens, in which grew strange, and to me unknown fruits. There was an inner wall about the Tower which itself was as if seven round towers had been built one by another, yet the middlemost was somewhat higher, and within they all entered one into another. Being come to the gates of the Tower, we were led a little aside on the wall, that so the coffins might be brought in without our notice, but of this the rest knew nothing. We were conducted into the Tower at the very bottom, which was an excellently painted laboratory, where we were fain to beat and wash plants, precious stones, and all sorts of things, extract their juice and essence, put up the same in glasses, and deliver them to be laid up. Our Virgin was so busie with us, and so full of directions, that she knew not how to give us employment enough, so that in this island we were meer drudges till we had atchieved all that was necessary for restoring the beheaded bodies. Meantime, as I afterwards learned, three Virgins were in the first apartment washing the corps with diligence. Having at length almost done our preparation, some broath, with a little draught of wine, was brought us, whereby I observed that we were not here for pleasure. When we had finished our day's work, everyone had a mattress laid on the ground for him, wherewith we were to content ourselves. For my part I was not much troubled with sleep, and walking out into the garden, at length came as far as the wall, where, the heaven being very clear, I could well give away the time in contemplating the stars. By chance I came to a great pair of stone stairs leading to the top of the wall, and because the moon shone very bright, I was so much the more confident, and, going up, looked too a little upon the sea, which was exceeding calm. Thus having good opportunity to consider better of astronomy, I found that this night there would happen such a conjunction of the planets, the like to which was not otherwise suddenly to be observed. Having looked a good while into the sea, and it being just about midnight, I beheld from far the seven Flames passing over sea hitherward, and betakeing themselves to the top of the spire of the tower. This made me somewhat affraid; for as soon as the Flames had settled themselves, the winds rose, and made the sea very tempestuous. The noon also was covered with clouds, and my joy ended with such fear that I had scarce time enough to hit upon the stairs again, and betake myself to the Tower, where I laid me down upon my mattress, and there being in the laboratory a pleasant and gently purling fountain, I fell asleep so much the sooner. And thus this fifth day too was concluded with wonders.

The Sixth Day.

Next morning, after we had awaked another, we sate together to discourse what might be the wont of things. Some were of opinion that the corps should all be inlivened again together. Others contradicted this, because the decease of the ancients was not only to restore life but increase too to the young ones. Some imagined that they were not put to death, but that others were beheaded in their stead. Having talked a pretty while, in comes the old man, and first saluting us, looks about to see if all things were ready. We had herein so behaved ourselves that he had no fault to find with our diligence, whereupon he placed all the glasses together, and put them into a case. Presently come certain youths, bringing ladders, roapes, and large wings, which they laid before us and departed. Then the old man began thus:--"My dear Sons, one of these three things must each of you this day constantly bear about with him. It is free for you to make choice of one of them, or to cast lots." We replied that we would choose. "Nay," said he, "let it rather go by lot. Hereupon he made three little schedules, writing on one Ladder, on the second Rope, on the third Wings. These he laid in an hat; each man must draw, and whatever he happened on was to be his. Those who got ropes imagined themselves in the best case; but I chanced on a ladder, which hugely afflicted me, for it was twelve-foot long, pretty weighty, and I must be forced to carry it, whereas the others could handsomely coyle their ropes about them, and as for the wings, the old man joyned them so neatly on to the third sort as if they had grown upon them. Hereupon he turned the cock, and the fountain ran no longer, and we were fain to remove it out of the way. After all things were carried off, he, taking with him the casket and glasses, took leave, and locked the door after him, so we imagined that we had been imprisoned in this Tower; but it was hardly a quarter of an hour before a round hole above was uncovered, where we saw our Virgin, who bad us good morrow, desiring us to come up. They with the wings were instantly through the hole; only they with the ropes were in an evil plight, for as soon as ever one of us was up, he was commanded to draw up the ladder to him. At last each man's rope was hanged on an iron hook, and he climbed up as well as he could, which indeed was not compassed without blisters. When we were all well up, the hole was again covered, and we were friendly received by the Virgin. This room was the whole breadth of the Tower itself, having six very stately vestries a little raised and reached by three steps. In these we were distributed to pray for the life of the King and Queen. Meanwhile the Virgin went in and out at the little door *a* till we had done. As soon as our process was absolved, there was brought in through the little door by twelve persons, which were formerly our musitians, a wonderful thing of longish shape, which my companions took to be a fountain, and which was placed in the middle. I well observed that the corps lay in it, for the inner chest was of an oval figure, so large that six persons might well lie therein one by another. After this they again went forth, fetched their instruments, and conducted in our Virgin, with her she-attendants, to a most delicate voice of musick. The Virgin carried a little casket, the rest only branches, and small lamps or lighted torches, which last were immediately given into our hands, and we stood about the fountain in this order.

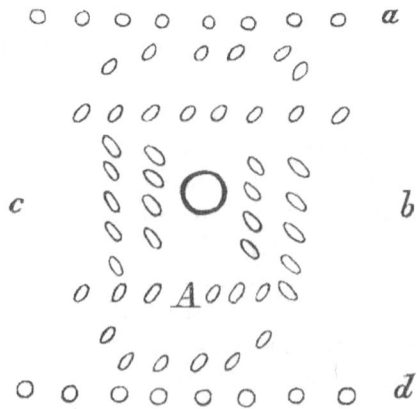

100

First stood the Virgin A, with her attendants in a ring round about, with the lamps and branches *c*. Next stood we with our torches *b*, then the musitians in a long rank; last of all, the rest of the Virgins *d*, in another long rank. Whence the Virgins came, whether they dwelt in the Castle, or were brought in by night, I know not, for their faces were covered with delicate white linnen. The Virgin opened the casket, in which was a round thing wrapped in a piece of green double taffata. This she laid in the uppermost kettle, and covered it with the lid, which was full of holes, and had besides a rim, on which she poured in some of the water which we had the day before prepared; the fountain began immediately began to run, and through four small pipes to drive into the little kettle. Beneath the undermost kettle were many sharp points, on which the Virgins stuck their lamps, that the heat might come to the kettle and make the water seeth, which, when it began to simper, by many little holes at a, fell in upon the bodies, and was so hot that it dissolved them all, and turned them into liquor. What the above-said round wrapt-up thing was, my companions knew not, but I understood that it was the Moor's head, from which the water conceived so great heat. At *b*, round about the great kettle, there were again many holes, in which they stuck their branches, but whether this was done of necessity or for ceremony I know not. However, these branches were continually sprinkled by the fountain, whence it afterwards dropt somewhat of a deeper yellow into the kettle. This lasted for near two hours, the fountain still running, but more faintly. Meantime the musitians went their way, and we walked up and down in the room, which truly was so made that we had opportunity enough to pass away our time. There were images, paintings, clock-works, organs, springing fountains, and the like. When it was near the time that the fountain ceased, the Virgin commanded a golden globe to be brought. At the bottom of the fountain was a tap, by which she let out all the matter dissolved by those hot drops (whereof certain quarts were then very red) into the globe. The rest of the water above in the kettle was poured out, and so this fountain was again carried forth. Whether it was opened abroad, or whether anything of the bodies that was useful yet remained, I dare not certainly say, but the water emptied into the globe was much heavier than six or more of us were able to bear, albeit for its bulk it should have seemed not too heavy for one man. This globe being with much ado gotten out of doors, we again sate alone, but I, perceiving a trampling over head, had an eye to my ladder. After one quarter of an hour, the cover above was lifted, and we commanded to come up, which we did as before, with wings, ladders, and ropes, and it did not a little vex me that whereas the Virgins could go up another way, we were fain to take so much toil; yet I could judge there must be some special reason for it, and we must leave somewhat for the old man to do too. The hole being again shut fast, I saw the globe hanging by a strong chain in the middle of the room, in which there was nothing but windows, with a door between every two, which was covered with a great polished looking-glass. These windows and looking-glasses were so optically opposed that although the sun, which now shined exceeding bright, beat only upon one door, yet (after the windows towards the sun were opened, and the doors before the looking-glasses drawn aside) in all quarters of the room there was nothing but suns, which by artificial refractions beat upon the whole golden globe hanging in the midst, which, being polished, gave such a lustre that none of us could open our eyes, but were forced to look out at windows till the globe was well heated, and brought to the desired effect. In these mirrors I saw the most wonderful spectacles that ever nature brought to light, for there were suns in all places, and the globe in the middle shined brighter yet. At length the virgin commanded to shut up the looking-glasses and make fast the windows to let the globe cool a little, wherefore we thought good, since we might now have leisure, to refresh ourselves with a breakfast. This treatment was again right philosophical, and we had no need to be afraid of intemperance, though we had no want, while the hope of the future joy, with which the virgin continually comforted us, made us so jocond that we regarded not any pains or inconvenience. I can truly say concerning my companions of high quality that their minds never ran after their kitchen or table, but their pleasure was only to attend on this adventurous physic, and hence to contemplate the Creator's wisdom and omnipotency. After our refection we settled ourselves to work, for the globe was sufficiently cooled, which with toil and labour we were to lift off the chain and set upon the floor. The dispute then was how we were to get the globe in sunder, for we were commanded to divide it in the midst. The conclusion was that a sharp-pointed diamond would be best to do it, and when we had thus opened the globe, there was no redness to be seen, but a lovely great snow-white egg, and it mightily rejoyced us that this was so well brought to pass, for the virgin was in perpetual care least the shell might still be too tender. We stood around about this egg as jocond as if we ourselves had laid it, but the Virgin made it presently be carried forth, and departed herself, locking the door behind her. What she did abroad with the egg, or whether it were privately handled, I know not, neither do I believe it. We were again to pause for one quarter of an hour, till the third hole opened, and we, by means of our instruments, came upon the fourth stone or floor. In this room we found a great copper kettle filled with silver sand, which was warmed with a gentle fire, and afterwards the egg was raked up in it, that it might therein come to perfect maturity. This kettle was exactly square. Upon one side stood these two verses writ in great letters--

O. BLI. TO. BIT. MI. LI.

KANT. I. VOLT. BIT. TO. GOLT. On the second side were these three words--

SANITAS. NIX. HASTA.

  The third had but this one word--

F.I.A.T.

  But on the hindmost part stood an entire inscription, running thus--

QUOD

Ignis: Aer: Aqua: Terra:

  SANCTIS REGUM ET REGINARUM NOSTR:

  Cineribus

Eripere non potuerunt.

  Fidelis Chymicorum Turba

  IN HANC URNAM

  Contulit.

Aó

Now, whether the sand or egg were hereby meant I leave the learned to dispute. Our egg, being ready, was taken out, but it needed no cracking, for the Bird soon freed himself, looking very jocond, though bloody and unshapen. We first set him on the warm sand, the Virgin commanding that before we gave him anything to eat we should be sure to make him fast, otherwise he would give us all work enough. This being done, food was brought him, which surely was nothing but the blood of the beheaded deluted with prepared water, by which the Bird grew so fast under our eye that we well saw why the Virgin gave such warning of him. He bit and scratched so devilishly that, could he have had his will upon any of us, he would soon have dispatched him. Now he was wholly black and wild, wherefore other meat was brought him, perhaps the blood of another of the Royal Persons, whereupon all his black feathers moulted and were replaced by snow-white ones. He was somewhat tamer too, and more tractable, though we did not yet trust him. At the third feeding his feathers began to be so curiously coloured that I never saw the like for beauty. He was also exceedingly tame, and behaved himself so friendly with us that, the Virgin consenting, we released him from captivity. "'Tis now reason," she began, "since by your diligence, and our old man's consent, the Bird has attained with his life and the highest perfection, that he be also joyfully consecrated by us." Herewith she commanded to bring in dinner, since the most troublesome part of our work was now over, and it was fit we should begin to enjoy our passed labours. We began to make merry together. Howbeit, we had still our mourning cloaths on, which seemed somewhat reproachful to our mirth. The Virgin was perpetually inquisitive, perhaps to find to which of us her future purpose might prove serviceable, but her discourse was, for the most part, about Melting, and it pleased her well when any one seemed expert in such compendious manuals as do peculiarly commend an artist. This dinner lasted not above three-quarters of an hour, which we yet, for the most part, spent with our Bird, whom we were fain constantly to feed with his meat, though he continued much at the same growth. After Dinner we were not long suffered to digest our food, for the Virgin, together with the Bird, departed from us, and the fifth room was opened, which we reached after the former manner, and tendred our service. In this room a bath was prepared for our Bird, which was so coloured with a fine white powder that it had the appearance of milk. It was cool when the Bird was set into it, and he was mighty well pleased with it, drinking of it, and pleasantly sporting in it. But after it began to heat, by reason of the lamps placed under it, we had enough to do to keep him in the bath. We, therefore, clapt a cover on the kettle, and suffered him to thrust out his head through a hole, till he had lost all his feathers in this bath, and was as smooth as a new-born babe, yet the heat did him no further harm. In this bath the feathers were quite consumed, and the bath was thereby turned into blew. At length we gave the Bird air, who of himself sprung out of the kettle, and was so glitteringly smooth that it was a pleasure to behold him. But because he was still somewhat wild, we were fain to put a collar, with a chain, about his neck, and so led him up and down the room. Meantime a strong fire was made under the kettle, and the bath sodden away till it all came to a blew stone, which we took out, and, having pounded it, we ground it on a stone, and finally with this colour painted the Bird's whole skin over, who then looked much more strangely, for he was all blew except the head, which remained white. Herewith our work in this story was performed, and we, after the Virgin with her blew Bird was departed from us, were called up a hole to the sixth story, where we were mightily troubled, for in the midst a little altar, every way like that in the King's hall, was placed. Upon it stood the six forementioned particulars, and he himself (the Bird) made the seventh. First of all the little fountain was set before him, out of which Ile drunk a good draught; afterwards he pecked upon the white serpent till she bled mightily. This blood we received in a golden cup, and poured down the Bird's throat, who was mighty averse from it; then we dipt the serpent's head in the fountain, upon which she again revived, and crept into her death's head, so that I saw her no more for a long time. Meanwhile the sphere turned constantly on until it made the desired conjunction. Immediately the watch struck one, upon which there was going another conjunction. Then the watch struck two. Finally, whilst we were observing the third conjunction, and the same was indicated by the watch, the poor Bird of himself submissively laid down his neck upon the book, and willingly suffered his head to be smitten off by one of us, thereto chosen by lot. Howbeit he yielded not one drop of blood till he was opened on the breast, and then the blood spun out so fresh and clear as if it had been a fountain of rubies. His death went to the heart of us, yet we might well judge that a naked bird would stand us in little stead. We removed the little altar, and assisted the Virgin to burn the body, together with the little tablet hanging by, to ashes, with fire kindled at the little taper, afterwards to cleanse the same several times, and to lay them in a box of cypress wood. Here I cannot conceal what a trick I, with three more, was served. After we had diligently taken up the ashes, the Virgin began to speak thus:--"My Lords, we are here in the sixth room, and have only one more before us, in which our trouble will be at an end, and we shall return home to our castle to awaken our most gratious Lords and Ladies. Now albeit I could heartily wish that all of you had behaved yourselves in such sort that I might have given your commendations to our most renowned King and Queen, and you have obtained a suitable reward, yet because, contrary to my desire, I have found amongst you these four"-- pointing at me and three others--"lazy and sluggish labourators, and yet according to my good-will to all, I am not willing to deliver them to condign punishment. However, that such negligence may not remain wholly unpunished, I purpose that they shall be excluded from the future seventh and most glorious action of all the rest, and so they shall incur no further blame from their Royal Majesties."

In what a case we now were I leave others to consider, for the Virgin so well knew how to keep her countenance that the water soon ran over our baskets, and we esteemed ourselves the most unhappy of all men. The Virgin by one of her maids, whereof there were many always at hand, caused the musitians to be fetcht, who were with cornets to blow us out of doors with such scorn and derision that they themselves could hardly sound for laughing. But it did particularly afflict us that the Virgin vehemently laughed at our weeping, and that there might be some amongst our companions who were glad of our misfortune. But it proved otherwise, for as soon as we were come out at the door the musitians bid us be of good cheere, and follow them up the winding staires to the eighth floor under the roof, where we found the old man standing upon a little round furnace. He received us friendly, and heartily congratulated us that we were hereto chosen by the Virgin; but after he had understood the fright we had conceived, his belly was ready to burst with laughing that we had taken such good fortune so hainously. "Hence," said he, "my dear sons, learn that man never knoweth how well God intendeth him." The Virgin also came running in, who, after she had sufficiently laughed at us, emptied her ashes into another vessel, filling hers again with other matter, saying, she must now cast a mist before the other artist's eyes, that we in the mean time should obey the old lord, and not remit our former diligence. Herewith she departed from us into the seventh room, whither she called our companions. What she first did with them I cannot tell, for they were not only most earnestly forbidden to speak of it, but we, by reason of our business, durst not peep on them through the cieling. Our work was to moisten the ashes with our fore-prepared water till they became like a very thin dough, after which we set the matter over the fire till it was well heated; then we cast it into two little forms or moulds, and so let it cool a little, when we had leisure to look on our companions through certain crevises in the floor. They were busie at a furnace, and each was himself fain to blow up the fire with a pipe, till he was ready to lose his breath. They imagined they were herein wonderfully preferred before us. This blowing lasted till our old man rouzed us to work again. We opened our little forms, and there appeared two bright and almost transparent little images, a male and a female, the like to which man's eye never saw, each being but four inches long, and that which most mightily surprised me was that they were not hard, but limber and fleshy as other human bodies; yet had they no life, so that I assuredly believe that Lady Venus' image was made after some such way. These angelically fair babes we laid upon two little sattin cushonets, and beheld them till we were almost besotted upon so exquisite an object. The old lord warned us to forbear, and continually to instil the blood of the bird, which had been received in a little golden cup, drop after drop into the mouths of the little images, from whence they apparently encreased, becoming according to proportion much more beautiful. They grew so big that we lifted them from the little cushonets, and were fain to lay them upon a long table covered with white velvet. The old man commanded us to cover them up to the breast with a piece of fine white double taffata, which, because of their unspeakable beauty, almost went against us. Before we had in this manner quite spent the blood, they were in their perfect full growth, having gold-yellow curled hair, and the figure of Venus was nothing to them. But there was not yet any natural warmth or sensibility in them; they were dead figures, yet of a lively and natural colour; and since care was to be taken that they grew not too great, the old man would not permit anything more to be given them, but covered their faces too with the silk, and caused the table to be stuck round about with torches. Let the reader imagine not these lights to have been of necessity, for the old man's intent was that we should not observe when the Soul entred into them, as indeed we should not have taken notice of it, in case I had not twice before seen the flames. However, I permitted the other three to remain in their belief, neither did the old man know that I had seen anything more. Hereupon he bid us sit down on a bench over against the table. The Virgin came in with the musick and all furniture, and carried two curious white garments, the like to which I had never seen in the Castle. I thought no other but that they were meer christal, but they were gentle and not

106

transparent. These she laid upon a table, and after she had disposed her Virgins upon a bench round about, she and the old man began many *leger-de-main* tricks about the table, which were done only to blind. All this was managed under the roof, which was wonderfully formed, for on the inside it was arched into seven hemispheres, of which the middlemost was somewhat the highest, and had at top a little round hole, which was shut and was observed by none but myself. After many ceremonies stept in six Virgins, each of which bare a large trumpet, rouled about with a green, glittering, and burning material like a wreath, one of which the old man took, and after he had removed some of the lights at top, and uncovered their faces, he placed one of the trumpets upon the mouth of one of the bodies in such manner that the upper and wider part of it was directed towards the fore-mentioned hole. Here my companions always looked upon the images, but as soon as the foliage or wreath about the shank of the trumpet was kindled, I saw the hole at top open and a bright stream of fire shoot down the tube and pass into the body, whereupon the hole was again covered, and the trumpet removed. With this device my companions were deluded into imagining that life came to the image by the fire of the foliage, for as soon as he received his Soul he twinckled his eyes though scarcely stirring. The second time he placed another tube upon its mouth, kindled it again, and the Soul was let down through the tube. This was repeated upon each of them three times, after which all the lights were extinguished and carried away. The velvet carpets of the table were cast together over them, and immediately a travelling bed was unlocked and made ready, into which, thus wrapped up, they were born, and, after the carpets were taken off them, neatly laid by each other, where, with the curtains drawn before them, they slept a good while. It was now time for the Virgin to see how the other artists behaved themselves; they were well pleased because they were to work in gold, which is indeed a piece of this art, but not the most principal, necessary, and best. They had too a part of these ashes, so that they imagined that the whole Bird was provided for the sake of gold, and that life must thereby be restored to the deceased. Mean time we sate very still, attending when our married couple would awake, and thus about half an hour was spent. Then the wanton Cupid presented himself, and, after he had saluted us all, flew to them behind the curtain, tormenting them till they waked. This happened to them with very great amazement, for they imagined that they had slept from the hour in which they were beheaded. Cupid, after he had awaked them, and renewed their acquaintance one with another, stepped aside and permitted them to recruit their strength, mean time playing his tricks with us, and at length he would needs have the musick fetcht to be somewhat the merrier. Not long after the Virgin herself comes, and having most humbly saluted the young King and Queen, who found themselves somewhat faint, and having kissed their hands, she brought them the two fore-mentioned curious garments, which they put on, and so stepped forth. There were already prepared two very curious chaires, wherein they placed themselves, and were by us with most profound reverence congratulated, for which the King in his own person most gratiously returned his thanks, and again re-assured us of all grace. It was already about five of clock, wherefore they could make no longer stay; but as soon as ever the chiefest of their furniture could be laden, we were to attend the young Royal Persons down the stairs, through all doors and watches unto the ship, in which they inbarqued, together with certain Virgins and Cupid, and sailed so swiftly that we soon lost sight of them, yet they were met, as I was informed, by certain stately ships, and in four hours time had made many leagues out at sea. After five of clock the musitians were charged to carry all things back to the ships, and to make themselves ready for the voyage, but because this was somewhat long a doing, the old lord commanded forth a party of his concealed soldiers, who had hitherto been planted in the wall so that we had taken no notice of any of them, whereby I observed that this tower was well guarded against opposition. These soldiers made quick work of our stuff, so that no more remained to be done but to go to supper. The table being compleatly furnished, the Virgin brings us again to our companions, where we were to carry ourselves as if we had truly been in a lamentable condition, while they were always smiling one upon another, though some of them too simpathized with us. At this supper the old lord was with us, who was a most sharp inspector over us, for none could propound anything so discreetly but that he knew how to confute or amend it, or at least to give some good document upon it. I learned most by this lord, and it were good that each would apply himself to him, and take notice of his procedure, for then things would not so often and untowardly miscarry. After we had taken our nocturnal refection, the old lord led us into his closets of rarities, dispersed among the bulworks, where we saw such wonderful productions of nature, and other things which man's wit in imitation of nature had invented, that we needed a year sufficiently to survey them. Thus we spent a good part of the night by candle-light. At last, because we were more inclined to sleep then see many rarities, we were lodged in rooms in the wall, where we had not only costly good beds but extraordinary handsome chambers, which made us the more wonder why we were forced the day before to undergo so many hardships. In this chamber I had good rest, and, being for the most part without care, and weary with continual labour, the gentle rushing of the sea helped me to a sound and sweet sleep, for I continued in one dream from eleven of clock till eight in the morning.

The Seventh Day.

After eight of clock I awaked, and quickly made myself ready, being desirous to return again into the tower, but the dark passages in the wall were so many that I wandered a good while before I could find the way out. The same happened to the rest, till we all meet in the nethermost vault, and habits intirely yellow were given us, together with our golden fleeces. At that time the Virgin declared o us that we were Knights of the **𝕲𝖔𝖑𝖉𝖊𝖓 𝕾𝖙𝖔𝖓𝖊**, of which we were before ignorant. After we had made ourselves ready, and taken our breakfast, the old man presented each of us with a medal of gold. On the one side stood these words--

AR. NAT. MI.

On the other these,

TEM. NA. F.

exhorting us to enterprize nothing beyond and against this token of remembrance. Herewith we went forth to the sea, where our ships lay so richly equipped that it was not well possible but that such brave things must first have been brought thither. The ships were twelve in number, six of ours and six of the old lord's, who caused his to be freighted with well-appointed soldiers. But he betook himself to us in our ship, where we were all together. In the first the musitians seated themselves, of which the old lord had also a great number. They sailed before us to shorten the time. Our flags were the twelve celestial signs, and we sate in Libra. Besids other things our ship had a noble and curious clock which showed us all the minutes. The sea was so calm that it was a singular pleasure to sail, but that which surpassed all was the old man's discourse, who so well knew how to pass away our time with wonderful histories that I could have been content to sail with him all my life long. The ships passed on, and before we had sailed two hours the mariner told us that he saw the whole lake almost covered with ships, by which we conjectured they were come out to meet us, which proved true, for as soon as we were gotten out of the sea into the lake of the forementioned river, there stood in to us five hundred ships, one of which sparkled with gold and pretious stones, and in it sate the King and Queen, with lords, ladies, and virgins of high birth. As soon as they were well in ken of us the pieces were discharged on both sides, and there was such a din of trumpets, shalms, and kettle-drums, that all the ships upon the sea capered again. As soon as we came near, they brought about our ships together and so made a stand. Old Atlas stepped forth on the King's behalf, making a short but handsom oration, wherein he wellcomed us, and demanded whether the royal Presents were in readiness. The rest of my companions were in an huge amazement whence this King should arise, for they imagined no other but that they must again awaken him. We suffered them to continue in their wonderment, and carried ourselves as if it seemed strange to us too. After Atlas' oration out steps our old man, making somewhat a larger reply, wherein he wished the King and Queen all happiness and increase, after which he delivered a curious small casket, but what was in it I know not. It was committed to the custody of Cupid, who hovered between them both. After the oration they again let off a joyful volle of shot, and so we sailed on a good time together, till we arrived at another shore, near the first gate at which I first entred. At this place there attended a great multitude of the King's family, together with some hundreds of horses. As soon as we were come to shore and disembarqued, the King and Queen presented their hands to all of us, one with another, with singular kindness, and so we were to get up on horseback. Here I desire to have the reader friendly entreated not to interpret the following narration to any vain glory of mine, but to credit me that had there been not a special necessity in it, I could well have concealed the honour which was shewed me. We were all distributed amongst the lords, but our old lord and I, most unworthy, were to ride even with the King, each of us bearing a snow-white ensign with a Red Cross. I indeed was made use of because of my age, for we both had long grey beards and hair. I had besides fastened my tokens round about my hat, of which the young King soon took notice, and demanded if I were he who could at the gate redeem these tokens. I answered yes in the most humble manner, but he laughed on me, saying there henceforth needed no ceremony, I was ms Father. Then he asked me wherewith I had redeemed them. I answered, "With Water and Salt," whereupon he wondred who had made me so wise, upon which I grew somewhat more confident, and recounted how it had happened to me with my Bread, the Dove, and the Raven; he was pleased with it, and said expressly, that it must needs be that God had herein vouchsafed me a singular happiness. Herewith we came to the first gate, where the porter with the blew cloaths waited, bearing in his hand a supplication. As soon as he spied me even with the king, he delivered me the supplication, most humbly beseeching me to mention his ingenuity before me towards the King; so, in the first place, I demanded of his majesty what the condition of this porter was, who friendly answered me, that he was a very famous and rare astrologer, always in high regard with the Lord his Father, but having on a time committed a fault against Venus, and beheld her in her bed of rest, this punishment was imposed upon him, that he should so long wait at the gate till some one should release him from thence. I replyed, "May he then be released?" "Yes," said the King, "if anyone can be Found that hath as highly transgressed as himself, he must stand in his stead, and the other shall be free. This word went to my heart; conscience convinced me that I was the offender, yet I held my peace and delivered the supplication. As soon as the King had read it, he was mightily terrified, so that the Queen, who, with our virgins and that other queen whom I mentioned at the hanging of the weights, rid behind us, asked him what the letter might signifie; but he, putting up the paper, began to discourse of other matters, till in about three hours we came quite to the Castle, where we alighted and waited upon the King into his hall, who called immediately for the old Atlas to come to him in a little closet, and showed him the writing. Atlas made no long tarrying, but rid out to the porter to take better cognizance of the matter, after which the young King, with his spouse and other Lords, Ladies, and Virgins sate down. Then began our Virgin highly to commend the diligence we had used, and the pains and labour we had undergone, requesting we might be royally rewarded, and that she henceforward might be permitted to enjoy the benefit of her commission. The old lord stood up too, and attested the truth of all that the Virgin had spoken, and that it was but equity that we should on both parts be contented. Hereupon we were to step out a little; it was concluded that each man should make some possible wish, and were to consider of it till after supper. Meantime the King and Queen, for recreation's sake, began to play together. It looked not unlike chesse, only it had other laws, for it was the vertues and vices one against another, where it might be ingeniously observed with what plots the vices lay in wait for the vertues, and how to re encounter them again. This was so properly and artificially performed that it were to be wished that we had the like game too. During the game in comes Atlas again, and makes his report in private, yet I blushed all over, for my conscience gave me no rest. The King presented me the supplication to read, the contents whereof were to this purpose: First, the writer wished the King prosperity and peace, and that his seed might be spread far and wide. Afterwards he remonstrated that the time was now come wherein, according to the royal promise, he ought to be released; because Yen us was already uncovered by one of his guests, for his observations could not lie to him, and that if his Majesty would please to make strict and diligent enquiry, in case this should not prove to be, he would remain before the gate all the days of his life. Then he humbly sued that, upon peril of body and life, he might be present at this night's supper, being in good hopes to spye out the offender and obtain his wished freedom. This was handsomly indited, and I could well perceive his ingenuity, but it was too sharp for me, and I could well have endured never to have seen it. Casting in my mind whether he might perchance be helped through my wish, I asked the King whether he might not be released some other way, but he replyed no, because there was special consideration in the business, but for this night we might gratifie his desire, so he sent one forth to fetch him in. Mean time the tables were prepared in a spatious room, in which we had never before been, which was so compleat that it is not possible for me to describe it. Into this we were conducted with singular ceremony. Cupid was not present, for the disgrace which had happened to his mother had somewhat angered him. In brieff, my offence, and the supplication which had been delivered, were the occasion of much sadness, for the King was in perplexity how to make inquisition amongst his guests. He caused the porter himself to make his strict surveigh, and showed himself as pleasant as he was able. Howbeit, at length they began again to be merry, and to bespeak one another with all sorts of recreative, profitable discourses. The treatment and other ceremonies then performed it is not necessary to declare, since it is neither the reader's concern nor serviceable to my design, but all exceeded more in invention than that we were overcharged with drinking. This was the last and noblest meal at which I was present. After the bancket the tables were suddainly taken away, and certain curious chairs placed round in circle, in which we, together with the King and Queen, both their old men, the Ladies and Virgins, were to sit. After this a very handsom Page opened the above mentioned glorious little book, when Atlas, immediately placing himself in the midst, bespoke us to the ensuing purpose:--That his Royal Majesty had not yet committed to oblivion the service we had done him, and therefore by way of retribution had elected each of us Knights of the Golden Stone. That it was, therefore, further necessary not only once again to, oblige ourselves towards his Royal Majesty, but to vow upon the following articles, and then His Royal Highness would likewise know how to behave himself towards his high people. Upon which he caused the Page to read over these articles:--

I. You, my Lords the Knights, shall swear that you will at no time ascribe your order either unto any Devil or Spirit, but only to God, your Creator, and His hand-maid Nature.

II. That you will abominate all whoredom, incontinency, and uncleanness, and not defile your order with such vices.

III. That you, through your talents, will be ready to assist all that are worthy and have need of them.

IV. That you desire not to employ this honour to worldly pride and high authority.

V. That you shall not be willing to live longer than God will have you.

At this last article we could not choose but laugh, and it may well have been placed there for a conceit. Now, being sworn them all by the King's scepter, we were afterwards, with the usual ceremonies, installed Knights, and, amongst other privileges, set over ignorance, poverty, and sickness, to handle them at our pleasure. This was afterwards ratified in a little chappel, whither we were conducted in procession, and thanks returned to God for it. There I also at that time, to the honour of God, hung up my golden fleece and hat, and left them for an eternal memorial. And because every one was to write his name there, I writ thus:--

Summa Scientia nihil Scire,

Fr. CHRISTIANUS ROSENCREUTZ.

Eques aurei Lapidis.

Anno. 1459.

Others writ differently, each as seemed him good; after which we were again brought into the hall, where, being sate down, we were admonished quickly to bethink ourselves what every one would wish. The King and his party retired into a little closet to give audience to our wishes. Each man was called in severally, so that I cannot speak of any man's proper wish; but I thought nothing could be more praiseworthy than, in honour of my order, to demonstrate some laudable vertue, and found that none at present could be more famous and cost me more trouble than gratitude; wherefore, not regarding that I might well have wished somewhat more agreeable to myself, I vanquished myself, and concluded, even with my own peril, to free the porter, my benefactor. Being called in, I was first demanded whether, having read the supplication, I had suspected nothing concerning the offendor, upon which I began undauntedly to relate how all the business had passed, how, through ignorance, I fell into that mistake, and so offered myself to undergo all that I had thereby demerited. The King and the rest of the Lords wondred mightily at so un-hoped for confession, and wished me to step aside a little; and as soon as I was called in again, Atlas declared to me that, although it were grievous to the King's Majesty that I, whom he loved above others, was fallen into such a mischance, yet, because it was not possible for him to transgress his ancient usages, he knew not how else to absolve me but that the other must be at liberty and I placed in his stead; yet he would hope that some other would soon be apprehended, that so I might be able to go home again. However, no release was to be hoped for till the marriage feast of his future son. This sentence near cost me my life, and I first hated myself and my twatling tongue in that I could not hold my peace; yet at last I took courage, and, because I considered there was no remedy, I related how this porter had bestowed a token on me and commended me to the other, by whose assistance I stood upon the scale, and so was made partaker of all the honour and joy already received. And therefore now it was equal that I should show myself grateful to my benefactor, and was willing gently to sustain inconvenience for his sake, who had been helpful to me in coming to so high place; but if by my wish anything might be effected, I wished myself at home again, and that so he by me, as I by my wish, might be at liberty. Answer was made me, that the wishing stretched not so far, yet it was very pleasing to his Royal Majesty that I had behaved myself so generously, but he was affraid I might still be ignorant into what a miserable condition I had plunged myself through this curiosity. Hereupon the good man was pronounced free, and I, with a sad heart, was fain to step aside. The rest were called for after me, and came jocundly out again, which was still more to my smart, for I imagined no other but that I must finish my life under the gate. I had also many pensive thoughts running in my head as to what I should yet undertake, and wherewith to spend the time. At length I considered that I was now old, and, according to the course of Nature, had few more years to live, that this anguish and melancholy life would easily dispatch me, and then my doorkeeping would be at an end, and that by a most happy sleep I might quickly bring myself into the grave. Sometimes it vexed me that I had seen such gallant things, and must be robbed of them; sometimes it rejoyced me that before my end I had been accepted to all joy, and should not be forced so shamefully to depart. Thus this was the last and worst shock that I sustained. During these my cogitations the rest were ready, wherefore, after they had received a good night from the King and Lords, each was conducted into his lodging, but I, most wretched man, had nobody to show me the way, and yet must suffer myself to be tormented. That I might be certain of my future function, I was fain to put on the Ring which the other had worn. Finally, the King exhorted me that, since this was the last time I was like to see him in this manner, I should behave myself according to my place, and not against the Order, upon which he took me in his arms and kissed me, all which I understood as if in the morning I must sit at my gate. After they had all spoken friendly to me, and at last presented their hands, committing me to the divine protection, I was by both the old men--the Lord of the Tower and Atlas--conducted into a glorious lodging, in which stood three beds, and each of us lay in one of them, where we yet spent almost two, &c.

Here are wanting about two leaves in quarto, and he (the author hereof), whereas he imagined he must in the morning be door-keeper, returned home.

CHAPTER VI. ON THE CONNECTION OF THE ROSICRUCIAN CLAIMS WITH THOSE OF ALCHEMY AND MAGIC.

THE guise of antiquity being almost indispensable to the pretensions contained in these singular documents, I have preferred presenting them to my readers in the archaic form of the original English translations, which, moreover, represent the Rosicrucian period in this country, than to undertake the somewhat superfluous task of a new version.

If the "Fama" and "Confessio Fraternitatis" are to be taken in their literal sense, the publication of these documents will not add new lustre to Rosicrucian reputations. We are accustomed to regard the adepts of the Rose-Cross as beings of sublime elevation and preternatural physical powers, masters of Nature, monarchs of the intellectual world, illuminated by a relative omniscience, and absolutely exalted above all weakness and all prejudice. We imagine them to be "holding no form of creed, but contemplating all" from the solitary grandeur of the Absolute, and invested with the "sublime sorrow of the ages as of the lone ocean." But here in their own acknowledged manifestoes they avow themselves a mere theosophical offshoot of the Lutheran heresy, acknowledging the spiritual supremacy of a temporal prince, and calling the pope Antichrist. We have gauged in these days of enlightenment and universal tolerance the intellectual capacities of all professors, past and present, of that art prophetic which is represented by Baxter and Cumming. We know the value of all the multitudinous speculations in the theological no-man's land of the Apocalypse. We do not expect a new Star of Jacob to rise out of the Galilee of religious intolerance, and out of the frantic folly of sectarian squabblings. We do not calculate the number of the beast, we do not denounce the Jesuits, we are not obsessed by an infectious terror of papal power and its possible agressions; on the contrary, we respect the associations connected with sovereign pontiffs, grand lamas, and chief patriarchs. We have, most of us, decided that the pope is neither God's vicar nor the Man of Sin; we persistently refuse our adherence to any theory which connects *the little horn* with Prince Jerome Napoleon, and we are not open to any positive convictions on the identity of the Scarlet Woman, or of the lost tribes of Israel. All persons possessed of such positive convictions we justifiably regard as fanatics, and after due and deliberate consideration of the Rosicrucian manifestoes, we do Dot feel able to make an exception in favour of this Fraternity, whose

"Manners have not that repose
Which marks the caste of Vere de Vere."

In other words, we find them intemperate in their language, rabid in their religious prejudices, and, instead of towering giant-like above the intellectual average of their age, we see them buffeted by the same passions and identified with all the opinions of the men by whom they were environed. The voice which addresses us behind the mystical mask of the Rose-Cross does not come from an intellectual throne, erected on the pinnacles of high thinking and surrounded by the serene and sunny atmosphere of a far-sighted tolerance; it comes from the very heart of the vexatious and unprofitable strife of sects, and it utters the war-cry of extermination. The scales fall from our eyes, the romance vanishes; we find ourselves in the presence of some Germans of the period, not of "the mystic citizens of the eternal kingdom."

We are dejected and disillusioned, but we are thankful, notwithstanding, to know the truth, as distinguished from the fictions of Mr Hargrave Jennings and the glamorous fables of professed romancers. In this spirit we proceed to a closer acquaintance with the Rosicrucians as represented by themselves.

I have already said that "The Universal Reformation" has little internal connection with the society which is supposed to have issued it in its Teutonic dress. The conclusion which is reached in that curious tract is, indeed, completely opposed to the expressed hopes of the Fraternity. It illustrates the ludicrous futility and abortiveness of the attempt to reform society, even when undertaken by the flower of the world's "literati." It bids the reformers begin their work at home, and reduces their Utopian scheming from the splendid scale of universal reconstruction to appraising sprats and cabbages. It considers mankind to be as good as his surroundings will allow him, and that "the height of human wisdom lies in the discretion to be content with leaving the world as they found it." On the other hand, the "Fama" and "Confessio" invite "the learned of Europe to co-operate with a secret society for the renovation of the age, the reform of philosophy," and to remedy "the imperfection and inconsistencies of all the arts." The discrepancy is singularly complete, and as "The Universal Reformation" throws no light upon the history or the claims of the Rosicrucians, it need not detain us. "The Chymical Marriage of Christian Rosencreutz" I shall also set aside for the present, because it is an allegorical romance--*pace* Professor Buhle, as De Quincey hath it--though otherwise of the first importance and interest.

From the "Fama" and "Confessio" we gather the religious opinions of the Rosicrucian Fraternity, and classify them as follows:--

a. They acknowledge Jesus Christ as the Son of God.

b. Man is born into life by the power of God, falls asleep in Jesus, and will rise again through the Holy Spirit.

c. They acknowledge a personal devil, the old enemy, who "hinders every good purpose by his instruments."

d. They "use two Sacraments, as they are instituted with all Formes and Ceremonies of the first and renewed Church."

e. It follows from this that they believe the Lutheran Reformation restored the Christian Church to its primitive purity.

f. They consider "that from the beginning of the world there hath not been given to man a more excellent, admirable, and wholesome book than the Bible," which is "the whole sum" of their laws.

g. They call the pope Antichrist, a blasphemer against Christ. They execrate him, and look forward to the time "when he shall be torn in pieces with nails." They foretell his "final fall," with the assurance of Brothers the prophet, and in the terminology of Mr Grattan-Guiness.

The philosophical and scientific opinions and pretensions of the Rosicrucian Society have more claim on our notice. As in their theological views, so in these they are simply the representatives of a certain school of thought current at their epoch. In its aspirations, as distinguished from its methods, this school was considerably in advance of the scientific orthodoxy of the moment. Looking with piercing glance

"Into great Nature's open eye,
To see within it trembling lie
The portrait of the Deity,"

they dreamed of a universal synthesis, and combining profound contemplation with keen observant faculties, the experimental with a priori methods, they sought to arrive at those realities which underlie phenomena, "in more common but more emblematic words," they sought for the substance which is at the base of all the vulgar metals. Mystics in an age of scientific and religious materialism, they were connected by an unbroken chain with the theurgists of the first Christian centuries; they were alchemists in the spiritual sense and the professors of a divine magic. Their disciples, the Rosicrucians, followed closely in their footsteps, and the claims of the "Fama" and "Confessio" must be viewed in the light of the great elder claims of alchemy and magic. In these documents we find--I. The doctrine of the *microcosmus*, which considers man as containing the potentialities of the whole universe, or *macrocosmus*. According to Paracelsus, who first developed this suggestive teaching from obscure hints in the Kabbalistic books, the *macrocosmus* and the *microcosmus* are one. "They are one constellation, one influence, one breath, one harmony, one time, one metal, one fruit." Each part of the great organism acts upon "the corresponding part of the small organism in the same sense as the various organs of the human body are intimately connected with and influence each other." Every change that takes place in the *macrocosmus* may be sensed by the spiritual body which surrounds the spirit of the *minutum mundum*. The forces composing the one are identical with those of the other. II. We find, in the next place, the doctrine of Elemental spirits, which it is a common error to suppose originated with the Rosicrucians. This graceful and fanciful hypothesis also owes its development, if not its invention, to the seer of

Hohenheim. It was naturalised on French soil by the author of the "Comte de Gabalis," and is known chiefly in England through the preface to "The Rape of the Lock," and of later years through the German "Romance of Undine," which has been many times translated. "When you shall be numbered among the Children of the philosophers," says the "Comte de Gabalis," "and when your eyes shall have been strengthened by the use of the most sacred medecine, you will learn that the Elements are inhabited by creatures of a singular perfection, from the knowledge of, and communication with, whom the sin of Adam has deprived his most wretched posterity. Yon vast space stretching between earth and Heaven has far nobler dwellers than the birds and the gnats; these wide seas hold other guests than the whales and the dolphins; the depths of the earth are not reserved for the moles alone; and that element of fire which is nobler than all the rest was not created to remain void and useless." According to Paracelsus, "the Elementals are not spirits, because they have flesh, blood, and bones; they live and propagate offspring; they eat and talk, act and sleep, &c. . . . They are beings occupying a place between men and spirits, resembling men and women in their organisation and form, and resembling spirits in the rapidity of their locomotion." They must not be confounded with the Elementaries which are the astral bodies of the dead. They are divided into four classes. "The air is replete with an innumerable multitude of creatures, having human shapes, somewhat fierce in appearance, but docile in reality; great lovers of the sciences, subtle, serviceable to the Sages, and enemies of the foolish and ignorant. Their wives and daughters are beauties of the masculine type. . . . The seas and streams are inhabited even as the air; the ancient Sages gave the names of Undines or Nymphs to these Elementals. There are few males among them, and the women are very numerous, and of extreme beauty; the daughters of men cannot compare with them. The earth is filled by gnomes even to its centre, creatures of diminutive size, guardians of mines, treasures, and precious stones. They furnish the Children of the Sages with all the money they desire, and ask little for their services but the distinction of being commanded. The gnomides, their wives, are tiny, but very pleasing, and their apparel is exceedingly curious. As to the Salamanders, those fiery dwellers in the realm of flame, they serve the Philosophers, but do not eagerly seek their company, and their wives and daughters are seldom visible. They transcend all the others in beauty, for they are natives of a purer element."III. In the third place, the Rosicrucian manifestoes contain the doctrine of the *signatura rerum*, which again is of Paracelsian origin. This is the "magical writing" referred to in the "Fama," and the mystic characters of that "Book of Nature" which, according to the "Confessio," stands open "for all eyes," but "can be read or understood by only a very few." These characters are the seal of God imprinted "on the wonderful work of creation, on the heavens,

118

the earth, and on all beasts." This "signature of things" is described by Paracelsus as "a certain organic vital activity," which is frequently "expressed even in the exterior form of things; and by observing that form we may learn something in regard to their interior qualities, even without using our interior sight. We see that the internal character of a man is often expressed in his exterior appearance, even in the manner of his walking and in the sound of his voice. Likewise the hidden character of things is to a certain extent expressed in their outward forms. As long as man remained in a natural state, he recognised the signatures of things and knew their true character; but the more he diverged from the path of Nature, and the more his mind became captivated by illusive external appearances, the more this power became lost." The same doctrine is developed by the most distinguished disciple of Paracelsus, the Kentish Rosicrucian, Robert Fludd. "There are other invisible writings, secretly impressed on the leaves of Nature's book, which are not to be read or comprehended save with the eyes of understanding, being traced by the Spirit of the living God on the hidden fleshly tablets of our own hearts. . . . These internal and spiritual characters, constituting the interior writing, may also to the bodily eyes be the cause and origin of the things which do appear." "It is manifest," he also remarks, "that those vivific letters and characters impressed on the Bible and on the great Book of Nature, and which we call arcane, because they are understood only by the few, are one thing, and that the dead, destroying letters of the same books, whose cortices contain the living and spiritual characters, are another."

IV. These speculative principles appear to have been united with some form of practical magic. Now magic is a term which conjures up into the mind of the ordinary reader some hazy notions either of gross imposture or diabolical compacts and hellish rites; it seems necessary, therefore, to state what it really was in the opinions of those who professed it. According to Paracelsus, magic is that great and hidden wisdom which discovers the interior constitution of everything. "It teaches the true nature of the inner man as well as the organization of his outward body." It includes "a knowledge of visible and invisible nature." It is the only true teacher of the art of healing. If physicians possessed it, their books might be burnt and their medicines be thrown into the ocean. "Magic and sorcery are two entirely different things, and there is as much difference between them as there is between light and darkness, and between white and black." The same authority teaches that the great agent in magic is the imagination confirmed by that faith which perfects will-power, and that the imagination thus strengthened can create its own objects. "Man has a visible and invisible workshop. The visible one is his body; the invisible one his imagination. . . . The imagination is a sun in the soul of man, acting in its own sphere as the sun of the earth acts in his. Wherever the latter shines, germs planted in the soil grow, and vegetation springs up; and the sun of the soul acts in a similar manner, and calls the forms of the soul into existence. . . . The spirit is the master, imagination the tool, and the body the plastic material. Imagination is the power by which the will forms sidereal entities out of thoughts. It is not *fancy*, which latter is the corner-stone of superstition and foolishness. . . . The power of the imagination is a great factor in medicine. It may produce diseases in man and in animals, and it may cure them." This theory covers all the phenomena of visions, ecstacies, evocations, and other pseudo-miracles, recognising that they are facts, and accounting for the futility of their results.

V. Whether the Rosicrucians pretended to manufacture material gold is a question which is difficult to decide from the materials contained in their manifestoes. They acknowledge the fact of transmutation, and call it a "great gift of God;" but "as it bringeth not always with it a knowledge of Nature, while this knowledge bringeth forth both that and an infinite number of other natural miracles, it is right that we be rather earnest to attain to the knowledge of philosophy, nor tempt excellent wits to the tincture of metals sooner then to the observation of Nature." Whatever may be thought of this reasoning, it definitely places the Rosicrucians in that school of alchemy to which I made reference at the close of the first chapter, and whose aim was to accomplish the spiritual side of the *magnum opus*, or great work of alchemical reconstruction. For them the transmutation of metals being no operation of common chemistry, both the "Fama" and "Confessio" appear to condemn indiscriminately all professors of the purely physical process, which they call "the ungodly and accursed gold-making." Here, as in their other opinions, they echo Paracelsus. "What shall I say to you about all your alchemical prescriptions, about all your retorts and bottles, crucibles, mortars, and glasses; about all your complicated processes of distilling, melting, cohibiting, coagulating, sublimating, precipitating, and filtering, all the tomfoolery for which you throw away your time and your money. All such things are useless, and the labour over them is lost. They are rather an impediment than a help to arrive at the truth." After the same fashion, the "Confessio" denounces the "monstrous symbols and enigmas" by which pseudo-chymists impose upon credulous curiosity. According to Dr Hartmann, "Paracelsus asserts that it is possible to make gold and silver by chemical means; still he condemns such experiments as useless, and it seems to be more than probable that even in such chemical experiments as may have succeeded, something more than merely chemical manipulations was required to make them successful." Éliphas Lévi, one of the most profound commentators on Paracelsus, declares that "there is light in gold, gold in light, and light in all things." Thus the first matter of the *magnum opus* is both within and about us, and "the intelligent will, which assimilates light, directs the operations of substantial form, and only employs chemistry as a very secondary instrument."At the same time the Rosicrucians claimed to be in possession of "great treasures of gold," and of the purse of Fortunatus. There seems no special reason to doubt that they intended this to be literally construed, and the "Fama" definitely states that it was a project of their founder, C. R., to institute a society in Europe "which might have gold, silver, and precious stones sufficient for to bestow them on kings."

VI. Closely connected with the secret of metallic transmutation is "the supreme medicine of the world," the life-elixir, which, according to Bernard-le-Trevisan (fifteenth century), is the reduction of the Philosophical Stone into mercurial water. It cures all diseases, and prolongs life beyond the normal limits. Without claiming to be actually in possession of this

"Wonderful Catholicon,
Of very subtle and magical powers,"

the Rosicrucians come before us as essentially, or at least primarily, a healing fraternity. "Their agreement was this . . . . That none of them should profess any other thing than to cure the sick, and that gratis." Professor Buhle, in his notice of the Rosicrucians and Freemasons, says that the evils of Germany at this period were immense, that the land was overswept by a "great storm of wretchedness and confusion." The science of medicine was still in its infancy, the Lutheran Reformation, by spoliating monasteries, had destroyed hospitals, and the diseases and miseries unavoidably consequent on unsanitary principles and medical guesswork, were undoubtedly very widely spread. The utter incompetence of the ancient methods led many others besides the Rosicrucians to disregard and denounce the traditional authority, and in the wide field of experimental research to lay the foundations of a new and rational hypothesis. The germs of this revolution are found in Paracelsus, and the practical theosophy--medicine itself being a branch of mysticism from the standpoint of orthodox mystics--practised by Rosicrucian adepts is their strongest claim on our favour, the one golden link which joins their dissonant commonplace with the Orphean harmonies of true and divine occultism.

It will be sufficient to enumerate only their belief in a secret philosophy, perpetuated from primeval times, in ever-burning lamps, in vision at a distance, and in the approaching end of the world. I have shown indisputably that there was no novelty in the Rosicrucian pretensions, and no originality in their views. They appear before us as Lutheran disciples of Paracelsus; and, returning for a moment to the problem discussed in the introduction, we find nothing in either manifesto to connect them with the typology of a remote period. It is, therefore, in modern, not ancient, times that we must seek an explanation of the device of the Rose-Cross. A passage contained in "The Chymical Marriage of Christian Rosencreutz" will assist in the solution of this important point.

121

CHAPTER VII. ANTIQUITY OF
THE ROSICRUCIAN FRATERNITY.

THE antiquity of the Rose in symbolism and of the Cross in symbolism, as I have already said, is no proof whatsoever of the antiquity of a society which we find to be using them at a period subsequent to the Renaissance; but, according to John Heydon, the Rosicrucians "have been since Christ;" they "inhabite the suburbs of Heaven," and are "as the eyes and ears of the great King, seeing and hearing all things." The existence of a "divine Fraternity" on the astral plane, or in. the fourth dimension, however "seraphically illuminated," and with whatever powers they may be invested by the "Generalissimo of the world," is a point which transcends the investigations of the merely human historian. His researches, however, have determined that, within his own limits--that is, on the physical plane of time and space--there are no vestiges of the Rosicrucians traceable before the beginning of the seventeenth century, and that the belief in their antiquity originates in à priori considerations which are concerned with the predilections and prejudices of thinkers whose faith and imagination have been favoured by evolution or environment at the expense of their judgment, and who determine historical questions by the illumination of their own understandings rather than by the light of facts.

Such persons are beyond the reach of criticism, and, as they are neither numerous nor important, may be left basking in the sunshine of a pleasing aberration, which is interesting in days of disillusion. But the existence and occasional prevalence in all ages of the world of those theosophical ideas, which are at the root of Rosicrucian philosophy, have caused even serious students to consider the Fraternity of an almost incredible antiquity--a hypothesis which wins golden opinions from those who delight in connecting the invisible threads of the secret societies and tracing them to a single primal source, of which one and all are ramifications more or less identical in ceremonies, secrets, and purposes.

Addressing myself to these students, I would say with Buhle that whoever adopts this hypothesis "is bound to show, in the first place, in what respect the deduction of this order from modern history is at all unsatisfactory; and secondly, upon his own assumption of a far elder origin, to explain how it happened that for sixteen entire centuries no contemporary writers have made any allusion to it."

Solomon Semler is one of the few writers whose erudition is unquestionable, and who have supported this view; but the facts which he cites are entirely inconclusive. He proves the existence in the fourteenth century of "an association of physicians and alchemists who united their knowledge and their labours to attain the discovery of the Philosophic Stone." It is this association to which the alchemist Raymond Lully apparently refers in his "Theatrum Chymicum," printed at Strasbourg in 1613, as a sec society existing during the fourteenth century in Italy, and the chief of which was called *Rex Physicorum*. Figulus states it to have been founded in 1410, and asserts it to have merged in the Rosicrucian Order about the year 1607. The same careful investigator cites an anonymous letter, published at the end of the sixteenth century, and stating the age of a certain secret society to be above two thousand years. It is also asserted that the alchemist Nicholas Barnaud conceived in 1591 a project of establishing a secret convention of theosophical mystics, who were to devote themselves to a determined investigation of all Kabbalistic sciences, and that he scoured both Germany and France with this object. Finally, the "Echo of the God-illuminated Order of the Brethren R. C." tells us that in 1597 an attempt was actually made to found such a society, apparently on the lines laid down by Barnaud, and it is a remarkable fact that the preface to the Christian Reader which is prefixed to this curious publication, is dated June 1597, while that which is addressed to the Brotherhood is dated 1 Nov. 1615, the book itself not having appeared till 1620.

These facts and statements are of the highest interest and of very considerable importance within their own, sphere, but the existence of secret associations even two thousand years old, much less the attempts occasionally made to establish others, affords no proof that they were in any way connected, or are to be identified, with the Rosicrucian Brotherhood, whose violent anti-Papal prejudices and ultra-Protestant principles are sufficient proof of a post-Lutheran origin.

The only sect or association with which the Rosicrucians may be pertinently compared, and which we hear of before the year 1610, is the *Militia Crucifera Evangelica* which assembled at Lunenburg in 1598 under the auspices of the mystic and theosophist, Simon Studion. Its proceedings are reported in an unprinted work from his pen entitled "Naometria, seu nuda et prima libri, intus et foris scripti, per clavem Davidis et calamum (virgæ similem) apertio; in quo non tantum ad cognoscenda tam S. Scripturæ totius, quam naturæ quoque universæ, mysteria, brevis fit introductio-- verum etiam Prognosticus (stellæ illius matutinæ, Anno Domini 1572, conspectæ ductu) demonstrator Adventus ille Christi ante diem novissimum secundus per quem homine peccati (Papa) cum filio sur perditionis (Mahomedo) divinitus devestato, ipse ecclesiam suam et principatus mundi restaurabit, ut in iis post hac sit cum ovili pastor unus. In cruciferæ militiæ Evangelicæ gratiam. Authore Simone Studione inter Scorpiones. Anno 1604." As this work exists only in manuscript, and as there is no transcript of this manuscript to be found in the English public libraries, my chief knowledge of its contents, and of the sect which it represents, is derived from an unsatisfactory notice by Professor Buhle, who describes the Militia as a Protestant sect heated by apocalyptic dreams, and declares the object of the assembly to have been apparently "exclusively connected with religion." But it is clear from the life of Studion that he was passionately devoted to alchemy, and the spiritual side of the *magnum opus* was probably the aim of these enthusiasts, who are otherwise identified in their views with the illuminati of the Rose-Cross. Like these they believed that the books of Revelation and of Nature were *intus et foris scripti*, written within and without, that is, they contain a secret meaning for the initiates of mystical wisdom; that the unaccountable appearance of new stars in the sky was significant of important events in the approximate future; that the last day was at hand; that the Pope was Anti-Christ and the Man of Sin; and finally, as Buhle himself confesses, the "Naometria" contains a great deal of mysticism and prophecy about the Rose and the Cross.

These points of resemblance are, I think, insufficient to establish a connection between the *Militia Crucifera Evangelica* and the Rosicrucians in a logical mind, but they are certainly curious and interesting. It will be shown in the next chapter why the symbolism of the Rose and the Cross was common to both associations.

The antiquity of the Rosicrucians, as I have hinted, finds few supporters at the present day, this view being chiefly confined to the members of pseudo-Rosicrucian societies, and to the pseudo-historian of the order, Mr Hargrave Jennings. From the fictitious importance unaccountably ascribed to the ill-considered and worthless work of this writer, it seems necessary to conclude with a short notice of the incoherent and visionary ramblings in "The Rosicrucians: their Rites and Mysteries." Mr Jennings may congratulate himself on being "that distinguished esoteric *littérateur*," who writes the worst English of this or any century, but he is a great man, a magician of the first order, in the important matter of titles. I freely confess that his work on this subject is so attractively labelled that it exercises an irresistible charm over the student. "The Rosicrucians: their Rites and Mysteries, with chapters on the ancient Fire and Serpent Worshippers, and explanations of the Mystic Symbols represented on the monuments and talismans of the Primeval Philosophers," is a label not otherwise than superb. It is a "strong delusion" which tempts the hesitating purchaser, and has often prompted the too credulous reader, by the subtlety of its mystic charm, "to believe"--at least the very opposite of what is true.

The book, so far as the Rosicrucians are concerned, begins with an account of an "historical adventure in Staffordshire," which is curiously distorted in the interests of an inexpensive sensationalism, and after much loquacity on "the insufficiency of worldly objects," we are introduced in the seventh chapter, without preface or apology, to the "Mythical history of the *Fleur-de-lys*," Druidic Cromlechs, and Gnostic Abraxas Gems. The rest of the work is Rosicrucian certainly, so far as the titles of the chapters are concerned, but not further. Thus we have "The Rosy-Cross in Indian,

Egyptian, Greek, Roman, and Mediaeval monuments," "Presence of the Rosicrucians in Christian Architecture," &c., but the chapters themselves are devoted to the lingam and the great pyramid, Persian fire-worship, phallic and serpent symbolism, and etymological speculations which would have astonished even Godfrey Higgins, and which Kenealy himself would disown. Doubtless these things are connected in the mind of Mr Hargrave Jennings with his mysterious and ubiquitous Brotherhood, for his diseased imagination perceives Rosicrucianism everywhere, "as those who believe in witchcraft see sorcery and enchantment everywhere." This connection, however, he nowhere attempts to establish, and it is incredible to suppose that the shallow pretence has ever imposed on anyone. The few statements which he makes concerning the Fraternity must be rejected as worthless; for example, he tells us that the alchemists were a physical branch of the Rosicrucians, whereas the Rosicrucians were a theosophical sect among the alchemists.

I have deemed it unnecessary to consider the alleged connection between the Templars and the Brethren of the Rose-Cross, for this hypothesis depends upon another, now generally set aside, namely, the connection of the Freemasons with the foregoing orders. It is sufficient to say that the Templars were not alchemists, that they had no scientific pretensions, and that their secret, so far as can be ascertained, was a religious secret of an anti-Christian kind. The Rosicrucians, on the other hand, were pre-eminently a learned society, and they were also a Christian sect.

ARMS OF ANDREAS.

CHAPTER VIII. THE CASE OF
JOHANN VALENTIN ANDREAS.

MOST existing theories as to the authorship of the Rosicrucian manifestoes are founded upon plausible assumptions or ingenious conclusions drawn from the doubtful materials of merely alleged facts. Each investigator has approached the subject with an ambitious determination to solve the problem connected with the mysterious Order, but, in the absence of adequate materials, has evolved a new hypothesis, where the supposititious has transfigured what is certain for the satisfaction of individual bias. As a simple historian working in the cause of truth, it is neither my inclination nor my duty to contrive a fresh theory, but rather to state the facts which are in conflict with all theories, and to draw no conclusion unwarranted by the direct evidence in hand.

The Rosicrucian theorists may be broadly divided into three bands--I. Those who believe that the history of Christian Rosencreutz is true in fact, and that the society originated in the manner recounted in the "Fama Fraternitatis." II. Those who regard both the society and its founder as purely mythical, and consider with Leibnitz, "*que tout ce que l'on a dit des Frères de la Croix de la Rose, est une pure invention de quelque personne ingenieuse.*" III. Those who, without accepting the historical truth of the story of Rosencreutz, believe in the existence of the Rosicrucians as a secret society, which drew attention to the fact of its existence by a singular and attractive fiction.

In the first division are gathered the men of large imagination and abundant faith, who, unawed by historical difficulties, unaffected by discrepancies of fact, and despising the *terra damnata* of frigid critical methods, are bewitched by romantic associations and the glamour of impenetrable mystery. They love to contemplate the adepts of the Rose-Cross moving silently among the ignorant and vulgar multitude, diffusing light and healing, masters of terrific secrets, having nothing in appearance and yet possessing all things, ever inscrutable, ever intangible, ever vanishing suddenly. The sublime dreams produced by their mystical hachish are undisturbed by the essential shallowness and commonplace of Rosicrucian manifestoes, for they reject authoritative documents, or interpret objectionable passages in an inverted sense.

Insuperable difficulties prevent us from supposing that the "Fama" and "Confessio Fraternitatis" emanated from a secret society whose literal history is contained in them. These difficulties are, for the most part, inherent in the nature of the alleged history, which I undertook in the introduction to prove mythical. It will be unnecessary for this purpose to consider the scientific foundation of Rosicrucian claims. The purse of Fortunatus--that is, the Stone of the Philosophers--the power of transmutation, the existence of elementary spirits, the doctrine of signatures, ever-burning lamps, and vision at a distance, may be possibilities, however remote on the horizon of natural science. There are many things in heaven and on earth which are undreamed of in the philosophy of Horatio, and occultism is venerable by its antiquity, interesting from its romantic associations, and replete with visionary splendours; but for all this, the fiction of the "Fama" is "monstrous, and betrays itself in every circumstance."Suspicion is immediately raised by the suppression of all names, and the concealment of the headquarters and all "local habitations" of the supposed Society. C. R. C., the hero of the history, journeys to a fabulous Oriental city, called Damcar, which is not Damascus, though the German originals continually confuse it therewith. A great part of this journey is performed alone by a boy of sixteen, who is described as possessing such "skill in physic" that he "obtained much favour of the Turks," and who, after five years' travelling, returns at the age of twenty-one years to Europe, fired with an inextinguishable ambition to correct the errors of all the arts and to reform the whole *philosophia moralis*. In Germany he erects a mysterious House of the Holy Spirit, situated apparently in space of three dimensions, besieged by the "unspeakable concourse of the sick," and yet, for the space of nearly two hundred years, completely unknown and unseen by the "wicked world" When the Society was incorporated, and its members despatched on their wanderings, two brethren always remained with the founder, and eight of them were present at his death, yet the secret of his burial-place was completely unknown to the third generation, till its discovery by a newly-initiated member when he was repairing his house, which, nevertheless, does not appear to be the House of the Holy Spirit. The sepulchre has been closed for one hundred and twenty years, and it is found to contain the *Vocabularium, Itinerarium*, and Life of Paracelsus. Taking 1614 as the year when the Fama" was published, and supposing the discovery of the burial-place to have ante-dated the manifesto by the shortest possible period, we are brought back to the year 1494, one year after the birth of Paracelsus, whose books it is supposed to contain. This point is, of course, conclusive, and it is unnecessary to comment on the mystery which surrounds the ultimate fate of the corpse of that "godly and high-illuminated Father, Brother C. R. C."

Thus it is obvious that the history of Christian Rosencreutz is not historically true, and that the Society did not originate in the manner which is described by the "Fama."

The theorists of the second and third divisions are in agreement upon several important points, and may, therefore, be considered together. Most of them unite in seeking the author of the Rosicrucian manifestoes among the literati of the period. On the one side they consider him a satirist, or the perpetrator of an imposture or elaborate jest; on the other, they hold him to be the founder of a secret society, or the mouthpiece of one which was already in existence, and to which they ascribe a various antiquity in accordance with their predilections and their knowledge of the true state of the case. The question of this antiquity has been discussed in the last chapter.

Several authors have been suggested, for the most part on very slender evidence. Some maintain that the manifestoes were written by Taulerus, the author of the German Theologia, an obscure writer not to be identified with the author of the Spiritual Letters, "Institutiones Divinæ," &c., others by Luther, others again by Wiegel. Joachim Junge, the celebrated philosopher of the seventeenth century, has secured several partisans. He was born at Lubeck in 1587, and became an M. A. of Giessen in 1609. At the very period when the "Fama Fraternitatis" first appeared, about 1614, he was holding numerous conferences with his friends on the methods of hastening the progress of philosophy, but his plans are supposed to have been without any immediate result. Subsequently, he sought to establish at Rostock an academy for the advancement of natural sciences; "but the rumour spread that this project concealed some evil designs, and people went so far as to accuse him of being one of the chiefs of the famous order of the Brothers of the Red-Cross, and he was forced to renounce a plan whose execution could only have had good results for his adopted country." He became rector of the University of Hamburg, and died of apoplexy, September 23, 1657. He was the author of "Geometria Empirica," "Harmonica Theoretica," &c., and appears to have been wholly unconnected with the alchemical pursuits of the period. A secretary of the Court of Heidelberg (according to Heidegger, the biographer of Johannes Ludovicus Fabricius) being, it is supposed, in the secret, is said to have confirmed in conversation the current report that Junge was the founder of the Fraternity and the writer of the "Fama Fraternitatis." No reference is made to this matter in the "Historia Vitæ et Mortis Joachimi Jungii Mathematici summi ceteraque Incomparabilis Philosophi," which was written by Martinus Fogelius in 1658. It contains, however, some account of his attempt to found a philosophical society, but the Leges Societatis Ereuneticæ which are to be found at the end of the pamphlet, sufficiently distinguish it from the Rosicrucian Brotherhood. The theosophist, Ægidius Gutmann, is claimed as the true author of the anonymous manifestoes by others--on what grounds I have not been able to ascertain; but, according to Buhle, this opinion is "supported by no other argument than that he was a distinguished mystic in that age of mysticism."

All these views have manifestly little to recommend them, but that which attributes the composition of the Rosicrucian manifestoes to Johann Valentin Andreas is supported by an extraordinary mass of evidence, which calls for very careful and impartial consideration. This interesting and singular personage, who is described by Brucker as very learned and of a very elegant genius, whom the "Bibliothèque Universelle" considers one of the most useful men which Germany produced in the seventeenth century, and whom all authorities unite in admiring for his talents and virtues, was a renowned theologian of Wirtemberg, and a multifarious *littérateur* not uncelebrated, even at this day, in his own country, as a poet and a satirist. He was born at Herrenberg, a town in the duchy of Wirtemberg, on the 17th of August 1586. He was the grandson of Jacob Andreas, also a celebrated theologian. His father was the pastor of Herrenberg, his mother, Mary Moseria. The delicacy of his early years characterised his maturer life, but he was of a shrewd and cheerful disposition. He received the rudiments of his education from Michael Beumler Subsequently he pursued his studies at Tubingen, Buhle informs us that, "besides Greek and Latin (in which languages he was distinguished for the elegance of his style), he made himself master of the French, Italian, and Spanish; was well versed in Mathematics, Natural and Civil History, Geography, and Historical Genealogy, without at all neglecting his professional study of divinity." "I so divided my time," he tells us, "that during the day I devoted myself to instruction in the arts; thereto I added long nocturnal studies, passed in the reading of various authors, and carried to such an extravagant extent that not only my eyesight suffered, but I made myself subject to the horrors of sleeplessness, and weakened the strength of memory."

He travelled much within the limits of his own country, visited France, Switzerland, Italy, including Venice, and twice journeyed into Austria. He was married on the second of August 1614, to Agnes Elizabeth, daughter of Josua Grüminger. He passed through various grades of ecclesiastical dignity, and became chaplain to the court at Stuttgart. "Here," says Buhle, "he met with so much thwarting and persecution, that, with his infirm constitution of body and dejection of mind from witnessing the desolation of Germany," the redress of the abuses and evils in which had been the main object of his life--"it is not to be wondered that he . . . sank into deep despondency and misanthropy." At his own earnest importunity he was permitted to resign his post, and died abbot of Adelberg and Lutheran almoner to the Duke of Wirtemberg in the year 1654, "after a long and painful illness."

All authorities are agreed upon one important point in the character of Andreas, and that is his predilection in favour of secret societies as instruments in the reformation of his age and country. According to Buhle, he had a profound and painful sense of the gross evils and innumerable abuses which afflicted the German fatherland, and which were revealed, not eradicated, by the lurid fire-brand of Luther's reformation. These abuses he sought to redress by means of "secret societies." The ambition of his boyhood appears to have been the labour of his after days. "The writings of

Andreas, issued during his life-time, are full of arguments on the necessity of forming a society solely devoted to the reformation of sciences and manners. . . . Three of his works, namely, 'Reipublicæ Christianopolitanæ Descriptio'; 'Turris Babel, sive Judiciorum de Fraternitate Rosaceæ Crucis Chaos'; 'Christianæ Societatis Idea,' all published at Strasbourg in the years 1619 and 1620, offer the clearest indications of his project to form a secret society. It is impossible not to perceive that he is always aiming at something of the kind. Some also appeal to his frequent travels as having no other object. A writer in the "Dictionnaire des Sciences Occultes" speaks with even greater emphasis. "The works of Andreas, to the number of one hundred, preach promiscuously the necessity of secret societies," and Louis Figuier, whose work, entitled "Alchemy and the Alchemists," though it does not betray much original research, represents in a French vestment the opinions and arguments of some high German authorities, calls Andreas "a fanatical partisan" of the doctrines of Paracelsus, declares him to have been fired with the ambition to fulfil certain predictions of his master which have been before referred to, and that he took upon himself to decide that the "Elias Artista," the robust child, to whom the magician refers, must be understood not of an individual but of a collective body or association.

It seems clear from these authorities, and from the facts of the case, that the mature, long-planned purpose of Andreas was the foundation of a society for the reformation of the age, and we find him cherishing this hope and apparently elaborating his designs at the very period when the first rumours of the Rosicrucian Fraternity began to be heard in Europe. It is, therefore, obviously and incontestably clear that if he had any hand in the foundation of this society, or in the authorship of the documents connected with it, that both were undertaken in all earnestness, and that the "Fama" and "Confessio Fraternitatis" are not pieces of frolicsome imposture, and satires on the credulity of the period. Such a supposition is wholly incompatible with Andreas' zeal and enthusiasm.

This point being definitely settled, I proceed to lay before my readers an abstract of those considerations which have induced several erudite investigators to accept Andreas as the author of the Rosicrucian documents.

I. I have said in the fifth chapter that the whole controversy to some extent centres in the "Chymical Marriage of Christian Rosencreutz," and since the publication of Seybold's "Autobiographies of Celebrated Men" in 1796, and which printed for the first time, albeit in a German version, the posthumous autobiography of Johann Valentin Andreas, there has been no room for doubt as its authorship. There he includes it among his earliest productions, states that it was written at the age of fifteen, and that it was one of a series of similar juvenilia which, for the most part, had perished. Now the "Chymical Marriage," having remained several years in manuscript, was printed at Strasbourg in 1616. The C. R. C. of the preceding manifestoes was immediately identified with the Christian Rosencreutz of the allegorical romance, and albeit the first edition of the "Confessio Fraternitatis," and seemingly also of the "Fama," do not describe the society as that of the Rosie Cross, the edition of 1615, printed at Francfurt, calls it the *Bruderschafft des Rosen-Creutzes* and it is, therefore, argued that the three works must have originated from a single source.

II. The "Chymical Marriage" contains the following passage:-- "Hereupon I prepared myself for the way, put on my white linnen coat, girded my loyns, with a blood-red ribbon bound *cross-ways* over my shoulder: In my hat I stuck *four roses.*" Elsewhere, he describes himself as a "brother of the Red-Rosie Cross," and a "Knight of the Golden Stone"-- *eques aurei lapidis.*

Now, the armorial bearings of the family of Andreas contain a St Andrew's Cross with four roses, one in each of its angles, which interesting piece of internal evidence indicates the authorship of this romance independently of the autobiographical statement, and points irresistibly, it is said, to the conclusion that the founder of the Rose-Cross Society was the man whose heraldic device was also the Rose and Cross.

III. The identity of the principles contained in the acknowledged work of Andreas, and in the pamphlets which it is sought to attribute to him, are considered too obvious to need enumeration, and it is sufficient to point out that all are equally directed against the charlatanic professors of the *magnum opus*, thriving in countless numbers upon the credulity and infatuation of the age.

IV. Arnold, in his "History of the Church and of Heretics," states that a comparison between Andreas' undoubtedly authentic writings and those of the Rosicrucian manifestoes do not allow any doubt that he is their author.

V. The earliest edition of Boccalini's "Ragguagli di Parnasso" was published at Venice in 1612. Andreas is known to have been an Italian scholar; he was also an omnivorous reader; he is said to have admired Boccalini, and to have imitated his style; and thence it is argued that he it was who translated Advertisement 77 of the first centuria, under the title of the "Universal Reformation of the Whole Wide World."

VI. An intimate friend of Andreas, Professor Besoldt, positively declares that the character of the Rosicrucian manifesto is plain enough, and considers it a marvellous and unexplainable circumstance that so many persons had mistaken that object. From this it is concluded that he was a repository of the secret concerning their authorship, and as he was in the confidence of Andreas, that Andreas was the author.

In this case, the question discussed in the introduction is, of course, definitely set at rest. The symbolism of the Rose-Cross is of no high significance as a badge of the secret society. It does not give expression to the arcana of the alchemical and celestial Dew of the Wise, nor contain the secret of the menstruum of the Red Dragon. It is simply the hereditary device of the founder, and its meaning is to be sought in German heraldry, and not in mysticism.

Those who accredit Andreas with the authorship of the Rosicrucian manifestoes interpret his reasons very variously. According to Arnold, he had already written many satirical pamphlets upon the corruptions and hypocrisy of the period and he considers that the "Fama" and "Confessio" were penned with the same purpose, namely to lay bare the follies of men's lives, and to set before them patterns of good and pious living. He quotes an unmentioned writer as stating that it was necessary that the brethren should be men of unblemished lives, and zealous preachers, who, under the appearance of a society, would try to lead the people to God. According to Figuier, as we have seen, Andreas established the order to fulfil certain prophecies of Paracelsus, and to pursue scientific researches on purely Paracelsian principles. But Buhle, with all his shortcomings, and weighted as he is by an extravagant Masonic hypothesis, is the best exponent of these views, and it will be necessary to cite his arguments at considerable length.

"From a close review of his life and opinions, I am not only satisfied that Andreä wrote the three works which laid the foundation of Rosicrucianism, but I see clearly *why* he wrote them. The evils of Germany were then enormous, and the necessity of some great reform was universally admitted. As a young man without experience, Andrea imagined that this reform would be easily accomplished. He had the example of Luther before him, the heroic reformer of the preceding century, whose memory was yet fresh in Germany, and whose labours seemed on the point of perishing unless supported by corresponding efforts in the existing generation. To organise these efforts and direct them to proper objects, he projected a society composed of the noble, the enlightened, and the learned--which he hoped to see moving, as under the influence of one soul, towards the redressing of public evils. Under this hope it was that he travelled so much: seeking everywhere, no doubt, for the coadjutors and instruments of his designs. These designs he presented originally in the shape of a Rosicrucian society; and in this particular project he intermingled some features that were at variance with its gravity and really elevated purposes. Young as he was at that time, Andreä knew that men of various tempers and characters could not be brought to co-operate steadily for any object so purely disinterested as the elevation of human nature: he therefore addressed them through the common foible of their age, by holding out promises of occult knowledge which should invest its possessor with authority over the powers of Nature, should lengthen his life, or raise him from the dust of poverty to wealth and high station. In an age of Theosophy, Cabbalism, and Alchemy, he knew that the popular ear would be caught by an account, issuing nobody knew whence, of a great society that professed to be the depository of Oriental mysteries, and to have lasted two centuries. Many would seek to connect themselves with such a society: from these candidates he might gradually select the members of the real society which he projected. The pretensions of the ostensible society were indeed illusions; but before they could be detected as such by the new proselytes, those proselytes would become connected with himself, and (as he hoped) moulded to nobler aspirations. On this view of Andreä's real intentions, we understand at once the ground of the contradictory language which he held about astrology and the transmutation of metals: his satirical works show that he looked through the follies of his age with a penetrating eye. He speaks with toleration then of these follies--as an exoteric concession to the age; he condemns them in his own esoteric character as a religious philosopher. Wishing to conciliate prejudices, he does not forbear to *bait* his scheme with these delusions: but he is careful to let us know that they are with his society mere παρεργα or collateral pursuits, the direct and main one being true philosophy and religion."

I fully concede the almost overwhelming force of some of the arguments I have enumerated, but, as a partisan of no particular theory, it is my duty to set before my readers a plain statement of certain grave difficulties.

I. The "Chymical Marriage" is called a *ludibrium* by its author, and Professor Buhle describes it as a comic romance, but those of my readers who are acquainted with alchemical allegories will discern in this singular narrative by a prepared student or artist who was supernaturally and magically elected to participate in the accomplishment of the *magnum opus*, many matters of grave and occult significance. They will recognise that the comic episodes are part of a serious design, and that the work as a whole is in strict accordance with the general traditions of alchemy. They will question the good faith of the author in the application of a manifestly incongruous epithet. Perhaps they will appear to be wise above what is written, but the position is not really unreasonable, for the passage in which reference is made by Andreas to the "Nuptiæ Chymicæ" is calculated to raise suspicion. He was a shrewd and keen observer; he had gauged the passions and the crazes of his period; he was fully aware that the rage for alchemy blinded the eyes and drained the purses of thousands of credulous individuals, who were at the mercy of the most wretched impostors, and that no pretence was too shallow and no recipe too worthless to find believers. He could not be ignorant that a work like the "Chymical Marriage of Christian Rosencreutz" was eminently liable to impose upon every class of theosophists. When, therefore, he supposes, and, by implication, expresses, astonishment that his so-called *ludibrium* became the object of earnest investigation and of high esteem, I freely confess that I, for one, cannot interpret him seriously; in other words, that I reject the statement. This, however, is only the initial difficulty. The same passage of the "Vita ab ipso Conscripta" contains another piece of incredible information, namely that Andreas wrote the "Nuptiæ Chymicæ" before he was sixteen, This story gives evidence of an acquaintance with the practice and purposes of alchemy which was absolutely impossible to the most precocious lad. Moreover, the boldness of its conception and the power which is displayed in its execution, setting aside the debateable question of its occult philosophical character, are things utterly transcending the *cacoethes scribendi* of a youngster barely attained to the age of puberty. I appeal to the discrimination of my readers whether the curious and ingenious perplexities propounded at the supper on the third day are in any way suggestive of "the light fire in the veins of a boy." The romance supposed to have been written in 1602-3 did not see the light till 1616, when it appeared in the full tide of the Rosicrucian controversy. Why did it remain in manuscript for the space of thirteen years at a period when everything treating of alchemy was devoured with unexampled avidity? The "Chymical Marriage," in its original draft, may have been penned at the age of fifteen, but it must have been subjected to a searching revision, though I confess that it betrays no trace of subsequent manipulation. These grave difficulties are enhanced by a fact which is wholly unknown to most Rosicrucian critics, and which was certainly not to be expected in the jest of a schoolboy, namely, that the barbarous enigmatical writings which are to be found in several places of "The Hermetick Wedding" are not an unmeaning hoax, but contain a decipherable and deciphered sense. The secretary of an English Rosicrucian Society says that the Supreme Magus of the Metropolitan College can read all three of the enigmas, and that he himself has deciphered two. Their secret is not a tradition, but the meaning dawns upon the student after certain researches. The last point is curious, and, outside the faculty of clairvoyance, the suggested method does not seem probable, but I give it to be taken at its worth, and have no reason to doubt the statement.

From these facts and considerations, the conclusion does not seem unreasonable, and may certainly be tolerated by an impartial mind, that in spite of the statement of Andreas, and partly because of that statement, the "Chymical Marriage" is not a *ludibrium*, that it betrays a serious purpose, and conceals a recondite meaning.

II. With this criticism the whole theory practically breaks down. We know that the "Fama Fraternitatis" was published in 1615 as a manifesto of the *Bruderschafft des löblichen Ordens des Rosen Creutses*. We have good reason to suppose that the original draft of the "Chymical Marriage" was tampered with; we do not know that previous to the year 1615 such a work was in existence as the "Chymical Marriage of Christian Rosencreutz." What we know to have existed was simply the "Nuptiæ Chymicæ." Now, supposing the "Fama Fraternitatis" to have emanated from a source independent of Andreas, he would be naturally struck by the resemblance of the mysterious Rosicrucian device to his own armorial bearings, and when in the year 1616 he published his so-called comic romance, this analogy may, not inconceivably, have led him to re-christen his hero, and to introduce those passages which refer to the Rose Cross. This, of course, is conjectural, but it is to be remarked that so far as can be possibly ascertained, the acknowledged symbol of the Fraternity never was a St Andrew's Cross with four Roses, but was a Cross of the ordinary shape, with a Red Rose in the centre, or a Cross rising out of a Rose. There is therefore little real warrant for the identification of the mystical and the heraldic badge. It is on this identification, however, that the Andrean claim is greatly based.

III. We find the "Chymical Marriage," like the "Fama" and "Confessio Fraternitatis," crusading against the "vagabond cheaters," "runagates and roguish people," who debased alchemical experiments in the interest of dishonest speculation; yet the one, under a thin veil of fiction, describes the proceedings in the accomplishment of the *magnum opus*, while the other terms transmutation a great gift of God. These points of resemblance, however, do not necessarily indicate a common authorship, for a general belief in the facts of alchemy was held at that period by many intelligent men, who were well aware, and loud in their condemnation, of the innumerable frauds which disgraced the science. On the other hand, it is plain that the history of C. R. C., as it is contained in the "Fama," is not the history, equally fabulous, of that Knight of the Golden Stone, who is the hero of the "Chymical Marriage."

IV. It is obviously easy to exaggerate the philological argument, or rather the argument from the identity of literary style, in the documents under consideration. This point indeed can only be adequately treated by a German. At present it rests on a single assertion of Arnold, which is uncorroborated by any illustrative facts. I think it will also be plain, even to the casual reader, that the "Chymical Marriage" is a work of "extraordinary talent," as Buhle justly observes, but that the "Fama Fraternitatis" is a work of no particular talent, either inventive or otherwise, while the subsequent "Confession," both in matter and manner, is simply beneath contempt. Yet we are required to believe that the first was produced at the age of fifteen, while the worthless pamphlets are the work of the same writer from seven to thirteen years subsequently.

V. The connection of the "Universal Reformation" with the other Rosicrucian manifestoes is so uncertain, that if Andreas could be proved its translator, his connection with the society would still be doubtful. The appearance of the "Fama Fraternitatis" and the "Universal Reformation" in one pamphlet no more proves them to have emanated from a single source, than the publication of the "Confessio" in the same volume as the

"Secretioris Philosophiæ Consideratio" proves Philippus à Gabella to have been the author of that document. The practice of issuing unconnected works within the covers of a single book was common at the period. But the argument which ascribes the "Universal Reformation" to Andreas is entirely conjectural.

VI. There is nothing conclusive in the statement of Professor Besoldt; it may have been simply an expression of personal opinion; those who interpret it otherwise in support of the claim of Andreas, to some extent base their interpretation on the very point which is in question, for unless Andreas were the author of the manifestoes, it is clear that Professor Besoldt is a person of no authority.

These difficulties are of themselves sufficient to cast grave doubt upon the Andrean theory, but when we pass to the consideration of the motives which are attributed to the reputed author by the chief supporter of his claims, we find them indefinitely multiplied. Buhle represents him as a young man without experience who imagined that the evils of his country, enormous as they confessedly were, could be eradicated easily. But if, by courtesy, we allow that the "Fama Fraternitatis" was published so early as 1612, then Andreas was twenty-six years of age, when a man of education and travel would be neither inexperienced nor Utopian.

What, however, is by implication assumed in this hypothesis is that the Rosicrucian manifestoes were written at the same age as the "Nuptiæ Chymicæ," for which there is not a particle of evidence, and that the object of Andreas' travels was to find "coadjutors and instruments for his designs," which is also wholly unsupported. The scheme which is fathered upon Andreas is a monstrous and incredible absurdity; it involves, moreover, a pious fraud which is wholly at variance with the known character of the supposed author. No sane person, much less a man who "looked through the follies of his age with a penetrating eye," could expect anything but failure to result from a gross imposition practised on the members of a projected association, who being assured of the possession of the Philosophical Stone, the life-elixir, and initiation into the secret mysteries of nature, were destined to receive, instead of these prizes, a barren and impossible commission to reform the age. What moral reformation could result from any scheme at once so odious and impracticable?

Let us accept however, for a moment, the repulsive hypothesis of Buhle. Suppose the Rosicrucian manifestoes to have been written in 1602. Suppose Andreas to have scoured Germany and also to have visited other countries in search of appropriate members for his society. It would then be naturally concluded that the publication of the "Fama Fraternitatis" signified that his designs were matured. The subsequent conduct of Andreas is, nevertheless, so completely in the face of this conclusion, that Buhle is obliged to assume

136

that the manifestoes were printed without the author's consent, than which nothing could be more gratuitous, and that the uproar of hostility which followed their publication made it necessary for Andreas to disavow them if he would succeed in his ultimate designs. The hostility provoked by the manifestoes bears no comparison with the welcome they received among all those classes to whom they were indirectly addressed, namely, the alchemists, theosophists, etc. Had Andreas projected a society upon the lines laid down by Buhle, nothing remained but to communicate with the innumerable pamphleteers who wrote in defence of the order during the years immediately succeeding the publication of the "Fama Fraternitatis," as well as with those other persons who in various printed letters offered themselves for admission therein, after which he could have proceeded in the accomplishment of his heartless design. That he did not do so when the circumstances were so favourable is proof positive that he had no such intention. In fact, at this very period, namely, in the year 1614, we find Andreas immersed in no dark and mysterious designs for the reformation of the age by means of a planned imposture, but simply celebrating his nuptials, and settling down into a tranquil domestic life.

One more gross and ineradicable blemish upon this hypothesis remains to be noticed. Not only is Andreas represented relinquishing his design at the very moment when it was possible to put it in force, but diverted at the universal delusion he had succeeded in creating, he is represented as endeavouring to foster it, "to gratify his satirical propensities," and when even in after life he becomes "shocked to find that the delusion had taken firm root in the public mind," he adopts no adequate measures to dispel it. Thus not only does Andreas wilfully turn the long-planned purpose of his life into a wretched fiasco, but to complete the libel on the character of a great and good man, he is supposed to delude his fellow creatures no longer for a lofty purpose, but from the lowest motive which it is possible to attribute to anyone,--a motive indefinitely meaner than any of personal gain.

The facts of the case untortured by any theory are these. The "Fama Fraternitatis" was published, say, in 1612. In 1613 a brief Latin epistle addressed to the venerable Fraternity R. C. is supposed to have appeared at Francfurt, supplemented the following year by an "Assertio Fraternitatis R. C. à quodam Fraterni ejus Socio carmine expressa." These two publications I have been unable to trace, though both are mentioned by Buhle, and are included by Langlet du Fresnoy in the Rosicrucian bibliography which is to be found in the third volume of his "Histoire de la Philosophie Hermétique." In 1615, the Latin original of the "Confessio Fraternitatis" appeared, as we have seen, in the alchemical quarto of Philip à Gabella. All these works are attributed to Andreas, and the year 1616 saw the publication of the "Chymical Nuptials of Christian Rosencreutz," which work is undoubtedly his. Taking this view, and comparing these persistent and successive attempts to draw attention to the secret society with the known character and the known ambitions of Andreas, we are evidently face to face with an earnest and determined purpose, not to be arrested by a little hostility and not likely to degenerate into a matter for jest and satire. We must therefore reject the Buhlean hypothesis, because it fails all along the line, "and betrays itself in every circumstance." We must reject also that view which attributes the manifesto to Andreas, but considers them an ingenious jest. It is universally admitted that this jest had a seriously evil effect, and Andreas, on this hypothesis, lived to see some of the best and acutest minds of his time, to say nothing of an incalculable number of honest and earnest seekers, misled by the vicious and wanton joke which had been hatched by the perverted talents of his youth. The wickedness and cruelty of persisting in concealment of the true nature of the case through all his maturer life, through all his age, and not even making a posthumous explanation in the "Vita ab ipso Conscripta," is enough to raise indignation in every breast, and is altogether, and too utterly, vile and mean to ascribe to any right-minded and honourable person, much less to a man of the known intellectual nobility of Johann Valentin Andreas. Buhle says that to have avowed the three books as his own composition would have defeated his scheme, and that "afterwards he had still better reasons for disavowing them." He had no such reasons. The bluntest sense of duty and the feeblest voice of manliness must have provided him with urgent and unanswerable reasons for acknowledging them--a course to which no serious penalties could possibly attach.

To dispose of the Andrean claim, a third hypothesis must be briefly considered. If Andreas was a follower of Paracelsus, a believer in alchemy, an aspirant towards the spiritual side of the *magnum opus*, or an adept therein, he would naturally behold with sorrow and disgust the trickery and imposture with which alchemy was then surrounded, and by which it has been indelibly disgraced, and it is not unreasonable to suppose that he may have attempted to reform the science by means of a secret society, whose manifestoes are directed against those very abuses. But in spite of the statement of Louis Figuier, I can find no warrant in the life or writings of Andreas for supposing that he was a profound student, much less a fanatical partisan of Paracelsus, and it is clear from his "Turris Babel," "Mythologia Christiana," and other works, that he considered the Rosicrucian manifestoes a reprehensible hoax. In the twenty-fifth chapter of the first of these books, the author proposes to supply the place of the fabulous Rosicrucian Society by his own Christian Fraternity. Indeed, wherever he speaks of it in his known writings, it is either with contempt or condemnation. *Nihil cum hac Fraternitate commune habeo*, says Truth in the "Mythologia Christiana." "Listen, ye mortals," cries Fama in the "Turris Babel," "you need not wait any longer for any brotherhood; the comedy is played out; Fama has put it up, and now destroys it. Fama has said Yes, and now utters No."

My readers are now in possession of the facts of the case, and must draw their own conclusions. If in spite of the difficulties which I .have impartially stated, Andreas has any claim upon the authorship of the Rosicrucian manifestoes, it must be viewed in a different light. According to Herder, his purpose was to make the secret societies of his time reconsider their position, and to shew them how much of their aims and movements was ridiculous, but not to found any society himself. According to Figuier, he really founded the Rosicrucian Society, but ended by entire disapproval of its methods, and therefore started his Christian Fraternity. But the facts of the case are against this hypothesis, for the "Invitatio Fraternitatis Christi ad Sacri amoris Candidatos" was published as early as 1617, long before the Rosicrucian Order could have degenerated from the principles of its master. It is impossible that Andreas should have projected two associations at the same time.

But in the face of the failure of all these hypotheses, one fact in the life of their subject remains unexplained. If Andreas did not write the "Fama" and "Confessio Fraternitatis," if he had no connection with the secret society from which they may be supposed to have emanated, if he did not study Paracelsus, and did not take interest in alchemy, how are we to account for the existence of the "Chymical Marriage," for its publication in the centre and heart of the Rosicrucian controversy, and for its apparently earnest purpose when he describes it as a jest or *ludibrium?* Without elaborating a new hypothesis, can we suggest a possible reason for this misnomer? Supposing Andreas to have been actually connected in his younger days with a certain secret society, which may have published the more or less misleading Rosicrucian manifestoes, the oath which all such societies impose upon their members, would for ever prevent him from divulging anything concerning it, though he may have withdrawn from its ranks at an early period. This society may have been identical, or affiliated, with the *Militia Crucifera Evangelica*, which, from the known character of its founder was probably saturated with alchemical ideas, in which case it offers at the end of the sixteenth century a complete parallel in its opinions with the Rosicrucian Fraternity. Both associations were ultra-Protestant, both were "heated with Apocalyptic dreams," both sought the *magnum opus* in its transfigured or spiritual sense, both abhorred the Pope, both called him Antichrist, both coupled him with the detested name of Mahomet, both expected the speedy consummation of the age, both studied the secret characters of nature, both believed in the significance of celestial signs, both adopted as their characteristic symbols the mystic Rose and Cross, and the reason which prompted this choice in the one probably guided it in the other. This reason is not to be sought in the typology of a remote period, nor even in the alchemical enigmas of mediæval times. It is not to be sought in the armorial bearings of Johann Valentin Andreas. They bore the Rose and Cross as their badge, not because they were Brethren of the Concocted and Exalted Dew, not because they had studied the book called Zohar, not because they were successors and initiates of the ancient Wisdom-Religion and the sublime hierarchies of Eld, but because they were a narrow sect of theosophical dissidents, because the monk Martin Luther was their idol, prophet, and master, because they were rabidly and extravagantly Protestant, with an ultra-legitimate violence of abusive Protestantism, because, in a single word, the device on the seal of Martin Luther was a Cross-crowned heart rising from the centre of a Rose, thus--

I am in a position to maintain that this was the true and esoteric symbol of the Society, as the Crucified Rose was the avowed, exoteric emblem, because in a professedly authoritative work on the secret *figuren* of the Order--"Geheime Figuren der Rosenkreuzer ans dem 16ten und 17ten Jahrhundert"--I find the following remarkable elaboration of the Lutheran seal, which practically decides the question.

Taking into consideration that the "Naometria" of Simon Studion and the original draft of the "Nuptiæ Chymicæ" both belong to nearly the same period, and that Andreas was undoubtedly acquainted with the work of the mystical teacher of Marbach, as a passage in the "Turris Babel" makes evident, it is not an impossible supposition that the young student of Tübingen came into personal communication with Studion, who was only some fifty miles distant in the cheapest days of travelling, and having a natural inclination to secret societies, became associated with the *Militia*

Crucifera Evangelica. Out of this connection the "Nuptiæ Chymicæ" might naturally spring, and the subsequent Rosicrucian society was the *Militia* transfigured after the death of Studion, and after the travels and experience of Andreas had divested him of his boyish delusions. Having proved the hollowness of their pretensions, but still bound by his pledge, he speaks of them henceforth as a deception and a mockery, and attempts to replace them by a practical Christian association without mysticism and symbols, making no pretension to occult knowledge, or to transcendant powers.

This view is not altogether a new one, and undoubtedly has its difficulties. It cannot account for the publication of the "Nuptiæ Chymicæ" in 1616, nor for the revision which it apparently underwent at the very period when Andreas was projecting the unalchemical Christian Fraternity; but so far as it extends, it does not torture the facts with which it professes to deal. I present it not in my character as a historian, but simply as a hypothesis which may be tolerated. To my own mind it is far from satisfactory, and, from a careful consideration of all the available materials, I consider that no definite conclusion can be arrived at. There is nothing in the internal character of the "Fama" and "Confessio Fraternitatis" to shew that they are a jest. On the other hand, they embody a fabulous story. There is no proof that they did or did not emanate from a secret society. The popular argument that the manifestoes were addressed to "the learned of Europe," but the earnest entreaties of the flower of theosophical literati for admission into the ranks of the Fraternity remained unanswered, is no proof that the Society itself did not exist, for the statement is vicious in the extreme. We have absolutely no means of ascertaining with whom it may have come into communication, or what letters and applications were answered, because inviolable secrecy would cover the whole of the proceedings, and those who might have the best reason to know that the Society existed would be most obliged to hold their peace. Thus "the meritorious Order of the R. C." still remains shrouded in mystery, but this mystery is destitute of romance and almost of interest. The avowed opinions of the Fraternity for ever prevent us from supposing that they were in possession of any secrets which would be worth disentombing. To have accomplished the *magnum opus* of the veritable adept, is to be master of the Absolute and the heir of Eternity, is to be above all prejudices, all fears, and all sectarian bitterness. By the aid of an ultra-Horatian philosophy we may conceive that such men have been, and still are, but they have passed above "material forms" and the clouded atmosphere of terrestrial ideas; they inhabit the ideal "city of intelligence and love." They have left the brawling gutter of religious squabbling, the identification of Antichrist, the destruction of the Pope by means of nails, and the number of the beast, to Baxter and Guinness, Cumming and Brothers the prophet, who may share its squalors and wretchedness with--the Rosicrucian Fraternity.

CHAPTER IX. PROGRESS OF ROSICRUCIANISM IN GERMANY.

THE immediate result of the "Fama" and "Confessio Fraternitatis" in Germany has been so well described by Professor Buhle that I cannot do better than transcribe this portion of his work as it is interpreted by Thomas De Quincey.

"The sensation which was produced throughout Germany . . . is sufficiently evidenced by the repeated editions . . . (of the manifestoes) which appeared between 1614 and 1617, but still more by the prodigious commotion which followed in the literary world. In the library at Göttingen there is a body of letters addressed to the imaginary order of Father Rosy Cross, from 1614 to 1617, by persons offering themselves as members. These letters are filled with complimentary expressions and testimonies of the highest respect, and are all printed, the writers alleging that, being unacquainted with the address of the society, they could not send them through any other than a public channel. As certificates of their qualifications, most of the candidates have enclosed specimens of their skill in alchemy and cabbalism. Some of the letters are signed with initials only, or with fictitious names, but assign real places of address. Many other literary persons there were at that day who forbore to write letters to the society, but threw out small pamphlets containing their opinions of the Order, and of its place of residence. Each successive writer pretended to be better informed on that point than all his predecessors. Quarrels arose; partisans started up on all sides; the uproar and confusion became indescribable; cries of heresy and atheism resounded from every corner; some were for calling in the secular power; and the more coyly the invisible society retreated from the public advances so much the more eager and amorous were its admirers, and so much the more bloodthirsty its antagonists. Meantime, there were some who, from the beginning, had escaped the general delusion, and there were many who had gradually recovered from it. It was remarked that of the many printed letters to the society, though courteously and often learnedly written, none had been answered; and all attempts to penetrate the darkness in which the order was shrouded by its unknown memorialist were successfully baffled. Hence arose a suspicion that some bad designs lurked under the ostensible purposes of these mysterious publications. Many vile impostors arose, who gave themselves out for members of the Rosicrucian order; and upon the credit which they thus obtained for a season, cheated numbers of their money by alchemy, or of their health by panaceas. Three in particular made a great noise at Watzlar, at Nuremburg, and at Augsburg; all were punished by the magistracy--one lost his ears in running the gauntlet, and one was hanged. At this crisis stepped forward a powerful writer, who attacked the supposed order with much scorn and homely good sense. This was Andrew Libau. He exposed the impracticability of the meditated reformation, the incredibility of the legend of Father Rosy Cross, and the hollowness of the pretended sciences which they professed. He pointed the attention of governments to the confusions which these impostures were producing, and predicted from them a renewal of the scenes which had attended the fanaticism of the Anabaptists."Andreas Libavius was born at Halle in Saxony about the year 1560. He was appointed professor of history and poetry at Jena in 1588, practised as a physician at Rotembourg on the Tauber from 1591 till 1605, when he became rector of the college of Casimir at Coburg in Franconia, where he died in 1616. He was the first writer who mentioned the transfusion of blood from one animal to another, and the property of oxide of gold to colour glass red. He also invented a chemical preparation, called the liquor of Libavius, "a highly concentrated muriatic acid, much impregnated with tin," and which has been long used in laboratories. He has been falsely represented by M. Hoefer as a follower of Paracelsus, but appears to have believed in the transmutation of metals, and in the medical virtues of various auriferous preparations. He is considered to rank among the first students of chemistry who pursued experimental researches upon the true method. His "Alchymia Recognita" and his "History of Metals" are among the best practical manuals of the period. Though seeking the Philosophick Stone, he attached no credit to the Rosicrucian manifestoes, and was one of the first writers who attacked them, in two Latin folios dated 1615, and in a smaller German pamphlet which appeared in the following year. The first of these works contains an exhaustive criticism of the Harmonico-Magical Philosophy of the mysterious Brotherhood. It is entitled "Exercitatio Paracelsica nova de notandis ex scripto Fraternitatis de Rosea Cruce," and forms part of a larger "Examen Philosophiæ Novæ, quæ veteri abrogandæ Opponitur."

Professor Buhle is one of those interesting literary characters, by no means uncommonly met with, whose luminous hypotheses completely transfigure every fact which comes within the range of their radiation. Few persons who have taken the pains to labour through the ponderous folios of Libavius would dream of terming him a powerful writer, and personally I have failed to discern much of that "homely good sense" which manifested itself so gratuitously before the discerning eyes of the acute German savant. The criticisms, on the contrary, are weak, verbose, and tedious, and the investigations, as a whole, appear to have little *raison d'être*. It may, in fact, be impartially declared that there is only one thing more barren and wearisome than the host of pamphlets, elucidations, apologies, epistles, and responses written on the Rosicrucian side, and that is the hostile criticism of the opposing party, and the dead level of unprofitable flatness which characterises its prosaic commonplace is an infliction which I honestly trust will be spared to all my readers.

Master Andreas Libavius, though he wrote upon Azoth, was a practical thinker, and he refused to contemplate the projected universal reformation through the magic spectacles of the Rosicrucian. He had not read Wordsworth, and he had no definite opinions as to "the light that never was on land or sea." So he penned what Professor Buhle might call a searching criticism; he was right in so far as the reformation is still to come, but in these days we have read Wordsworth, and we prefer the vague poetry of Rosicrucian aspirations to the perditional dulness of Master Libavius' prose. Still we respect Professor Buhle, chiefly because we love De Quincey, and we have a thin streak of kindly feeling for his alchemical *protégé*, so we recommend him as an antidote to Mr Hargrave Jennings, who has doubtless never read him, and seems only to have heard by report of such documents as the Fame and Confession of the meritorious order of the Brethren R. C.

Though he disbelieved in the universal reformation, Libavius did not reject the signs of the times. "No one doubts that we are in the last age of the world, by reason of the signs which have preceded nearly every important event, and are still at this day repeatedly appearing." He takes exception to the philosophical peregrination of the high illuminated C. R. C. in Arabia, because it was superfluous to seek magicians in the east when they abounded at home. Some of his objections are, however, sufficiently pertinent. "If the society hath been ordained and commissioned of God, it ought to be in a position to prove its vocation in some conclusive manner." Incidentally he denounces astrology. "We have heard and read innumerable astrological theories, but we have not discovered their rational basis. On the contrary, we are daily deceived by lying predictions." With regard to the secrecy of the Order, he flings at it the following text--*Omnis qui male agit, odit lucent et non venit ad lucem, ne arguantur opera ejus.* Condemning their anonymous mystery, he asks--"Is their danger greater than Luther's, threatened by the proscription of the Pope and the Emperor both?" Representing the Rosicrucians as promising a new Theologia, Physica, and Mathematica, he asks--"What manner of new theology is this, seeing there is nothing new under the sun? Again, where is its novelty, if it be that of the primitive Church? Is it of the Gentile, Mahometan, Jew, Papist, Arian, Anabaptist, Lutheran, or disciple of Paracelsus? Make unto yourselves also a new God, with a new heaven, and beware lest you are plunged into the old perdition! On our part, we will cling to the antiquity of the canonical Scriptures." And then in regard to the new physics, "If it be after the fashion of Parcelsus, chew the cud of your own reflections in silence, and slumber placidly in your absurdity. . . . If ye come with the cabalistic calculations concerning the fifty gates of understanding, scrutinising the *mysteriarcham Dei,* take care that ye are not consumed by the fire which is therein, for those who will become searchers of majesty shall be overwhelmed with glory."

The "Analysis Confessionis Fraternitatis de Rosea Cruce pro admonitione et Instructione eorum, qui, quia judicandum sit de ista nova factione scire cupiant," extracts, after the author's own fashion, the thirty-seven "reasons of our purpose and intention" which are to be found hidden in that Rosicrucian manifesto, and criticises the *Viæ accedendi,* or methods of approaching the Order, which are—I. By a written petition. II. By the study of the Scriptures and their interpretation in the cabilistico-magical manner of the Paracelsists. III. By the writings and precepts of Paracelsus. IV. By the symbolical characters inscribed on the Macrocosmos.

These two Latin treatises were supplemented by a less tedious German pamphlet, which appeared at Francfurt in 1616 under the title of "Well-wishing objections concerning the Fame and Confession of the Brotherhood of the R. C., and their universal reformation of the whole world before the day of Judgment, and transformation thereof into an Earthly Paradise, such as was inhabited by Adam before the fall, and the restitution of all arts and wisdom as possessed by Adam, Enoch, Salomon, &c. Written with great care, by desire and command of some superior persons, by Andrew Libavius." It claims to be inspired by a spirit of friendly criticism, decides that the Order does exist, advises the accomplishment of a limited and private reformation, leaving the universal one to God, as the world is far too corrupt for improvement before the judgment day, and that a pretension so large will never by any possibility be carried out. Though posing as a critic, he advises all persons to join the Order, because there is much to be learned and much wisdom to be attained by so doing. He praises their sound doctrine in matters of religion, particularly the denunciation of the Pope and Mahomet, the value they set upon the Bible, &c. It is evident, in fact, that in spite of his "homely good sense" he had radically changed his ground. The treatise is divided into forty-three chapters, and among the subjects discussed are the Spheric Art, the *Lapis Philosophorum,* and the Magical Language.

What we seek as vainly in the most authoritative Rosicrucian apologists as in their critics, is any additional information concerning the society, its members, or its whereabouts. Such information is promised frequently on the title-pages of the innumerable pamphlets of the period, but it is not given, and the proffered proofs of the existence of the Order are confined to abstract considerations devoid of historical value.

Professor Buhle considers that the attacks of Libavius joined to other writings "of the same tendency" might possibly have dispelled the delusion, except for the conduct of Andreas, whom he represents as doing his best to increase it by the publication of other documents, and for that of the

Paracelsists. "With frantic eagerness they had sought to press into the imaginary order; but, finding themselves lamentably repulsed in all their efforts, at length they paused; and, turning suddenly round, they said to one another, 'What need to court this perverse order any longer? We are ourselves Rosicrucians as to all the essential marks laid down in the three books. We also are holy persons of great knowledge; we also make gold, or shall make it; we also, no doubt, give us but time, shall reform the world: external ceremonies are nothing: substantially it is clear that we are the Rosicrucian Order.' Upon this they went on in numerous books and pamphlets to assert that they were the identical Order instituted by Father Rosycross, and described in the 'Fama Fraternitatis.' The public mind was now perfectly distracted; no man knew what to think; and the uproar became greater than ever."

Here is a dramatic situation well conceived and described; its only fault is the very slender foundation of actual fact on which it appears to be based. I have failed altogether to discover those numerous books and pamphlets wherein the Paracelsists assert that they are to all intents and purposes identical with the invisible and unapproachable Brotherhood. Their anxiety to be admitted into its ranks may be freely granted, but it is remarkable how few of the pamphleteers who wrote favourably on the Rosicrucian mystery made any claim to be personally connected therewith.

In the pages which follow I shall give a brief account, arranged in chronological order, of the most important and interesting publications that appeared in elucidation of this mystery. A work of considerable interest was printed in 1615, under the title "Echo of the God-illuminated Brotherhood of the Worthy Order R. C., to wit, an absolute proof that not only all which is stated in the 'Fama' and 'Confessio' of the R. C. Brotherhood is possible and true, but that it has been known already for nineteen years and more to a few God-fearing people, and has been laid down by them in certain secret writings; as it has all been stated and made public in an excellent magical letter and pamphlet by the Worshipful Brotherhood R. C., in print in the German language." The accredited author was Julius Sperber of Anholt, Dessau. This work was printed at Dantzig by Andreas Huenfeldts. It maintains that there have been only a few human beings who have been worthy to become recipients of the wisdom of God, the reason being that so few have sought it with the necessary earnestness. When Christ was on the earth he had innumerable listeners, of whom only a small portion could discern the significance of His teachings. It was for this cause that He said to his disciples--"To you it is given to know the mysteries of the Kingdom of Heaven, but to them it is not given." Peter, James, and John were the only three of His apostles to whom he revealed these mysteries, and to them He showed the same sight that had been vouchsafed by God to Elias and Moses. Only those who renounce the world and their own fleshly lusts

146

can become worthy to know such secrets. Nobody who is addicted to mundane wisdom can ever attain them, for the wisdom of God and the wisdom of this world are contradictory.

The preface is addressed to the R.C. Brotherhood. It admonishes the members to persevere in the way they have chosen, and to get possessed of the secrets of God. It praises their wisdom and knowledge, but says that much of what is stated in the "Fama" and "Confessio" must appear foolish to the worldly wise. It calls upon the Brethren to meet together in the name of the Holy Trinity, and to teach the true light to the world, as it is contained in the secret meaning of Holy Scripture and of Nature. Some curious information, not always relevant to the main object, is scattered throughout the volume. The second preface mentions a certain Petrus Wirtzigh of Presslau as one of the greatest and wisest men of his time, who, being by profession a medical man, studied the secret arts with such zeal that he became master of many wonderful mysteries. He was the author of many large unpublished volumes which the writer of the "Echo," being his great friend, has been allowed to dip into, and he avers that they contain much wisdom and curious lore. Another wise and God-loving man was Ægidius Guttmann in Suaria, who wrote a book which he divided into twenty-four volumes. The author of the "Echo" compares this work, having regard to the wisdom of its contents, with the seventy volumes which God dictated by His angel to the prophet.

Like other writers on the Rosicrucian side, the author of the "Echo" deals in vague generalities, and even the Laws of the Fraternity which he publishes are worthless as regards information. They run as follows:--

1. Love your neighbour.
2. Talk not badly of him, neither hold him in contempt.
3. Be faithful.
4. Be modest and obedient.
5. Do not ridicule the secret studies.
6. Keep silent about what you learn from these studies.
7. Share your fortune with your fellow-creatures. According to this apologist of the secret order, "Adam was the first Rosicrucian of the Old Testament and Simeon the last." The golden chain of the esoteric tradition was not broken by Christ, who established "a new college of magic."

In 1615, Julianus de Campis published an "open letter or report," addressed to all who have read anything concerning the new Brotherhood of R. C., or have heard anything of the position of this matter. It accounts for the Rosicrucians not revealing their whereabouts, "and not answering the letters addressed to them. He was himself," he said, "a member of the Order; but in all his travels he had met but three other members, there being (as he presumed) no more persons on the earth worthy of being entrusted with its mysteries." It is needless to say that an initiate of the

Fraternity would be accurately acquainted with its numerical strength, and that the writer's statement on this point contradicts the "Fama Fraternitatis." The pamphlet otherwise is not of great importance. "There are many who run for, but few who gain, the jewel. Therefore I, Julianus de Campis, admonish all who are governed by a fortunate disposition not to be made obstinate by their own diffidence, nor by the judgments of ignorant people." Many great secrets are concealed by Nature, and those who study them are worthy of every praise. The R. C. are defended against various accusations, and the theologians who attack them are reminded that the questions raised are without their province, because they are *theologi* and not *theosophi*. The secret art of the R. C. is declared to be a matter of fact, and not an abstract or fanciful thing; and the *profanum vulgus* are assured that those who are in the possession of such an imperial secret can dispense with the praise of the world. The "Fama Remissa ad Fratres Roseæ Crucis," which appeared in 1616, is to a great extent an anonymous pamphlet written against the pretensions and ideas of the Brethren, principally denouncing their impracticable and Utopian ambition to reform the whole world. It complains bitterly of their religious opinions, and absolutely declines to acknowledge them as a good society until they openly accept and subscribe to the Confession of Augsbourg. A brief Latin appendix incidentally discusses the doctrine of transubstantiation and to reconcile the words of Jesus, "*Hoc est corpus meum*," with the statement of this Evangelist, *et ascendit in cœlum*, it speculates on the distance which intervenes between the earth and the Empyrean. According to Pencerus the eighth sphere is distant 20081 1/28 semidiameters of the earth, and the distance, according to the "Fama Remissa," from the Mount of Olives to the Empyrean Heaven is, in its *summa tota*, 17,266,001 *milliaria Germania!*The following year beheld the publication of Brotoffer's curious and perverse alchemical interpretation of the Universal Reformation, another edition of the Rosicrucian manifestoes, with additions by Julianus de Campis and Georg Molthers, and two works from the pen of Michael Maier, which will be noticed in the next chapter. Among the curious pamphlets of this year professing to treat of the mysterious Order, must be included the "'Fraternitatis Rosatæ Crucis Confessio Recepta,' to wit: A short and well-wishing report concerning the Confession or Faith of the Brethren of the Rosy Cross, useful to all readers who not only consider their well-being in this world, but their salvation in the next. Written by A. O. M T. W." This appeared in defence of the Order, and maintains that it is a good and useful Society, which is not merely in possession of many and great secrets, but is righteous in the eyes of Almighty God. The author distinguishes at length between the different ways whereby God makes Himself known, and declares that it requires much study and careful research, as well as personal sacrifice, to become the possessor of transcendental secrets, but that anyone can do so by following the Divine counsels. He concludes with an admonition to "the highly-wise and God-beloved R. C." to press on with their sublime work.

About this time a somewhat vicious attack was made on the supposed Society by a writer calling himself Fredericus G. Menapius, but whose real name was Johann Valentin Alberti, and who is associated by Buhle with Irenæus Agnostus as a personal friend of Andreas. It is clear, however, from the evidence of all the pamphlets, that Agnostus and Menapius are one and the same person. "Epitimia, F. R. C., to wit: The final manifestation or discovery and defence of the worthy and worshipful Order R. C. Also of the true and well-known confession addressed to all classes of literati and illustrious persons in Europe. Written by command of the above-mentioned society by Irenaeus Agnostus (Menapius)." The only edition of this work which I have seen is dated 1619, but it seems to have been originally published about two years previously. It is a skit written against the R. C. by Menapius, but pretends to be printed and published by the command of the Order. The principal purpose of the pamphlet is to prove that the Rosicrucian Fraternity was founded by the Jesuits for the purpose of the secret propaganda of their doctrines in opposition to the Protestant religion. It begins with a lengthy and pseudo-authoritative laudation of the writer, who is declared to be an eminently learned and godly man, having saved the lives of a number of persons in a miraculous manner, and disputed victoriously with the most learned Catholic divines. It proceeds to a vigorous denunciation of the Roman Church for its manifold corruptions and abuses, citing a good many historical examples of princes who have expressed themselves in similar terms, and concluding with an admonition to live well and act uprightly. Speaking in his own person, the author addresses his supposed *confrères* in the following fashion:--"I know not, my Brothers of the R. C., what manner of men to consider you. T have troubled my mind about you this long time, but can attain to no conclusion, because all that you set down in your writings has been so long familiar. Could you tell me anything of the unicorn, or anything more trustworthy than has emanated from Andreas Baccius, your productions would be much more valuable. A number of hooks have been written by you, or have appeared in your name, but they teem with such violent contradictions that I should imagine you were yourselves in doubt as to who or what you are, and as to your own performances." Afterwards he very reasonably declares that if the Rosicrucians are the depositaries of a beneficial knowledge, they ought to proclaim it publicly in their own persons and not in anonymous pamphlets. He upbraids them as magicians who falsely pretend to great power, says that he has travelled in many countries without hearing anything concerning them, and concludes by expressing his conviction that their supposed wisdom is a shallow pretence, and that they are in reality ignorant people.

This attack was presently followed by a tract entitled "I. Menapius Roseæ Crucis, to wit: Objections on the part of the unanimous Brotherhood against the obscure and unknown writer, F. G. Menapius, and against his being classed among the true brethren. II. A Citation of the same person to our final Court at Schmejarien contra Florentinus de Valentia. III. Finally, a convocation of the R. C. Fratres to the same invisible place. By order of the worshipful society. Written and published by Theophilus Schweighart. 1619." Here Menapius presents himself under another name, and poses as his own opponent. The pamphlet contains a sort of legal process, with citation, defence, &c. One of the arguments used against the Rosicrucian Fraternity, who believed in the manufacture of gold from ignoble metals, is as follows:--"A grown up man is a reasoning being; so is a young boy. A cow is an unreasoning being; so is a calf. But this does not prove that the cow is a calf; and the transmutation of ignoble metals into gold is just as easy as to transform a cow into a calf. of you ask why there is so little gold, it is for the same reason that there are so few cows, namely, in the one case, because the young calves are killed, and in the other, because the ignoble metals are not left long enough in the earth, but are extracted by avaricious people." Menapius is the most entertaining of the dull race of Rosicrucian critics, but his analogical arguments are not of a convincing nature. He concludes with an admonition to all and several-- literati, nobles, merchants, peasants, &c.--to live well and to do their duty.

Menapius, as I have said, is represented by Buhle as a friend of Andreas, and Andreas is accredited with two Rosicrucian pamphlets which appeared under the name of "Florentinus de Valentia." The authority may be questionable or not, but the reference is somewhat suicidal to the Buhle-Andrean hypothesis, for not only do we discover the pseudonymous author attacking his personal friend, but hurrying forward full of zeal to the defence of the Rosicrucian pretensions. "Rosa Florescens contra F. G. Menapii Calumniis, to wit: A short notice and refutation of the libels published on June 3, 1617, in Latin, and on July 15 of the same year in German by F. G. Menapius, against the Rosicrucian Society. Written by Florentinus de Valentia in great zeal." It is a reply to the first pamphlet of Menapius, the Latin original of which I have been unable to trace. It begins by blaming Menapius for his extravagant self-laudation, then refers to the attack on the secresy of the Society, and on the anonymous publication of their manifestoes. It declares any other method than that of secresy to be contrary to the will of God, and in other ways dangerous, asserting that nobody suffers by the concealment of their names and places of abode. The writer further accuses Menapius of blind hatred of the Rosicrucians, when he compares them to the devils, for the whole intent of the Society is the welfare of all humanity. He says:--"The opinion of the Fraternity is not that all men should be made or become equal, because the majority are too hard and sinful, but that the few who love God, and live to please Him, should be like Adam in Paradise." The desire of the Order is to serve God as faithfully as possible, to discover the secrets of Nature, and to use them in diffusing a true belief in Christ, and for the glory of God. Therefore, the author requests Menapius to desist from blaming and libelling the members of the Fraternity, but rather to turn round and to love them, because they are true seekers of the veritable wisdom.

In a Latin appendix to a tract entitled "Fons Gratiæ," by Irenæus Agnostus, Johann Valentin Alberti, *alias* F. G. Menapius, *alias* Theophilus Schweighart, *alias* Irenæus Agnostus, published a short rejoinder in prose and verse to the defence of Valentia.

"Judicia de Statu Fraternitatis de Rosea Cruce" is a *mélange* of prose and verse, with addresses *ad venerandos, doctissimos, et illuminatissimos, viros Dom. Fratres S. Roseæ Crucis conjunctissimos*, and as the judgment is professedly that of an outsider seeking initiation, it does not throw any light upon the proceedings of the Society. It is crammed with extravagant adulation of the pious, learned, and illuminated Brothers, but is otherwise not inelegantly written, and has apt classical quotations. A lofty ambition is claimed by the aspirant to association, who avers that he is in search of no common and metallic gold, but that Philosophical and Spiritual Treasure, one particle of which is sufficient to transmute and perfectionise the soul, and conduct it from illumination to illumination. This is that veritable gold, says the alchemical enthusiast, none other than the first and all-containing knowledge, whereby

Mens pura et nullo mortali pondera pressa,

Libera terrenis affectibus, atria cœli

Scandit, et ætherea cum diis versatur in aula.

None can expect to attain it unless he shall first have expelled--

A sese omne nefas, purgatus crimine ab omni,

Quippe habitare negat fœdum Sapientia pectus,

Impurasque odit, cum sit purissima, mentes. Those who believe in the existence and magical endowments of the Rosicrucian Brethren will hope that this promising pupil received the recompense so undoubtedly due to the beauty of his aspirations. The Latin Epistle is supplemented by a *post datum*, which refers to the "Nuptiæ Chymicæ" as containing "the whole chymical artifice enigmatically delineated."

"Responsum ad Fratres Rosaceæ Crucis Illustres" is a printed letter addressed to the Fraternity in the year 1618, by Hercules Ovallodius, Alsatus; Heermannus Condesyanus; and Martinus à Casa Cegdessa Marsiliensis. It is a piece of piteous pleading for admission into the ranks of the Brethren by three writers who believe themselves to have fallen upon evil times, and know that there is no entrance into the mystic temple which is filled with the glory and power of God, till the seven last plagues have been poured out upon the earth. They acknowledge the *Viri Fratres* as the instruments of the Divine vengeance in the consummation of the age. *Ipse est malleus noster et arma, vos ipsius servi.*

A curious Rosicrucian reverie, entitled "F. R. C. Fama e scanzia Redux," written in execrable Latin, and printed in a style corresponding with its literary merits, appeared Anno Christi M.DC.XVIII., as the title has it. It professes to be the trumpet *Jubilei ultimi,* that is, presumably, of the last jubilee year among the Jews, and bears for one of its mottoes, "One woe hath passed; behold, there come yet two other woes after this one." It is precisely one of those mysterious and problematical productions which are sometimes supposed to conceal deep secrets, because they are completely unintelligible and barbarous. It professes to contain a *Judicium de Fraternitatis R. C. Sigillo et Buccina et futuræ Reformationis Mysterie,* and is mystically separated into seven parts or chapters, each terribly intituled. Thus the seventh is the "voice of the dove speaking concerning the jawbone of the ass," and the "Judgment" itself is averred to proceed from a similar quarter "*ex asini mandibula.*" The statement is apparently serious, for this extraordinary local habitation is parenthetically explained to be the *fons vitæ,* or fount of life. The whole pamphlet is a raving chaos of scriptural quotations concerning the Corner Stone, the Keys of David, and the proximity of the *Regnum Dei.* It concludes with the following triumphant admonition to the reader:--

Quisquis de Roseæ dubitas Crucis ordine Fratrum,

Hoc lege, perlecto carmine certus eris.

It is needless to say that the whole pamphlet does not contain a single reference to the Rosicrucians.

"φλενσθιουρεδας. Hoc est Redintegratio," addressed to the "Brotherhood of the Rose-Cross," appeared in 1619, with the motto, Omnes de Saba veniunt, aurum et thus deferentes, et laudem Domini annunciantes, and prefaced by the following lines

O Roseæ Fratres crucis, O pia turba sophorum,
Vestro præsentes esse favore mihi.
Fama velut cunctis vos respondere paratos
Exhibet; Ah ne sint irrita vota precor.
Fidus amicus ero, fidos quoque gestit amicus
Mens mea de musis conciliare novem.
At, si scripta fient quædam minus apta, flabello
Fratrum non Momi sint abigenda, pio.
Usus enim Famæ potiori ex parte loquelis
Fratres propitios hinc mage spero mihi.

This little pamphlet compares different expressions of opinions by opposed parties, and concludes that any person may take part with a good conscience in the Brotherhood, and without prejudice to their Christianly convictions. It cites the common reproaches cast at the Order, to wit: that they are enemies of all lawful government, Jesuits, or Calvinists, also the suspicion that there is no order at all, but that the whole business is a farce, written for some undefined purpose. It maintains that there is such an order, and that it is in possession of great secrets, because it consists of preeminently learned men. Finally, the author exhorts all to join it.

Among the acknowledged works of Andreas which contain satirical references to the Rosicrucian mystery may be mentioned "Menippus, sive, Dialogorum Satyricorum Centuria, inanitatum nostratium speculum," 1673, 8vo; "Institutio Magica pro curiosis," and "Turris Babel, sive, Judicium de Fraternitatis Roseæ crucis Chaos." Argentorati, 1619, 12mo. They contain absolutely nothing which can be tortured into a confession of the authorship of the manifestoes, nor any gleam of light on any subject connected with the Society. They express simply the personal opinions of Andreas, and those who make a contrary assertion have read their own hypotheses between the lines of their author.

By the year 1620, the subject of the Rosicrucians was completely exhausted in Germany. It had been discussed from all standpoints by men of the most various character, but, in the absence of ascertainable facts, no man was wiser; and as the Rosicrucians, supposing them to have existed, kept silent amidst the confusion of opinions and the unproductive clamour which they had created, making no further sign, the interest concerning them gradually died away. Seekers for the *magnum opus*, and persons imbued with the ambition to reform the world, looked elsewhere for light and assistance. Pseudo-Rosicrucian societies, of course, appeared on the field, and gangs of miserable tricksters who traded on individual credulity by the power of the magical name. Buhle cites from the "Occulta Philosophia" of Ludovicus Conradus Orvius, the unhappy personal experience of that writer concerning such a society, "pretending to deduce themselves from Father Rosy-Cross, and who were settled at the Hague in 1622. After swindling him out of his own and his wife's fortune, amounting to eleven thousand dollars, they kicked him out of the order, with the assurance that they would murder him if he revealed their secrets, 'which secrets,' says he, 'I have faithfully kept, and for the same reason that women keep secrets-- viz., because I have none to reveal; for their knavery is no secret.'"

Vague rumours of veritable Rosicrucian adepts were occasionally heard, but in spite of their boasted powers, in spite of their projected reformation of all the world, and in spite of the seven years' strife of tongues which they occasioned, they had no influence whatsoever upon the thought of their age. An isolated and doubtful transmutation is occasionally ascribed to them, which is the sum total of their alchemical achievements. They posed principally as a healing fraternity, yet their influence on the medical science of their century is less still than that which they exerted upon alchemy. "In medicine," says Figuier, "that art which they were pledged to practise wherever they wandered, according to the first commandment of their master, the catalogue of their triumphs is speedily exhausted. We have already seen that they boasted of having cured the leprosy in an English count. They also claimed to have restored life to a Spanish King after he had been dead for six hours. Apart from these two cures, the second of which is doubtless a miracle, but can boast only of their own testimony, their whole medical history consists in vague allegations and a few unimportant facts, as, for instance, that which Gabriel Naudé cites in the following terms:--

"In the year 1615 a certain pilgrim suddenly appeared in a German town, and assisted, as a doctor, at the prognostication of the death of a woman whom he had helped by some of his remedies; he assumed to be proficient in several languages, related what had occurred in the town during his sojourn at this house; in a word, apart front the doctrine in which he shone still more, he was in every way similar to that Wandering Jew described by Cayot in his "Histoire Septenaire"--moderate, reserved, carelessly clad, never willingly remaining a long time in any one place, and still less desirous to be taken for what he nevertheless claimed to be, the third brother of the R.C., as he testified to the doctor Moltherus, who could not be so certainly persuaded to give credence to his statements, but has presented us with this history, leaving our judgment free to decide if it could establish a certain proof of the existence of this Company." According to Sprengel, a true Rosicrucian had only to gaze fixedly on a person, and however dangerous his disease, he was instantaneously healed; the Brethren claimed to cure all diseases, without the help of drugs, by means of imagination and faith. But the matter remains at this day just where the claim originally left it, wholly unsupported by fact.

CHAPTER X. ROSICRUCIAN APOLOGISTS: MICHAEL MAIER.

THIS celebrated German alchemist was born at Ruidsburg, in Holstein, about the year 1658. In his youth, says the "Biographie Universelle," he applied himself to the study of medicine, and establishing himself at Rostoch, he practised that art with so much success that he became physician to the Emperor Rudolph II., by whom he was ennobled for his services. Some adepts, notwithstanding, succeeded in wiling him from the practical path he had followed so long; *il se passionna pour le grand œuvre*, and scoured all Germany to hold conferences with those whom he thought to be in possession of transcendent secrets. Another account declares that he sacrificed his health, his fortune, and his time to these "ruinous absurdities." According to Buhle, he travelled extensively, particularly to England, where he made the acquaintance of Robert Fludd. He finished by accepting the post of physician at Magdebourg, where he died in 1622.

Michael Maier is one of the most important and interesting persons connected with the Rosicrucian controversy. He was the first to transplant it into England, "and as he firmly believed in the existence of such a sect, he sought to introduce himself to its notice; but finding this impossible," says Buhle, "he set himself to establish such an order by his own efforts; and in his future writings he spoke of it as already existing--going so far even as to publish its laws." He was a voluminous and ingenious writer, and, according to Langlet du Fresnoy, all his treatises were excessively rare, even in the eighteenth century. "They contain much curious material," says this writer, "and I am astonished that the German booksellers, who publish innumerable worthless works, have not condescended to perceive that a complete collection of the writings of Michael Maier would be more useful and command a larger sale than the trash with which they overwhelm scholars and the public generally."

This task still remains to be accomplished, and considerations of space will prevent me from even supplying a bibliography of these singular works. The most curious of all is "Atalanta Fugiens," which abounds with quaint and mystical copperplate engravings, emblematically revealing the most unsearchable secrets of Nature. This production, with the "Tripus Aureus," or three tracts of Basil Valentin, Thomas Norton, and Cremer, the Abbot of Westminster, all of which were unearthed by the diligence of Maier, seem to have appeared before he had immersed himself in the insoluble Rosicrucian mystery. The "Silentium Post Clamores," however, published at Francfurt in 1617, professes to account not only for the speech in season uttered by the Fraternity in its priceless manifestoes, but for the silence which followed when it declined even to reply to the pamphlets and epistles of persons seeking initiation. The author asserts that from very ancient times philosophical colleges have existed among various nations for the study of medicine and of natural secrets, and that the discoveries which they made were perpetuated from generation to generation by the initiation of new members, whence the existence of a similar association at that present time was no subject for astonishment. The philosophical colleges referred to are those of old Egypt, whose priests in reality were alchemists, "seeing that Isis and Osiris are sulphur and *argentum vivum*"; of the Orphic and Eleusinian mysteries, of the Samothracian Cabiri, the Magi of Persia, the Brachmans of India, the Gymnosophists, Pythagoreans, &c. He maintains that one and all of these were instituted, not for the teaching of exoteric doctrines, but the most arcane mysteries of Nature. Afterwards he argues that if the German Fraternity had existed, as it declares, for so many years, it was better that it should reveal itself, than be concealed for ever under the veil of silence, and that it could not manifest itself otherwise than in the "Fama" and "Confessio Fraternitatis," which contain nothing contrary to reason, nature, experience, or the possibility of things. Moreover, the Order rightly observes that silence which Pythagoras imposed on his disciples, and which alone can preserve the mysteries of existence from the prostitution of the vulgar. The contents of the two manifestoes are declared to be true, and we are further informed that we owe a great debt to the Order for their experimental investigations, and for their discovery of the universal Catholicon. The popular objections preferred against it are disposed of in different chapters, *e.g.*, the charges of necromancy and superstition. The explicit statement of the Society, that all communications addressed to it should not fail to reach their destination, although they were unknown and anonymous, proving apparently false, was a special cause of grievance; those who sought health and those who coveted treasures at their hand were equally disappointed, and, according to Michael Maier, appear to have been equally enraged. He expostulates with them, saying *Non omnis ad omnia omnibus horis paratus est*, but his arguments as a whole can hardly be deemed satisfactory. *Locorum absentia, personarum distantia*, &c., could scarcely prove obstacles to men who were bound by no considerations of space and time, and readers of the inmost heart would have discovered some who were worthy among the host of applicants.

A much larger work, "Symbola Aureæ Mensæ," published in the same year as the "Silentium Post Clamores" also contains some references to the "College of German Philosophers of R. C." The story of the founder is reprinted, and Apollo with the twin muses are represented as contributing various vexatious metrical enigmas for the benefit of those enquirers who desired to be directed to the local habitation of the Order. Neither of these works represents their author as personally connected with the Rosicrucians, nor do they convey any information respecting them. The same must be said of "Themis Aurea, hoc est, De Legibus Fraternitatis R.

C. Tractatus," which Maier published at Francfurt in 1618. It maintains that the laws in question are good, dilates upon the pre-eminent dignity of the healing art, declares that all vices are intolerable in physicians, and that the Rosicrucians are free from all. The most curious and important point in the whole "Apologia" is that Maier declares the "Universal Reformation" to have no connection with the manifestoes of the Society, but to be a tract translated from the Italian, and simply bound up with the "Fama." Moreover, he earnestly endeavours to free the Order from the imputation that it desired to reform the world. *Reformatio omnium hæresum potius ad Deum, quam hominem spectat, nec a Fratribus affectatur.* But whether the *Communis et Generalis Reformatio* had any connection with the Rosicrucians, or not, it is evident from the documents about which there is no doubt or question, and particularly from the "Fama Fraternitatis," that they believed a general revolution to be at hand, and that they would be concerned therein.

A posthumous tract of Michael Maier was published in 1624 by one of his personal friends, who explicitly states that he is ignorant whether the departed alchemist, who so warmly and gratuitously defended the cause of the Rosicrucians, was ever received into their number, but that it is certain he was a Brother of the Christian Religion, or a Brother of the Kingdom of Christ. This statement may simply mean that he was a Christian and a man of God, or, on the other hand, it may signify that he was a member of the Christian Fraternity of Andreas. However this may be, two Latin tracts, being translations from the German made by the same friend of Maier, follow the posthumous pamphlet of the alchemist. The first is a colloquy on the Society by personages respectively called Quirinus, Polydorus, Tyrosophus, Promptutus, and Politicus. The second is an "Echo Colloquii" by Benedict Hilarion, who professes to write "Mandato superiorum," to represent the order, and to be himself a Rosicrucian. There are two mottoes on the title page of this work--the one is *per augusta ad augusta*, the other

Augustis, Augusta, viis petit ardua virtus,
Non datur, ad cœlum currere lata via.

The writer refers in a kindly manner to the propagandist labours of Michael Maier, and assures the anonymous but illustrious Tyrosophus that his Rosicrucian apologies were not written in vain, and hints broadly that he was at length admitted into their Order, which still holds out the promise of initiation to others when the proper time shall have arrived. This publication is singularly free from the sectarian bitterness of the first manifestoes. It recognises that all have erred, including Luther himself, and seems animated by a reasonable and conciliatory spirit. At the end there are published some "Declaratory Canons" of the Order, which define God to be the Eternal Father, incorruptible fire, and everlasting light, discuss the generation of the invisible and incomprehensible Word of God, and the tetradic manifestation of the elements.

In none of these works does the statement of Professor Buhle, concerning the foundation of a Rosicrucian society, and the publication of its laws, receive a particle of corroboration. The other works of Michael Maier are of a purely alchemical nature, save and except some obscure pamphlets which are not in the Library of the British Museum, which I have therefore been unable to consult, and which may contain the information in question; but from my knowledge of Professor Buhle and his romantic methods, I suspect his imagination has been unconsciously at work on some doubtful passages in the writings which have already been noticed, more especially as the personal but anonymous friend who edited Maier's posthumous tract entitled "Ulysses," knew nothing apparently of such a pseudo-association, nor is it likely that the author of the "Echo Colloquii" would hint at his initiation into the genuine order if Maier had instituted a rival society, shining by the borrowed lustre of its name and its symbols.

However this may be, with the death of Michael Maier the Rosicrucians disappear from the literary horizon of Germany till the year 1710, when a writer, calling himself S. R., that is, Sincerus Renatus, otherwise Sigmund Richter, published at Breslau his "Perfect and True Preparation of the Philosophical Stone, according to the Secret of the Brotherhoods of the Golden and Rosy Cross," to which is annexed the "rules of the above-mentioned Order for the initiation of new members" and their enrolment among the Sons of the Doctrine. This extraordinary publication was followed, in 1785-88, by the "Secret Symbols of the Rosicrucians of the Sixteenth and Seventeenth Centuries," which, though published at Altona, seem to have emanated from the same source. The latter work is also of an alchemical nature, and no information of a historical kind is to be found in either. I shall conclude this account of the results of the Rosicrucian manifestoes in Germany with the

Laws of the Brotherhood, as published by Sincerus Renatus.

It is certain, says Semler, that the long series of regulations enumerated by this writer were not adopted before 1622, for Montanus (Ludov. Conr. von Berger), who was supposed to have been expelled from the Order in that year, was not acquainted with them.

I. The brotherhood shall not consist of more than sixty-three members.

II. The initiation of Catholics shall be allowed, and one member is prohibited to question another about his belief.

III. The ten years' office of the Rosicrucian imperator shall be abolished, and he shall be elected for life.

IV. The imperator shall keep the address of every member on his list, to enable them to help each other in case of necessity. A list of all names and birthplaces shall likewise be kept. The eldest brother shall always be imperator. Two houses shall be erected at Nurenberg and Ancona for the periodical conventions.

V. If two or three brethren meet together, they shall not be empowered to elect a new member without the permission of the imperator. Any such election shall be void.

VI. The young apprentice or brother shall be obedient unto death to his master.

VII. The brothers shall not eat together except on Sundays, but if they work together they shall be allowed to live, eat, and drink in common.

VIII. It is prohibited for a father to elect his son or brother, unless he shall have proved him well. It is better to elect a stranger so as to prevent the Art becoming hereditary.

IX. Although two or three of the brethren may be gathered together, they shall not permit anyone, whomsoever it may be, to make his profession to the Order unless he shall have previously taken part in the Practice, and has had full experience of all its workings, and has, moreover, an earnest desire to acquire the Art.

X. When one of the brethren intends to make an heir, such an one shall confess in one of the churches built at our expense, and afterwards shall remain about two years as an apprentice. During this probation he shall be made known to the Congregation, and the Imperator shall be informed of his name, country, profession, and origin, to enable him to despatch two or three members at the proper time with his seal to make the apprentice a brother.

XI. When the brethren meet they shall salute each other in the following manner:--The first shall say, *Ave Frater!* The second shall answer, *Roseæ et Aureæ.* Whereupon the first shall conclude with *Crucis.* After they have thus discovered their position, they shall say one to another, *Benedictus Dominus Deus noster qui dedit nobis signum,* and shall also uncover their seals, because if the name can be falsified the seal cannot.

XII. It is commanded that every brother shall set to work after he has been accepted in our large houses, and has been endowed with the Stone (he receives always a sufficient portion to ensure his life for the space of sixty years). Before beginning he shall recommend himself to God, pledging himself not to use his secret Art to offend Him, to destroy or corrupt the empire, to become a tyrant through ambition or other causes, but always to appear ignorant, invariably asserting that the existence of such secret arts is only proclaimed by charlatans.

XIII. It is prohibited to make extracts from the secret writings, or to have them printed, without permission from the Congregation; also to sign them with the names or characters of any brother. Likewise, it is prohibited to print anything against the Art.

XIV. The brethren shall only be allowed to discourse of the secret Art in a well-closed room.

XV. It is permitted for one brother to bestow the Stone freely upon another, for it shall not be said that this gift of God can be bought with a price.

XVI. It is not permissible to kneel before any one, under any circumstances, unless that person be a member of the Order.

XVII. The brethren shall neither talk much nor marry. Yet it shall be lawful for a member to take a wife if he very much desire it, but he shall live with her in a philosophical mind. He shall not allow his wife to practise over-much with the young brethren. With the old members she may be permitted to practise, and he shall value the honour of his children as his own.

XVIII. The brethren shall refrain from stirring up hatred and discord among men. They shall not discourse of the soul, whether in human beings, animals, or plants, nor of any other subject which, however natural to themselves, may appear miraculous to the common understanding. Such discourse can easily lead to their discovery, as occurred at Rome in the year 1620. But if the brethren be alone they may speak of these secret things.

XIX. It is forbidden to give any portion of the Stone to a woman in labour, as she would be brought to bed prematurely.

XX. The Stone shall not be used at the chase.

XXI. No person having the Stone in his possession shall ask a favour of any one.

XXII. It is not allowable to manufacture pearls or other precious stones larger than the natural size.

XXIII. It is forbidden (under penalty of punishment in one of our large houses) that anyone shall make public the sacred and secret matter, or any manipulation, coagulation, or solution thereof.

XXIV. Because it may happen that several brethren are present together in the same town, it is advised, but not commanded, that on Whitsuntideday any brother shall go to that end of the town which is situated towards sunrise and shall hang up a green cross if he be a Rosicrucian, and a red one if he be a brother of the Golden Cross. Afterwards, such a brother shall tarry in the vicinity till sunset, to see if another brother shall come and hang up his cross also, when they shall salute after the usual manner, make themselves mutually acquainted, and subsequently inform the imperator of their meeting.

XXV. The imperator shall every ten years change his abode, name, and surname. Should he think it needful he may do so at shorter periods, the brethren to be informed with all possible secresy.

XXVI. It is commanded that each brother, after his initiation into the Order, shall change his name and surname, and alter his years with the

Stone. Likewise, should he travel from one country to another, he shall change his name to prevent recognition.

XXVII. No brother shall remain longer than ten years out of his own country, and whenever he departs into another he shall give notice of his destination, and of the name he has adopted.

XXVIII. No brother shall begin to work till he has been one year in the town where he is residing, and has made the acquaintance of its inhabitants. He shall have no acquaintance with the *professores ignorantes*.

XXIX. No brother shall dare to reveal his treasures, either of gold or silver, to any person whomsoever; he shall be particularly careful with members of religious societies, two of our brethren having been lost, anno 1641, thereby. No member of any such society shall be accepted as a brother upon any pretence whatever.

XXX. While working, the brethren shall select persons of years as servants in preference to the young.

XXXI. When the brethren wish to renew themselves, they must, in the first place, travel through another kingdom, and after their renovation is accomplished, must remain absent from their former abode.

XXXII. When brethren dine together, the host, in accordance with the conditions already laid down, shall endeavour to instruct his guests as much as possible.

XXXIII. The brethren shall assemble in our great houses as frequently as possible, and shall communicate one to another the name and abode of the Imperator.

XXXIV. The brethren in their travels shall have no connection nor conversation with women, but shall choose one or two friends, generally not of the Order.

XXXV. When the brethren intend to leave any place, they shall divulge their destination to no one, neither shall they sell anything which they cannot carry away, but shall direct their landlord to divide it among the poor, if they do not return in six weeks.

XXXVI. A brother who is travelling shall carry nothing in oil, but only in the form of powder of the first projection, which shall be enclosed in a metallic box having a metal stopper.

XXXVII. No brother should carry any written description of the Art about him, but should he do so, it must be written in an enigmatical manner.

XXXVIII. Brethren who travel, or take any active part in the world, shall not eat if invited by any man to his table unless their host has first tasted the food. If this be not possible, they shall take in the morning, before leaving home, one grain of our medicine in the sixth projection, after which they can eat without fear, but both in eating and drinking they shall be moderate.

XXXIX. No brother shall give the Stone in the sixth projection to strangers, but only to sick brethren.

XL. If a brother, who is at work with anyone, be questioned as to his position, he shall say that he is a novice and very ignorant. XLI. Should a brother desire to work, he shall only employ an apprentice in default of securing the help of a brother, and shall be careful that such an apprentice is not present at all his operations.

XLII. No married man shall be eligible for initiation as a brother, and in case any brother seeks to appoint an heir, he shall choose some one unencumbered by many friends. If he have friends, he must take a special oath to communicate the secrets to none, under penalty of punishment by the imperator.

XLIII. The brethren may take as an apprentice anyone they have chosen for their heir, provided he be ten years old. Let the person make profession. When the permission of the imperator is obtained, whereby anybody is really accepted as a member, he can be constituted heir.

XLIV. It is commanded that a brother who by any accident has been discovered by any prince, shall sooner die than initiate him into the secret; and all the other brethren, including the imperator, shall be obliged to venture their life for his liberation. If, by misfortune, the prince remain obstinate, and the brother dies to preserve the secret, he shall be declared a martyr, a relative shall be received in his place, and a monument with secret inscriptions shall be erected in his honour.

XLV. It is commanded that a new brother can only be received into the Order in one of the churches built at our expense, and in the presence of six brethren. It is necessary to instruct him for three months, and to provide him with all things needful. Afterwards he must receive the sign of Peace, a palm-branch, and three kisses, with the words--"Dear brother, we command you to be silent." After this, he must kneel before the imperator in a special dress, with an assistant on either side, the one being his magister, and the other a brother. He shall then say I, N. N., swear by the eternal and living God not to make known the secret which has been communicated to me (here he uplifts two fingers) to any human being, but to preserve it in concealment under the natural seal all the days of my life; likewise to keep secret all things connected therewith as far as they maybe made known to me; likewise to discover nothing concerning the position of our brotherhood, neither the abode, name, or surname of our imperator, nor to shew the Stone to anyone; all which I promise to preserve eternally in silence, by peril of my life, as God and His Word may help me."

Afterwards his magister cuts seven tufts of hair from his head and seals them up in seven papers, writing on each the name and surname of the new brother, and giving them to the imperator to keep. The next day the brethren proceed to the residence of the new brother, and eat therein without speaking or saluting one another. When they go away, however, they must say, "*Frater Aureæ (vel Roseæ) Crucis Deus sit tecum cum perpetuo silentio Deo promisso et nostræ sanctæ congregationi.*" This is done three days in succession.

XLVI. When these three days are passed, they shall give some gifts to the poor, according to their intention and discretion.

XLVII. It is forbidden to tarry in our houses longer than two months together.

XLVIII. After a certain time the brethren shall be on a more familiar footing with the new brother, and shall instruct him as much as possible. XLIX. No brother need perform more than three projections while he stays in our large house, because there are certain operations which belong to the magisters.

L. The brethren shall be called, in their conversation with each other, by the name they received at their reception.

LI. In presence of strangers they shall be called by their ordinary names.

LII. The new brother shall invariably receive the name of the brother then last deceased; and all the brethren shall be obedient to these rules when they have been accepted by the Order, and have taken the oath of fidelity in the name of the Lord Jesus Christus.

CHAPTER XI. ROSICRUCIAN APOLOGISTS: ROBERT FLUDD.

THE central figure of Rosicrucian literature, towering as an intellectual giant above the crowd of *souffleurs*, theosophists, and charlatanic professors of the *magnum opus*, who, directly or otherwise, were connected with the mysterious Brotherhood, is Robertus de Fluctibus, the great English mystical philosopher of the seventeenth century, a man of immense erudition, of exalted mind, and, to judge by his writings, of extreme personal sanctity. Ennemoser describes him as one of the most distinguished disciples of Paracelsus, but refuses to number him with "those consecrated theosophists who draw all wisdom from the fountain of eternal light." He does not state his reasons for this depreciatory judgment, and the brief and inadequate notice which he gives of Fludd's system displays such a cursory acquaintance with the works in which it is developed, that it is doubtful whether he had taken pains to understand his author. I should rank the Kentish mystic second to none among the disciples of the "divine" Theophrastus, while in the profundity and extent of his learning, there can be no question that he far surpassed his master, who is said to have known little but to have divined almost everything, and who is, therefore, called *divinus*, in the narrower sense of that now much abused term. Robert Fludd was born at Milgate House, in the parish of Bersted, Kent, during the year 1574. By his mother's side he was descended from the ancient family of Andros of Taunton in Somerset. His father, Thomas Fludd, was a representative of a Shropshire stock, and successively occupied several high positions. He was victualler of Bewick, and then of Newhaven in France; afterwards he was made Receiver of Kent, Sussex, and Surrey, and being appointed treasurer of the army sent under Lord Willoughby to Henry IV. of France, "he behaved so honourably that he was knighted, and on his return to England was made treasurer of all her Majesty's forces in the Low Countries." This was in the reign of Queen Elizabeth; he was constantly a justice of the peace where he resided, and was also treasurer of the Cinque ports. "He bore for his arms--vert, a chevron between three wolves' heads erased, argent, which coat, with his quarterings, was confirmed to him by Robert Cook, Clar., Nov. 10, 1572."I have succeeded in compiling from various sources the following scanty genealogy of the Fludd family:-- According to this genealogy, Robert Fludd was the youngest of five sons. He was entered of St John's College in the year 1591, at the age of seventeen. Having graduated both in arts and medicine, he appears to have travelled extensively, for the space of six years, in France, Germany, Italy, and Spain. On his return to England, he was made a member of the London College of Physicians, and took his degree of Master in Arts in the year 1605. His first published work appeared in 1616, about which time he was visited by Michael Maier, by whom he was probably acquainted with the Rosicrucian controversy, and with whom he corresponded after the renowned German alchemist had returned to his own country. Fludd appears to have resided chiefly in London, then as now the great intellectual centre of England. He had a house in Fenchurch Street, according to Fuller, and another in Coleman Street, where he died in the year 1637, on the 8th day of September. He was buried in the chancel of Bersted Church, under a tomb which he had previously erected--"An oblong square of dark, slate-coloured marble, occupying a large space of the chancel wall on the left as you stand before the altar, looking up the body of the small church towards the door. There is a seated half-length figure of Fludd, with his hand on a book, as if just raising his head from reading to look at you. Upon the monument are two marble books inscribed *Misterium Cabalisticum* and *Philosophia Sacra*. There were originally eight books. The inscription to his memory is as follows:--

"'VIII. Die Mensis VII. A° Dᵐ, M.D.C.XXXVII. O doribus vrua vaporat crypta tegit cineres nec speciosa tvos ovod mortale minvs tibi. Te committimus vnvm ingenii vivent hic monumenta tui nam tibi qui similis scribit moriturque sepulchrum pro tota eternum posteritate facit. Hoc monumentum Thomas Flood Gore Court in oram apud Cantianos armiger infoelissimam in charissimi patrin sui memoriam nexit, die Mensis Augusti M.D.C.XXXVII.'"Bersted Church is situated on high ground, at a small distance south of Bersted Green. It is dedicated to the Holy Cross, and, according to Hasted, is a handsome building, consisting of two aisles and two chancels, with a square beacon tower at the west end of it. This is in the Perpendicular style, and at three angles of the summit are three rude figures, said to be three dogs or bears seiant, but so defaced by time that they cannot well be distinguished.

The list of Fludd's works is as follows:--

Apologia Compendiaria Fraternitatem de Rosea Cruce suspicionis et infamiæ maculis aspersam, veritatis quasi Fluctibus abluens et abstergens. Leyden, 1616. 8vo.

Tractatus Apologeticus integritatem Societatis de Rosea Cruce defendens. Lugduni Batavorum, 1617. 8vo. A duplicate of the preceding with a new title.

Utriusque Cosmi majoris scilicet et minoris metaphysica, physica atque technica historia in dua volumina secundum cosmi differentiam divisa. 2 tom. Oppenheimii, Francofurti, 1617-24. Fol.

Veritatis Proscenium . . . seu demonstratio quædam analytica, in qua cuilibet comparationis particulæ, in appendice quadam à J. Kepplero, nuper in fine Harmoniæ suæ Mundanæ edita, factæ inter Harmoniam suam mundanam et illam R. F. ipsissimis veritatis argumentis respondetur. Francofurti, 1621. Fol. Monochordum Mundi Symphoniacum, seu,

Replicatio R. F. . . . ad apologiam . . . J. Kepleri adversus demonstrationem suam analyticam nuperrime editam in qua Robertus validioribus Joannis objectionibus Harmoniæ sum legi repugnantibus, comiter respondere aggreditur. Francofurti, 1622. 4to.

Anatomiæ Amphitheatrum effigie triplici, more et conditione varia designatam. Francfurte, 1623. Fol.

Philosophia Sacra et vere Christiana, seu Meteorologica Cosmica. Francofurti, 1626. Fol.

Medecina Catholica, seu mysticum artis medicandi sacrarium. 5 parts. Francofurti, 1629-31.

Sophiæ cum moria certamen, in quo, lapsis Lydius a falso structore . . . M. Mersemio . . . reprobatus, celeberrima voluminis sui Babylonici figmenta accurate examinat (Summum bonum, quod est verum subjectum veræ magicæ, cabalæ, alchymiæ fratrum Roseæ Crucis verorum in dictarum scientiarum laudem, et insignis calumniatoris . . . M. Mersenni dedecus publicatum, per J. Frizium). 2 pt. Francofurti, 1629. Fol.

Doctor Fludd's Answer unto M. Foster, or the squesing of Parson Foster's Sponge, ordained by him for the wiping away of the weapon-salve. London, 1631. 4to.

Clavis Philosophiæ et Alchymiæ. (A Reply to Father Gassendi.) Francofurti, 1633. Fol.

Phylosophia Mosaica. In qua Sapientia et Scientia creationis et creaturarum sacra vereque Christiana . . . ad amussim et enuncleate explicatur. Goudæ, 1638. Fol.

It will be seen from this list that the Rosicrucian manifestoes found an immediate defender in Robert Fludd, that is, if the "Apologia" which bears his name is to be considered his work. There is some uncertainty on this point, but it has been disputed on insufficient grounds, As a maiden effort, it will not of course bear comparison with the dialectical skill of his mature productions, but the principles it propounds are those of the "Mosaicall Philosophy" and the "Tractatus Varii." "What was the particular occasion of his own first acquaintance with Rosicrucianism is not recorded," says Buhle. "All the books of Alchemy or other occult knowledge, published in Germany, were at that time immediately carried over to England--provided they were written in Latin; and if written in German, were soon translated for the benefit of English students. He may therefore have gained his knowledge immediately from the Rosicrucian books, but it is more probable that he acquired it from his friend Maier. . . . At all events, he must have been initiated into Rosicrucianism at an early period."

By whomsoever written, the "Tractatus Apologeticus" is an exceedingly curious work, so astonishing occasionally in the nature of its arguments that it is difficult to suppose that they were put forward seriously. It was called for by Andrew Libavius' "searching and hostile analysis" of the Rosicrucian

Confession, and was written to clear the Society from the *Infamiæ maculæ* cast on it by the accusations then brought forward, and above all from the charges of detestable magic and diabolical superstition. It is divided into three parts, and various chapters are illustrated by appropriate quotations from the manifesto it is defending, whose underlying principles are developed and explained. The first part treats of the various departments of magical science, of the Cabala, of the Books of God, both visible and invisible, of the secret characters of Nature, and of the value of astrological portents. The second part is devoted to a lugubrious consideration of the impediments and degeneracy of the arts and sciences in modern times--*de scientiarum hodierno die in scholis vigentium impedimentis*. It enlarges on the urgent necessity for a reformation in Natural Philosophy, Medicine, and Alchemy.

Concerning the first, the author declares it to be impossible for any one to attain to the supreme summit of the natural sciences unless he be profoundly versed in the occult meaning of the ancient philosophers, but the minute and most accurate observer who does achieve this height will not find it difficult to adapt the materials which are prepared by Nature in such a manner as to produce, by the application of actives to passives, many marvellous effects before the time ordained by Nature; and this, he adds, will be mistaken by the uninitiated for a miracle.

Like others of his school, he insists on the uncertainty of *à posteriori* and experimental methods, to which he unhesitatingly attributes all the errors of the natural sciences. "Particulars are frequently fallible, but universals never. Occult philosophy lays bare Nature in her complete nakedness, and alone contemplates the wisdom of universals by the eyes of intelligence. Accustomed to partake of the rivers which flow from the Fountain of Life, it is unacquainted with grossness and with clouded waters."

In Medicine he laments the loss of that universal panacea referred to by Hippocrates:--"But absolutely nothing remains of that one and only medicament of which Hippocrates makes mention (darkly and mystically, I admit) in several places, and still less are its operations understood, inasmuch as no one now searches with lynx-like eyes into the profound depths of true natural philosophy, to gain an accurate knowledge of its composition and its virtues." Concerning Arithmetic, he asks mournfully, and with apparent earnestness, "Which of us has, at this day, the ability to discover those true and vivific numbers whereby the elements are united and bound to one another?" And then, with regard to music, which, as he remarks, *non aliter succedit Arithmeticæ quàm medicina Philosophiæ Naturali*, he cries after the same fashion:--"But, good God, what is this when compared with that deep and true music of the wise, whereby the proportions of natural things are investigated, the harmonical concord and the qualities of the whole world are revealed, by which also connected things are bound together, peace established between conflicting elements, and whereby each star is perpetually suspended in its appointed place by its weight and strength, and by the harmony of its lucent spirit." It is impossible to read without a smile when the author urges the necessity for a musical reformation, on the ground that we have lost that art of Orpheus by which he moved insensible stones, and that of Arion by which the fishes were charmed.

The cursory review of alchemy is equally gloomy:--"The art, also, of alchemy or chemistry is surrounded with such insoluble enigmas that we can scarcely gain anything but ignorance therefrom, and *ignotum per ignotius.*" He enlarges on its fictitious vocabulary, and quotes Maricinus as follows:-- "The magisterium of the philosophers is hidden and concealed, and wherever found is known by a thousand names; moreover, it is surrounded by symbols and is revealed to the wise alone, yet this is, notwithstanding, the one, only, and lineal way of the whole operation." Then he himself continues:--"Neither common fire, but Nature herself, neither artificial furnaces, but natural matrices, are needed in this work, which is the work of Nature only, and wherein nothing is required save the brief co-operation of her minister, by whom things natural to things also natural, and species to their congruents, are duly and accurately applied." Mathematics, optics, and astronomy he treats after the same fashion, comparing their tame and commonplace frivolities with the sublime knowledge of the ancients.

The third part is entitled "De Naturæ Arcanis," and treats of the mysteries of Light, &c., developing in a small space a curious and profound philosophy. It describes God as the *ens entium,* eternal form, inviolable, purely igneous, without any intermixture of material, unmanifested before the creation of the universe, according to the maxim of Mercurius Trismegistus, "*Monas generat molem, et in seipsum reflectit ardorem suam.*" Earth is defined to be a gross water, water a gross air, air a gross fire, fire a gross ether, while the ether itself is the grosser part of the empyrean, which is distinguished from the ethereal realm, and is described as a water of extreme tenuity, constituted of three parts of luminous substance to one aqueous part; it is the purest essence of all substances, and is identical with the luminiferous ether of the latest scientific hypothesis. Its place is the medium mundi, wherein is the *sphæra æqualitatis,* in which the sun performs its revolution. The sun itself is composed of equal parts of light and water. Light is the cause of all energies--*nihil in hoc mundo peractum fuerit, sine lucis mediatione aut actu divino.* "It is impossible for man to desire more complete felicity than the admirable knowledge of light and its virtues," by which the ancient magi constructed their ever-burning lamps, forced fire out of stones and wood, kindled tapers from the rays of stars, and naturally, by means of its reflections, produced many wonders in the air, such as phantom writing, and, more than all, by the true use of the *lux invisibilis,* made men themselves invisible.

168

The information scattered through the various parts of the apology on the different departments of magic is also noteworthy. It distinguishes between natural, mathematical, venific, necromantic, and thaumaturgie magic. "That most occult and secret department of physics by which the mystical properties of natural substances are extracted, we term Natural Magic. The wise kings who (led by the new Star from the East) sought the infant Christ, are called Magi, because they had attained a perfect knowledge of natural things, whether celestial or sublunar. This branch of the Magi also includes Salomon, since he was versed in the arcane virtues and properties of all substances, and is said to have understood the nature of every plant from the cedar to the hyssop. Magicians who are proficient in the mathematical division construct marvellous machines by means of their geometrical knowledge; such were the flying dove of Archytas, and the brazen heads of Roger Bacon and Albertus Magnus, which are said to have spoken. Venific magic is familiar with potions, philtres, and with the various preparations of poisons; it is in a measure included in the natural division, because a knowledge of the properties of natural things is requisite to produce its results. Necromantic Magic is divided into goëtic, maleficient, and Theurgic. The first consists in diabolical commerce with unclean spirits, in rites of criminal curiosity, in illicit songs and invocations, and in the evocation of the souls of the dead. The second is the adjuration of the devils by the Virtue of Divine Names. The third pretends to be governed by good angels and the Divine Will, but its wonders are most frequently performed by evil spirits, who assume the names of God and of the angels. This department of Necromancy n can, however, be performed by natural powers, definite rites and ceremonies, whereby celestial and divine virtues are reconciled and drawn to us; the ancient Magi promulgated in their secret books many rules of this doctrine. The last species of magic is the thaumaturgie, begetting illusory phenomena; by this art the Magi produced their phantasms and other marvels."

When speaking of the wonders wrought mechanically by Roger Bacon, Albertus Magnus, and Boëtius, the apologist of the Rosicrucians tells us that he himself, by his assiduity in mechanical arts, constructed a wooden bull which lowed and bellowed after the fashion of the living animal; a dragon which flapped its wings, hissed, and vomited forth fire and flames upon the bull; and a lyre which played melodies without human intervention, as well as many other things, which by the simple mathematical art, apart from natural magic, could not have been accomplished.

The scientific and philosophical principles of Robert Fludd were attacked by Father Mersenne, with special reference to his belief in the Rosicrucian Society. Some twelve years had passed since the appearance of the "Tractatus Apologeticus," which he probably no longer valued. He replied to the attack in the work entitled "Sophiæ cum Moriâ Certamen," without mentioning the Rosicrucians. But the "Summum Bonum," by Joachim Fritz, which accompanied this reply, contains an elaborate defence of the Order, to which, in one of its phases, Fludd is said to have belonged. The authorship of this defence he is supposed to have disavowed. Buhle, however, points out that as "the principles, the style, the animosity towards Mersenne, the publisher, and the year, were severally the same as in the 'Sophiæ cum Moriâ Certamen' which Fludd acknowledged, there cannot be much reason to doubt that it was his." But as I am unwilling to consider that a man of Fludd's high character would be guilty of deliberate falsehood, and as it was not his habit to write either anonymously or pseudonymously, I prefer the alternative offered by the German critic when he says, "If not Fludd's, it was the work of a friend of Fludd's." In either case, his opinions are represented. On the title-page of the "Summum Bonum," there is a large Rose on which two bees have alighted, with this motto above--*Dat Rosa mel apibus*. The book treats of the noble art of magic, the foundation and nature of the Cabala, the essence of veritable alchemy, and of the *Causa Fratrum Roseæ Crucis*. It identifies the palace or home of the Rosicrucians with the Scriptural house of wisdom. *Ascendamus ad montem rationabilem, et ædificemus domum Sapientiæ.* The foundation of the mountain thus referred to is declared to be the *Lapis angularis*, the corner-stone, cut out of the mountain without hands. This stone is Christ. It is the spiritual palace which the Rosicrucians desire to reveal, and is therefore no earthly or material abode. There is a long disquisition on the significance of the Rose and the Cross, a purely spiritual interpretation being adopted. At the conclusion, the writer anticipates the question whether he himself is a brother of the Rose Cross, since he has settled all questions as to their religion and symbolism. His answer is that he least of any has deserved such a grace of God; if it have pleased God to have so ordained it, it is enough. To satisfy, however, the curiosity of his readers, he supplies them with a curious letter supposed to have emanated from the society, and which has been quaintly translated in a manuscript of the seventeenth century.

This Epistle was written and sent by ye Brethren of R. C. to a certaine Germaine, a coppy whereof Dr Flud obtained of a Polander of Dantziche his friend, which he since printed in Latin at ye end of his tract, intituled, *De Summo Bono.*

Venerable and Honourable Sr.

Seeing that this will be ye first yeare of thy nativity, wee pray that thou mayst have from ye Most High God, a most happy entrance into and departure from out of thy life, and because thou hast hitherto been with a good mind a constant searcher of holy philosophy, well done! Proceed, fear God, for thus thou mayest gaine Heaven. Get to thyself the most true knowledge, for it is God who hath found out every way; it is God who alone is circumference and centre. But draw thee neere, listen, take this to thee ✠ , for he who increaseth knowledge increaseth sorrow, because that in much knowledge is much griefe, wee speake by experience. For all worldlings, and vaine-glorious, vauntinge boasters, gorgious men, talkers, and vaine people doe unworthily scandalize, yea, and curse us for an unknown matter. But we wonder not that ye ungrateful world doe persecute ye professors of ye true Arts, together with ye truth itself. Yett for thy sake wee shall briefly answer to these questions, viz.: What wee doe? What can wee doe? Or whether are any such as wee? In John, therefore, wee reade that God is ye Supreme Light, and in light wee walke, so that wee exhibit light (although in a lanthern) to ye world. But thou man of ye world that deniest this, thou knowest not or seest not it behoves thee to know that in thy vile boddy Jesus dwelleth. This thou hast from ye apostle. "And Jesus knew all their thoughts," to whom if thou adherest, thou are at length made one spirit with Him, and being such, who prohibeteth thee with Solomon to know as well ye wicked as good contentions of men. And this thou mayest take from me out of ye premises. And hence it is that wee doe not answer to all, viz., because of the deceitfull minds of some. For whosoever are alienated from God are contrary to us, and who is so foolish as to permit a new-come stranger to enter into another man's house? But if thou objectest that this union is onely to be expected in ye world to come, behold now in this thou showest thyself for a worldling who extinguishest light by thy ignorance. Also thou are not ashamed to make ye apostle a liar, in whom those things are more clearly manifested in these wordes--"So that you may be wanting in no grace, expectinge ye Revelation of our Lord Jesus Christ." But thou sayest that this is not to be understood of this inferiour life. What therefore does ye followinge verse intend? "Who shall confirme you even to the end," for in the Kingdome of God there is noe end, therefore in this temporall state will appear ye glory of ye Lord, and Jesus glorified. If any thinge is further demanded concerning our office, our endeavoure is to leade backe lost sheepe to ye true sheepefold. You labore therefore in vaine, O miserable mortals, who enter upon another way than that ye apostle wills by putinge off your tabernacle, which way is not walked in through dyinge, but as Peter willeth when he saith: "As Christ hath taught mee," viz., when he was transfigured in ye mount, which laienge down, if it had not bine secret and hidden, ye apostle had not saide, "as Jesus taught mee," neither had ye Supreme Truth saide: "Tell this to no man," for accordinge to ye vulgar way, vulgarly to die was known to all men from ye beginninge of ye world. Be yee changed therefore, be yee changed from dead stones into livinge philosophical stones. The apostle shews ye way when he saith: "Lett the same minde be in you as is in Jesus." Also he explains that minde in ye followinge words, viz., when as beinge in ye form of God, he thought it no robbery to be equal to God. Behould these things, O all you that search into ye abstruse secrets of nature! Yee heare these matters, but you believe them not, O miserable mortals, who doe so anxiously run into youre own ruine, but wilt thou be more happy, O thou most miserable, wilt thou be elevated above ye circles of ye world, O thou proud one, wilt thou command in Heaven above, this earth, and thy darke body, O thou ambitious, will yee performe all miracles, O yee unworthy? Know yee, therefore, ye rejected, of what nature it is, before it is sought. But thou, O Brother, hearken! I will speake with S. John, that thou mayest have fellowshippe with us, and indeed our fellowshippe is with ye Father and with Jesus, and wee write unto you that yee may rejoyce because God is light, and in Him there is no darkness at all. But that thou mayest come unto us, behould this light, for it is impossible for thee to see us (unless when wee will) in another light. In this, therefore, follow us, whereby thou mayest be made happy with us, for our most immoveable pallace is ye centre of all things, likewise is it much obscured, because covered with many names. Enter, enter into ye glory of God and thy own salvation, ye gates and Schoole of Philosophicall Love, in which is taught everlastinge charity and fraternall love, and that some resplendent and invisible castle which is built upon the mountaine of ye Lord, out of whose roote goeth forth a fountaine of livinge waters, and a river of love! Drinke, drinke, and againe drinke, that thou mayest see all hidden things, and converse with us! Againe beware! But what? For thou knowest very well that nature receives nothing for nutriment but that which is subtile, the thick and fœculent is cast out as excrements. It is also well disputed by thyself, that those who will live in ye minde, rather than in ye body, take in nourishment by ye spirit, not by ye mouth. As for example, it is lawful to know Heaven by Heaven, not by earth, but ye virtues of this by ye other, and if you understand me aright, no man ascends into Heaven, which thou seekest, except He who descended from Heaven, which thou seekest not, enlighteneth him first. Whatsoever therefore is not from Heaven is a false immage, and cannot be called a virtue. Therefore, O Brother, thou canst not be better confirmed then by virtue itselfe, which is ye Supreame Truth, which if thou wilt religiously, and with all thy might, endeavour to follow in all thy wordes and workes, it will confirm thee, daily more and more, for it is a fiery spirite, a glisteninge sparke, a graine impossible, never diinge, subliminge his own body, dwellinge in every created beeinge, sustaininge and governinge it, gold burninge, and by Christ purged, pure in ye fire, allwaye more glorious and pure, jubilatinge without diminution, this shall (I say) confirme thee daily, untill (as a certaine learned man saith) thou art made like a lion in battle, and canst take away all ye strength of ye world, and fearest not death, nor any violence whatsoever a divellish tyranny can invent, viz., seeinge thou art become such a one as thou desirest, a stone and a worke. And that God may bless thy labours which thou shalt receive in most approved authors under a shaddow, for a wise man reads one thinge and understands another. Art thou imperfect? Aspire after a due perfection. Art thou foul and unclean? Purge thyself with teares, sublime thyselfe with good manners and virtues, adorn and beautify thyselfe with sacramentall graces! Make thy soule sublime and subtile for ye contemplation of heavenly thinges, and conformable to angelicall spirits, that it may vivify thy vile ashes and vulgar body, and make it white, and render it altogether incorruptible and impassible by ye resurrection of our Lord Jesus Christ. Doe these thinges, and thou wilt confess that no man hath wrote more plainly then I. These thinges the Lady Virtue hath commended should be told to thee, from (or by) whom, accordinge to thy deserts, thou shalt hereafter be more largely taught, these read, if thou wilt, as the apostle willeth, keepe that which is committed to thy trust. Farewell.

F. T. F., in Light and C.

By his talents and intellectual ability, Robert Fludd is a character so important in English Rosicrucian literature, that I propose to give a short sketch or syllabus of his singular cosmical philosophy. The substance will be taken from the "Mosaicall Philosophy," and the folio volume entitled *Tractatus Varii*, and it will be rendered as far as possible in the philosopher's own words.

The author distinguishes in several places between the Divine σοφία, the eternal sapience, the heavenly wisdom, which is only mystically revealed to mankind, and the wisdom which is derived from the invention and tradition of men. He declares the philosophy of the Grecians, or the ethnick philosophy, to be based only on the second, and to be terrene, animal, and diabolical, not being founded on the deific corner-stone, namely, Jesus Christ, who is the essential substance and foundation of the true science.

The original fountain of true wisdom is in God, the *natura naturans*, the infinite, illimitable Spirit, beyond all imagination, transcending all essence, without name, all wise, all-clement, the Father, the Word, and the ineffable, Holy Spirit, the highest and only good, the indivisible Trinity, the most splendid and indescribable light. This Wisdom is the *vapor virtutis Dei*, and the stainless mirror of the majesty and beneficence of God. All things, of what nature and condition soever, were made in, by, and through this Divine Word or emanation, which is God Himself, as it is the Divine Act, whose root is the Logos, that is, Christ. This Eternal Wisdom is the fountain or corner-stone of the higher arts, by which also all mysterious and miraculous discoveries are effected and brought to light.

Before the spagirical separation which the Word of God, or divine Elohim, effected in the six days of creation, the heavens and earth were one deformed, rude, undigested mass, complicitly comprehended in one dark abyss, but explicitly as yet nothing. This nothing is compared by St

Augustine to speech, which while it is in the speaker's mind is as nothing to the hearer, but when uttered, that which existed complicitly in *animo loquentis*, is explicitly apprehended by the hearer. This *nihilum* or nothing is not a *nihilum negativum*. It is the First Matter, the infinite, informal. primordial Ens, the *mysterium magnum* of the Paracelsists. It existed eternally in God. If God had not produced all things essentially out of Himself, they could not be rightly referred to Him. The primeval darkness is the *potentia divina* as light is the *actus divinus*--the *Aleph tenebrosum* and *Aleph lucidum*. Void of form and life, it is still a material developing from potentiality into the actual, and was informed by the Maker of the world with a universal essence, which is the Light of Moses, and was first evolved in the empyrean heaven, the highest and supernatural region of the world, the *habitaculum fontis lucidi*, the region not of matter but of form--form simple and spiritual beyond all imagination. There is a second spiritual heaven, participating in the clarity and tenuity of the first, of which it is the base; this is the medial heaven, called the *sphæra æqualitatis* and it is corporeal in respect of the former. The third heaven is the locality of the four elements. The progression of the primordial light through the three celestial spaces was accomplished during the first three days of creation. Christ the Wisdom and Word of God, by His apparition out of darkness, that is, by the mutation of the first principle from dark Aleph to light Aleph, revealed the waters contained in the profound bosom of the abyss, and animated them by the emanation of the spirit of eternal fire, and then by his admirable activity distinguished and separated the darkness from the light, the obscure and gross waters from the subtle and pure waters, disposing the heavens and spheres, as above stated, and dividing the grosser waters into sublunary elements. These elements are described as follows:--Earth is the conglomeration of the material darkness and the refuse of the heavens; Water is the more gross spirit of the darkness of the inferior heaven, nearly devoid of light; Air is the spirit of the second heaven; Fire, the spirit of the darkness of the Empyrean heaven.

Fludd's theory of the Macrocosmus is enunciated in the following manner. According to Fludd's philosophy, the whole universe was fashioned after the pattern of an archetypal world which existed in the Divine ideality, and was framed out of unity in a threefold manner. The Eternal Monad or Unity, without any egression from his own central profundity, compasses complicitly the three cosmical dimensions, namely, root, square, and cube. If we multiply unity as a root, in itself, it will produce only unity for its square, which being again multiplied in itself, brings forth a cube which is one with root and square. Thus we have three branches differing in formal progression, yet one unity in which all things remain potentially, and that after a most abstruse manner. The archetypal world was made by the egression of one out of one, and by the regression of that one, so emitted, into itself by emanation. According to this ideal image, or archetypal world, our universe was subsequently fashioned as a true type and exemplar of the Divine Pattern; for out of unity in his abstract existence, viz., as it was hidden in the dark chaos, or potential mass, the bright flame of all formal being did shine forth, and the Spirit of Wisdom, proceeding from them both, conjoined the formal emanation with the potential matter, so that by the union of the divine emanation of light and the substantial darkness, which was water, the heavens were made of old, and the whole world.

God, according to these abstruse speculations, is that pure, catholic unity which includes and comprehends all multiplicity, and which before the objective projection of the cosmos must be considered as a transcendent entity, reserved only in itself, in whose divine puissance, as in a place without end or limit, all things which are now explicitly apparent were then complicitly contained, though in regard to our finite faculties it can only be conceived as nothing--*nihil, non finis, non ens, aleph tenebrosum*, the Absolute Monad or Unity.

Joined to the cosmical philosophy of Robert Fludd, there is an elaborate system of spiritual evolution, and the foundation of both is to be sought in the gigantic hypotheses of the Kabbalah. His angelology is derived from the works of pseudo-Dionysius on the celestial hierarchies, and he teaches the doctrine of the pre-existence of human souls, which are derived from the vivifying emanation dwelling in the *Anima Mundi*, the world's spiritual vehicle, the catholic soul, which itself is inacted and preserved by the Catholic and Eternal Spirit, sent out from the fountain of life to inact and vivify all things.

These mystical speculations, whatever their ultimate value, are sublime flights of an exalted imagination, but they are found, in the writings of Robert Fludd, side by side with the crudest physical theories, and the most exploded astronomical notions. He denies the diurnal revolution of the earth, and considers the light of all the stars to be derived from the one "heavenly candle" of the sun. Rejecting the natural if inadequate explanations of Aristotle and his successors, he presents the most extravagant definitions of the nature of winds, clouds, snow, &c. The last is described as a meteor which God draweth forth of His hidden treasury in the form of wool, or as a creature produced out of the air by the cold breath of the Divine Spirit to perform his will on earth. Thunder is a noise which is made in the cloudy tent or pavilion of Jehovah, lightning a certain fiery air or spirit animated by the brightness and burning from the face or presence of Jehovah. Literally interpreting the poetic imagery of Scripture, he perceives the direct interference of the Deity in all the phenomena of Nature, and denounces more rational views as "terrene, animal, and diabolical."

CHAPTER XII. ROSICRUCIAN
APOLOGISTS: THOMAS VAUGHAN.

EUGENIUS PHILALETHES, the author of the renowned "Introitus apertus ad occlusum Regis Palatium," the "Entrance opened to the Closed Palace of the King," is so far connected with the Rosicrucians that he published a translation, as we have seen, of the "Fama" and "Confessio Fraternitatis," and his philosophical doctrines are very similar to those of the mysterious Brotherhood, of which he has been erroneously, and despite his express and repeated denials, represented as a member. Like them, he expected the advent of the artist Elias who was foretold by Paracelsus, represents his most important alchemical work as his precursor, and declares that problematical personage to be already born into the world. The entire universe is to be transmuted and transfigured by the science of this artist into the pure mystical gold of the Spiritual City of God, when all currencies have been destroyed.

"A few brief years," he cries in his prophetic mood, "and I trust that money will be despised as completely as dross, and that we shall behold the destruction of this vile invention, so opposed to the spirit of Jesus Christ. The world is bewitched by it, and the infatuated nations adore this vain and gross metal as a divinity. Is it this which will help towards our coming redemption and our lofty future hopes? By this shall we enter that New Jerusalem when its ways are paved with gold, and its gates are of pearls and precious stones, and when the Tree of Life, planted in the centre of Paradise, will dispense health to the whole of humanity? I foresee that my writings will be esteemed as highly as the purest gold and silver now are, and that, thanks to my works, these metals will be as despised as dung."

The date of this author's birth was 1612; he is supposed to have been a native of Scotland, but the fact of his placing a Welsh motto on the title of one of his books, together with his true name, Thomas Vaughan, which is pure Welsh, is a strong argument of his Welsh nationality. He adopted various pseudonyms in the different countries through which he passed in his wanderings as an alchemical propagandist. Thus in America he called himself Doctor Zheil, and in Holland Carnobius. According to Herthodt, his true name was Childe, while Langlet du Fresnoy writes it Thomas Vagan, by a characteristic French blunder. His nom de plume was Eugenius not Irenæus Philalethes, as Figuier states. The life of this adept is involved in an almost Rosicrucian uncertainty; he was a mystery even to his publishers, who received his works from "an unknown person." Nearly all that is ascertained concerning him, and concerning his marvellous transmutations, rests on the authority of Urbiger, who has been proved inaccurate in more than one of his statements. His sojourn in America is an established fact, according to Louis Figuier, and the projections which he there accomplished in the laboratory of George Starkey, an apothecary, were subsequently published by the latter in London. His writings shew him to be a supreme adept of spiritual alchemy, and he despised the gold which he claimed to be able to manufacture. The history of this man who roamed from place to place, performing the most lavish transmutations, but always anonymous, always obliterating his personality, often disguised to conceal his identity, by his own representation in continual dangers and difficulties through the possession of his terrific secret, and gaining nothing by his labours, is a curious study of the perversity of human character for those who disbelieve in alchemy, and some ground for the faith of those who believe in it. The essential elements of fraud are wanting, and the intellectual nobility of the man, illuminated, moreover, by lofty religious aspirations, is conspicuous in all his works.

The list of his writings is as follows:--

"Anthroposophia Magica;" or a Discourse of the Nature of Man and his State after Death. "Anima Magica Abscondita;" or a Discourse of the Universall Spirit of Nature. London, 1650. 8vo.

"Magia Adamica;" or the Antiquities of Magic, and the descent thereof from Adam downwards proved. Whereunto is added a perfect and full discovery of the "Cœlum Terræ." London, 1650. 8vo.

The Man-Mouse taken in a Trap . . . for Gnawing the Margins of Eugenius Philalethes. (A satire on Henry More, who attacked him in a pamphlet entitled "Observations upon 'Anthroposophia Magica,'" etc.) London, 1650. 8vo.

"Lumen de Lumine;" or a New Magicall Light discovered and communicated to the World, with the Aphorismi Magici Eugenianii." London, 1651. 8vo.

The Second Wash; or The Moore Scour'd once more, being a charitable cure for the distractions of Alazonomastix (i.e., Henry More). London, 1651. 8vo.

The Fame and Confession of the Fraternity of R. C., with a Preface annexed thereto, and a short declaration of their physicall work. London, 1652. 8vo.

Euphrates; or The Waters of the East; being a short discourse of that great fountain whose water flows from Fire, and carries in it the beams of the Sun and Moon. London, 1655. 8vo.

A Brief Natural History, intermixed with variety of Philosophical Discourses and Observations of the Burnings of Mount Etna, &c. London, 1669. 8vo.

Introitus Apertus ad Occlusum Regis Palatium. Philalethæ Tractatus Tres. I. Metallorum Metamorphosis. II. Brevis Manductio ad Rubrium Cœlestem. III. Fons Chymicæ Veritatis. 1678. 4to.

It is only in the introduction to the "Fame and Confession" that Philalethes makes any important reference to the Rosicrucian Society. There his opinions are expressed in the following manner:--"I am in the humour to affirm the essence and existence of that admired chimæra, the Fraternitie of R. C. And now, gentlemen, I thank you, I have aire and room enough; methinks you sneak and steal from me, as if the plague and this Red Cross were inseparable. Take my Lord have mercy along with you, for I pitty your sickly braines, and certainly as to your present state the inscription is not unseasonable. But in lieu of this, some of you may advise me to an assertion of the Capreols of del Phæbo, or a review of the library of that discreet gentleman of La Mancha, for in your opinion those knights and these brothers are equally invisible. This is hard measure, but I shall not insist to disprove you. If there be any amongst the living of the same bookish faith with myself, they are the persons I would speak to."

The preface proceeds to discourse upon the contempt which magic has undergone in all ages, and then the author distinctly denies his personal acquaintance with the Rosicrucian Society. "As for that Fraternity, whose History and Confession I have here adventured to publish, I have, for my own part; no relation to them, neither do I much desire their acquaintance. I know they are masters of great mysteries, and I know withal that nature is so large they may as wel receive as give. I was never yet so lavish an admirer of them as to prefer them to all the world, for it is possible, and perhaps true, that a private man may have that in his possession whereof they are ignorant. It is not their title and the noise it has occasioned which makes me commend them. The acknowledgment I give them was first procured by their books, for there I found them true philosophers, and therefore not chimæras, as most think, but men. Their principles are every way correspondent to the ancient and primitive wisedome--nay, they are consonant to our very religion, and confirm every point thereof. I question not but most of their proposals may seem irregular to common capacities, but when the prerogative and power of Nature is known, there they will quickly fall even, for they want not order and sobriety. It will be expected, perhaps, that I should speak something as to their persons and habitations, but in this my cold acquaintance will excuse me, or, had I any familiarity with them, I should not doubt to use it with more discretion. As for their existence (if I may speak like a schoolman), there is great reason we should believe it; neither do I see how we can deny it, unless we grant that Nature is studied, and books also written and published, by some other creatures then men. It is true, indeed, that their knowledg at first was not purchased by their own disquisitions, for they received it from the Arabians, amongst whom it remained as the monument and legacy of the children of the East. Nor is this at all improbable, for the eastern countries have been always famous for magical and secret societies."

He compares the habitation of the Brachmans, as it is described by Philostratus in his life of Apollonius, with the Rosicrucian Locus Sancti Spiritus, concerning which he quotes the following curious passage by a writer whom he does not name:--"*Vidi aliquando Olympicas domos, non procul a Fluviolo et Civitate notâ, quas S. Spiritus vocari imaginamur. Helicon est de quo loquor, aut biceps Parnassus, in quo Equus Pegasus fontem aperuit perennis aquæ adhuc stillantem, in quo Diana se lavat, cui Venus ut Pedissequa et Saturnus ut Anteambulo, conjunguntur. Intelligenti nimium, inexperto minimum hoc erit dictum.*" Quoting afterwards the description of the Elysium of the Brachmans--"I have seen (saith Apollonius) the Brachmans of India dwelling on the earth and not on the earth; they were guarded without walls, and possessing nothing, they enjoyed all things"--this is plain enough, says Philalethes, "and on this hill have I also a desire to live, if it were for no other reason but what the sophist applyed to the mountains--

Hos primum sol salutat, ultimosque deserit,

Quis locum non amet, dies longiores habentem?

But of this place I will not speak any more, lest the readers should be so mad as to entertain a suspicion that I am of the Order." He attempts, however, to show "the conformity of the old and new professors,"--namely, the Rosicrucians and the Indian initiates. "When we have evidence that magicians have been, it is proof also that they may be. . . . I hold it then worth our observation that even those magi who came to Christ Himself came from the East; but as we cannot prove they were Brachmans, so neither can we prove they were not. If any man will . . . contend for the negative, it must follow that the East afforded more magical societies then one. . . . The learned will not deny but wisdom and light were first manifested in the same parts, namely, in the East. From this fountain also, this living, oriental one did the Brothers of R. C. draw their wholesom waters."

He concludes by reiterating his previous statement--"I have no acquaintance with this Fraternity as to their persons."

CHAPTER XIII. ROSICRUCIAN APOLOGISTS: JOHN HEYDON.

THE last of the line of apologists who has any claim on our notice is the extraordinary Royalist mystic and geomancer, John Heydon, who, in the preface to "The Holy Guide," has left us the following interesting and curious fragment of autobiography:--

"I was descended from a noble family of London in

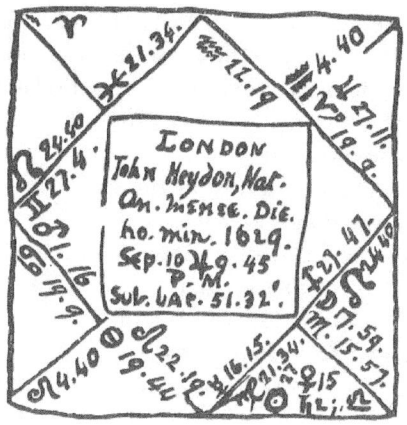

England, being born of a complete tall stature, small limbs, but in every part proportionable, of a dark flaxen haire, it curling as you see in the Effigies, and the above figures of Astrologie at the time I was born: this is also the Character of my Genius Malhitriel, and Spirit Taphza Benezelthar Thascraphimarah. I had the small pox and rickets very

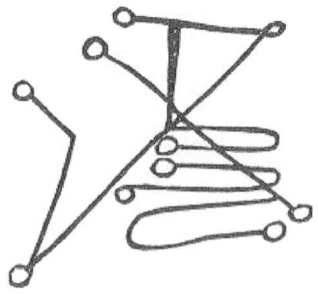

young--Ascendent to Conjunction, Mars, and Sol to the quartile of Saturn. I was at Tardebich in Warwickshire, neer Hewel, where my mother was borne, and there I learned, and so carefull were they to keep me to the book and from danger, that I had one purposely to attend me at school and at home. For, indeed, my parents were both of them honourably descended. They put me to learn the Latine tongue to one Mr George Linacre, the minister of the Gospel at Golton; of him I learned the Latine and Greek perfectly, and then was fitted for Oxford. But the Warrs began, and the Sun came to the body of Saturn and frustrated that design; and whereas you are pleased to stile me a noble-natured, sweet gentleman, you see my nativity:--Mercury, Venus, and Saturn are strong, and by them the Dragon's head and Mars, I judge my behaviour full of rigour, and acknowledge my conversation austere. In my devotion I love to use the civility of my knee, my hat, and hand, with all those outward and sensible motions which may express or promote invisible devotion. I followed the army of the King to Edgehill, and commanded a troop of horse, but never violated any man, &c., nor defaced the memory of saint or martyr. I never killed any man wilfully, but took him prisoner and disarmed him; I did never divide myself from any man upon the difference of opinion, or was angry with his judgment for not agreeing with me in that from which, perhaps, within a few dayes, I should dissent myself. I never regarded what religion any man was of that did not question mine. And yet there is no Church in the world whose every part so squares unto my conscience, whose articles, constitutions, and customs seem so consonant unto reason, and, as it were, framed to my particular devotion as this whereof I hold my belief, the Church of England, to whose faith I am a sworn subject, and therefore in a double obligation subscribe unto her articles, and endeavour to observe her constitutions. Whatsoever is beyond, as points indifferent, I observe according to the rules of my private reason, or the humour and fashion of my devotion, neither believing this because Luther affirmed it, or disproving that because Calvin hath disfavoured it. Now as all that dye in the war are not termed souldiers, neither can I properly term all those that suffer in matters of religion martyrs. And I say, there are not many extant that in a noble way fear the face of death lesse than myselfe; yet from the moral duty I owe to the commandement of God, and the natural respects that I tender unto the conversation of my essoine and being, I would not perish upon a ceremony, politique points, or indifferency; nor is my belief of that untractable temper, as not to bow at their obstacles or connive at matters wherein there are not manifest impieties. The leaves, therefore, and ferment of all, not only civil, but religious actions, is wisdome, without which to commit ourselves to the flames is homicide, and, I fear, but to passe through one fire into another. I behold, as a champion, with pride and spirites, and trophies of my victories over my enemies, and can with patience embrace this life, yet in my best meditations do often defie death; I honour any man that contemns it, nor can I love any that is afraid of it--this makes me naturally love a souldier that will follow his captain. In my figure you may see that I am naturally bashful. Yet you may read my qualities on my countenance. About the time I travelled into Spain, Italy, Turkey, and Arabia, the Ascendent was then directed to the Trine of the Moon, Sextile of Mercury and Quartile of Venus. I studied philosophy and writ this treatise, and the 'Temple of Wisdome,' &c. Conversation, age, or travell hath not been able to affront or enrage me, yet I have one part of the modesty which I have seldom discovered in another, that is (to speak truly), I am not so much afraid of Death as ashamed thereof. It is the very disgrace and ignominy of our natures, that in a moment can so disfigure us that our beloved friends stand afraid and start at us; the birds and beasts of the field that before in a naturall feare obeyed us, forgetting all allegiance, begin to prey upon us. This very thought in a storm at sea hath disposed and left me willing to be swallowed up in the abyss of waters, wherein I had perished unseen, unpitied, without wondering eyes, tears of pity, lectures of morality, and none had said;--*Quantum mutatus ab illo*. Not that I am ashamed of the anatomy of my parts, or can accuse Nature of playing the pupil in any part of me, or my own vitious life for contracting any shameful disease upon me, whereby I might not call myself a compleat bodyed man, free from all diseases, sound, and, I thank God, in perfect health.

"I writ my 'Harmony of the World,' when they were all at discord, and saw many revolutions of kingdomes, emperours, grand signiours, and popes; I was twenty when this book was finished, but me thinks I have outlived myself, and begin to be weary of the Sun, although the Sun now applies to a Trine of Mars. I have shaken hands with delight and know all is vanity, and I think no man can live well once but he that could live twice, yet for my part I would not live over my howres past, or begin again the minutes of my dayes, not because I have lived them well, but for fear I should live them worse. At my death I mean to take a total adieu of the world, not caring for the burthen of a tombstone and epitaph, nor so much as the bare memory of my name to be found anywhere, but in the Universal Register of God. I thank God that with joy I mention it, I was never afraid of Hell, nor never grew pale at the mention of Sheol, or Tophet, &c., because I understand the policy of a pulpit, and fix my contemplations on Heaven.

"I writ the 'Rosie Crucian Infallible Axiomata,' in foure books, and study not for my own sake only but for theirs that study not for themselves. In the Law I began to be a perfect clerk; I writ the 'Idea of the Law,' &c., for the benefit of my friends and practice in the King's Bench. I envy no man that knows more than myself, but pitty them that know lesse. For Ignorance is rude, uncivill, and will abuse any man, as we see in bayliffs, who are often killed for their impudent attempts; they'll forge a warrant and fright a fellow to fling away his money, that they may take it up; the devill, that did but buffet St. Paul, playes me thinks at Sharpe with me. To do no injury nor take none, was a principle which to my former years and impatient affection seemed to contain enough of morality, but my more settled years and Christian constitution have fallen upon severer resolutions. I hold there is no such thing as injury, and if there be, there is no such injury as revenge, and no such revenge as the contempt of an injury. There be those that will venture to write against my doctrine, when I am dead, that never durst answer me when alive. I see Cicero is abused by Cardan, who is angry at Tully for praising his own daughter; and Origanus is so impudent, that he adventures to forge a position of the heavens and calls it Cornelius Agrippa's nativity, and they say that Cornelius was borne to believe lyes and to broach them. Is not this unworthiness to write such lyes, and shew such reasons for them? His nativity I could never finde, I believe no man knows it, but by a false figure thus they scandalize him. And so they may use me, but behold the scheam of my nativity in Geomancy,

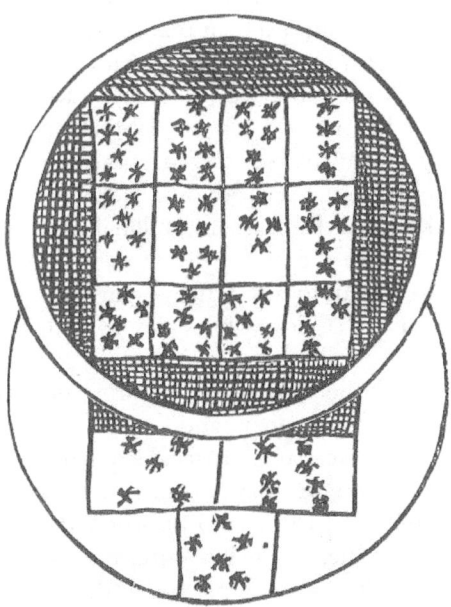

and the character of my spirit Taphzabnezeltharthaseraphimarah,

183

projected by a learned lord for the honour (? hour) of birth. Now let any astrologer, geomancer, philosopher, &c., judge my geniture; the figures are right according to the exact time of my birth, rectified by accidents and verified by the effects of directions. Now in the midst of all my endeavours, there is but one thought that dejects me--that my acquired parts mast perish with myself, nor can be legacyed amongst my dearly beloved and honoured friends. I do not fall out or contemn a man for an errour, or conceive why a difference in opinion should divide an affection; for a modest reproof or dispute, if it meet with discreet and peaceable natures, doth not infringe the laws of charity in all arguments.

"When the mid heaven was directed to the Trine of the Moon, I writ another book, and entituled it, 'The Fundamental Elements of Philosophy, Policy, Government and the Laws,' &c. After this time I had many misfortunes, and yet I think there is no man that apprehends his own miseries less than myself, and no man that so nearly apprehends another's. I could lose an arm without a tear, and with few groans, methinks, be quartered into pieces, yet can I weep seriously, with a true passion, to see the merciless Rebels in England forge a debt against the King's most loyall subjects, purposely to put them in the Marshalsey, or other Houses of Hell to be destroyed in prison, or starved, or killed by the keepers, and then two or three poore old women for as many shillings shall perswade the Crowner and the people to believe the men dyed of consumptions. It is a barbarous part in humanity to add unto any afflicted parties' misery, or endeavour to multiply in any man a passion whose single nature is already above his patience.

"The Ascendent to the Quartile of Saturn, and part of Fortune to the Sextile of the Moon came next; and it is true I had loved a lady in Devonshire, but when I seriously perused my nativity, I found the seventh House afflicted, and therefore never resolve to marry; for, behold, I am a man, and I know not how: I was so proportioned 1 and have something in me that can be without me, and will be after me, and here is the misery of a man's life; he eats, drinks, and sleeps to-day that he may do so tomorrow, and this breeds diseases, which bring death, 'for all flesh is grass.' And all these creatures we behold are but the herbs of the field digested into flesh in them, or more remotely carnified in ourselves; we are devourers not onely of men but of ourselves, and that not in an allegory but a positive truth, for all this masse of flesh which we behold came in at our mouths; this frame we look upon hath been upon our trenchers, and we have devoured ourselves, and what are we? I could be content that we might raise each other from death to life as Rosie Crucians doe without conjunction, or that there were any way to perpetuate the world without this trivial and vain way of coition as Dr Brown calls it. It is the foolishest act a wise man commits all his life, nor is there anything that will more

184

deject his cold imagination than to consider what an odd errour he hath committed. Had the stars favoured me, I might have been happy in that sweet sex.

"I remember also that this Quartile of Saturn imprisoned me at a messenger's house for contending with Cromwell, who maliciously commanded I should be kept close in Lambeth House, as indeed I was two years. My person he feared, and my tongue and pen offended him, because, amongst many things, I said particularly, such a day he would die, and he dyed. It is very true Oliver opposed me all his life, and made my father pay seventeen-hundred pounds for his liberty; besides, they stole, under pretence of sequestering him, two thousand pounds in jewels, plate, &c., and yet the King's noblest servants suffer upon suspition of death.

"When the moon was directed to the Quartile of Sol, and the M. C. to the opposition of Sol, I was by the phanatick Committee of Safety committed to prison, and my books burnt, yet I would not entertain a base design, or an action that should call me villain, for all the riches in England; and for this only do I love and honour my own soul, and have, methinks, two arms too few to embrace myself. My conversation is like the Sun with all men, and with a friendly aspect to good and bad. Methinks there is no man bad, and the worst best, that is, while they are kept within the circle of those qualities wherein there is good. The method I should use in distributive justice I often observe in commutation, and keep a geometrical proportion in both, whereby becomming equal to others, I become unjust to myself, and suberogate in that common principle, 'Doe unto others as thou wouldst be done unto thy self'; yet I give no alms to satisfie the hunger of my brother, but to fulfil and accomplish the will and command of God. This general and indifferent temper of mine doth nearly dispose me to this noble virtue amongst those million of vices I do inherit and hold from Adam. I have escaped one and that a mortal enemy to charity, the first and father sin, not onely of man, but of the devil, Pride--a vice whose name is comprehended in a monosyllable, but in its nature not circumscribed with a world. I have escaped it in a condition that can hardly avoid it; these petty acquisitions and reputed perfections that advance and elevate the conceits of other men add no feather unto mine. And this is the observation of my life--I can love and forgive even my enemies."

The materials supplied in this singular fragment of an autobiography are supplemented by a "Life of John Heydon," from the pen of Frederick Talbot, Esq., which was prefixed to "The Wise Man's Crown," and which I shall present to my readers in a compressed form, to avoid the prolixity and irrelevance of much of the original.

John Heydon, the son of Francis and Mary Heydon, now of Sidmouth in Devonshire, is not basely but nobly descended. Antiquaries derive them from Julius Heydon, King of Hungary and Westphalia, that were descended from the noble family of Cæsar Heydon in Rome, and since this royal race the line runs down to the Hon. Sir Christopher Heydon of Heydon, near Northwick; Sir John Heydon, late lord-lieutenant of the king's Tower of London, and the noble Chandlers in Worcestershire of the mother's side, which line spread by marriage into Devonshire, among the Collins, Ducks, Drues, and Bears. He had one sister, named Anne Heydon, who dyed two years since, his father and mother being yet living. He was born at his father's house in Green-Arbour, London, and baptized at S. Sepulchre's, and so was his sister, both in the fifth and seventh years of the reign of King Charles I. He was educated in Warwickshire, among his mother's friends, and so careful were they to keep him and his sister from danger, and to their books, that they had one continually to wait upon them, both to the school and at home.

He was commended by Mr John Dennis, his tutor in Tardebick, to Mr George Linacre, priest of Cougheton, where he learned the Latine and Greek tongues. The war at this time began to molest the universities of this nation. He was then articled to Mr Michael Petty, an attorney at Clifford's Inn, with eighty pound, that at five years' end he should be sworn before Chief Justice Roll. Being very young, he applyed his minde to learning, and by his happy wit obtained great knowledge in all arts and sciences. Afterwards he followed the armies of the King, and for his valour commanded in the troops. When he was by these means famous for learning and arms, he travelled into Spain, Italy, Arabia, Ægypt, and Persia, gave his minde to writing, and composed, about twenty years since, "The Harmony of the World," and other books, preserved by the good hand of God in the custody of Mr Thomas Heydon, Sir John Hanmer, Sir Ralph Freeman, and Sir Richard Temple. During the tyrant's time first one had these books, then another, and at last, at the command of these honourable, learned, and valiant knights, they were printed. He wrote many excellent things, and performed many rare experiments in the arts of astromancy, geomancy, &c., but especially eighty-one--the first upon the King's death, predicted in Arabia by him to his friends; the second upon the losses of the King at Worcester, predicted at Thauris, in Persia; the third predicted the death of Oliver Cromwell in Lambeth House, to many persons of honour, mentioned in his books; the fourth he wrote of the overthrow of Lambert, and of the Duke of Albymarle his bringing again of the King to his happy countries, and gave it to Major Christopher Berkenhead, a goldsmith at the Anchor, by Fettes Lane End in Holborn; the fifth precaution or prediction he gave to his Highness the Duke of Buckingham, two months before the evil was practised, and his enemy, Abraham Goodman, lies now in the Tower for attempting the death of that noble prince; the sixth, for Count Grammont, when he was banished into England by the King of France; and he predicted, by the art of astromancy and geomancy, the King's receiving of him again into favor, and his marriage to the Lady Hamelton; the seventh, for Duke Minulaus, a peer of Germany, that, the Emperour sent to him when the Turk had an army against him, and of the death of the pope. The rest are in his books. By these monuments the name of Heydon, for the variety of his learning, was famous not onely in England, but also in many other nations into which his books are translated. He hath taught the way to happiness, the way to long life, the way to health, the way to wax young, being old; the way to resolve all manner of questions, present and to come, by the rules of astromancy and geomancy, and how to raise the dead.

He is a man of middle stature, tending to tallness, a handsome straight body; an ovall, ruddy face, mixed with a clear white, his hair of a dark flaxen-brown colour, soft, and curling in rings gently at the ends of the locks; his hands and fingers long and slender, his legs and feet well proportioned, so that to look upon he is a very compleat gentleman. But he never yet cast affection on a woman, nor do I find him inclined to marry. He is very often in great ladies' chambers, and, I believe, his modest behaviour makes them the more delighted in his company. The princes and peers, not only of England but of Spain, Italy, France, and Germany, send to him dayly, and upon every occasion he sheweth strong parts and a vigorous brain. His wishes and aimes speak him owner of a noble and generous heart; his excellent books are admired by the world of lettered men as prodigies of these later times; indeed (if I am able to judge anything), they are full of the profoundest learning I ever met withal'. if any man should question my judgement, they may read the comendations of both universities, besides the learned Thomas White and Thomas Revell, Esquires, both famous in Rome and other parts beyond sea, that have highly honoured this gentleman in their books. Yet he hath suffered many misfortunes. His father was sequestered, imprisoned, and lost two thousand pounds by Cromwell; this Oliver imprisoned this son also two years and a half, or thereabout, in Lambeth House, for he and his father's family were always for the king, and endeavoured to the utmost his restoration; and indeed the tyrant was cruel, but John Thurloe, his secretary, was kind to him, and pittied his curious youth. Joshua Leadbeater, the messenger, kept him (at his request and Mr John Bradley's) at his own house, and gave him often leave to go abroad, but being yet zealous and active for the king, he was again taken and clapt up in Lambeth House. In these misfortunes it cost him £1000 and upwards. After this, some envious villains forged actions of debt against him, and put him in prison. It seems at the beginning of these misfortunes a certain harlot would have him marry her, but denying her suit, or that he ever promised any such thing, and that he ever spake to her in his life good or evil, she devised, with her confederates, abundance of mischief against him. Many courted him to marry, but he denyed. Now there was left amongst a few old almanacks and scraps of other men's wits, collected and bequeathed unto the world by Nicholas Culpeper, his widdow, Alice Culpeper; she hearing of this gentleman that he was an heir to a great fortune, courts him by letters of love to no purpose. The next saint in order was she that calls herself the German princess; but he flies high and scorns such fowl, great beasts. The first of these two blessed birds caused Heath to arrest him, and another after him laid actions against him that he never knew or heard of.

In this perplexity was he imprisoned two years, for they did desire nothing but to get money or destroy him, for fear, if ever he got his liberty, he might punish them; but he, being of a noble nature, forgave them all their malice, and scorns to revenge himself upon such pittiful things. God indeed hath done him justice, for this Heath consumes to worse then nothing; and, indeed, if I can judge or predict anything, his baudy-houses will be pawned, and he will die a miserable, diseased beggar. Heydon's mistris, when he was very young, and a clerk, desired him to lye with her; but he, like Joseph, refusing, she hated him all her life. God preserved him, although one of these three lewd women swore this gentleman practised the art magick. She told Oliver Cromwell she saw familiar spirits come and go to him in the shape of conies, and her maid swore she had often seen them in his chamber when he was abroad, and sometimes walking upon the house top in a moonshine night, and sometimes vanishing away into a wall or aire; yet she never saw him in her life, nor could she tell what manner of man he was. These stories were not credited, and for all these, and many more, afflictions and false accusations, I never saw him angry, nor did he ever arrest or imprison any man or woman in all his life, yet no client of his was ever damnyfied in his suit.

He was falsly accused but lately of writing a seditious book, and imprisoned in a messenger's custody; but his noble friend, the duke of Buckingham, finding him innocent and alwaies for the king, he was discharged, and indeed this glorious duke is a very good and just judge; although some speak slightly of him, he studies the way to preserve his king and country in peace, plenty, and prosperity. It is pitty the king hath no more such brave men as he; a thousand such wise dukes as this,

"Like marshall'd thunder, back'd with flames of fire,"

would make all the enemies of the King and Christendome quake, and the Turk fly before such great generals. In all submission we humbly pray for this great prince, and leave him to his pleasure, and return to our subject.

John Heydon hath purposely forsaken Spittle-Fields, and his lodgings there, to live a private life, free from the concourse of multitudes of people that daily followed him; but if any desire to be advised, let them by way of letter leave their business at his booksellers, and they shall have answer and counsel without reward, for he is neither envious nor enemie to any man;

what I write is upon my own knowledge. He writes now from Hermeupolis, a place I was never at. It seems, by the word, to be the City of Mercury, and truly he hath been in many strange places, among the Rosie Crucians, and at their castles, holy houses, temples, sepulchres, sacrifices; all the world knows this gentleman studies honourable things, and faithfully communicates them to others; yet, if any traduce him hereafter, they must not expect his vindication. He hath referred his quarrel to the God of Nature; it is involved in the concernments of his truths, and he is satisfied with the peace of a good conscience. He hath been misinterpreted in his writing; with studied calumnies, they disparage his person whom they never saw, nor perhaps will see. He is resolved for the future to suffer, for he says, "God condemns no man for his patience." His enemies are forced to praise his vertue, and his friends are sorry he hath not ten thousand pounds a year. He doth not resent the common spleen; and when the world shall submit to the general tribunal, he will find his advocate where they shall find their judge. When I writ this gentleman's life, God can bear me witness, it was unknown to him, and for no private ends. I was forced to it by a strong admiration of the mistery and majesty of Nature written by this servant of God and secretary of Nature. I began his life some years since, and do set it down as I do finde it. If any man oppose this I shall answer; if you are for peace, peace be with you; if you are for war, I have been so too (Mr Heydon doth resolve never to draw sword again in England, except the King command him). Now, let not him that puts on the armour boast like him that puts it off. *Gaudet patientia duris* is his motto, and thus I present myself a friend to all artists, and enemy to no man. The list of Heydon's published works is as follows:--

Eugenius Theodidactus, The Prophetical Trumpeter . . . illustrating the Fate of Great Britain. (A celestial vision in heroic verse) . . . By the Muses' most unworthy John Heydon. London, 1655.

A New Method of Rosie Crucian Physick; wherein is shewed the cause and . . . cure of all diseases. London, 1658. 4to.

Advice to a Daughter in opposition to advice to a Son, or directions for your better conduct through the various and most important events of this life. London, 1658. 12mo.

The Idea of the Law charactered from Moses to King Charles. London, 1660. 8vo.

The Rosie Crucian Infallible Axiomata; or, generall rules to know all things past, present, and to come. London, 1660. 12mo.

The Holy Guide, Leading the Way to the Wonder of the World: A Compleat Phisitian, teaching the knowledge of all things, past, present, and to come. London, 1662. 8vo.

Theomagia; or, The Temple of Wisdome. In three parts spirituall, celestiall, and elementall. London, 1662-3-4. 8vo.

The Harmony of the World, being a discourse of God, Heaven, Angels, Stars, Planets, Earth, &c., whereunto is added the State of the New Jerusalem. . . . London, 1662. 8vo.

Psonthonpanchia; Being a Word in Season to the Enemies of Christians, and an appeal to the natural faculties of the mind of man, whether there be not a God. London, 1664. 8vo.

The Wise Man's Crown; or, The Glory of the Rosie-Cross . . . with the full discovery of the true *Cœlum Terræ*, or first matter of the Philosophers. . . . With the *Regio Lucis*, and Holy Household of Rosie Crucian Philosophers. London, 1664. 8vo.

El Havarevna; or, the English Physitian's Tutor in the Astrobolismes of Mettals Rosie Crucian. London, 1665. 8vo.

The philosophical principles of John Heydon need hardly detain us long. That Typhon is the adversary of Beata Pulchra, that Hyle is the spirit of the cold and dry earth, that Beata Pulchra is the vivifying spirit of Nature, that the bodies of the dead rebellious angels became a fruitless and unprofitable chaos, are matters which will scarcely interest the serious student. His alchemical theories and experiments belong to the lowest dregs of this much degraded science, except in those parts which are bodily stolen from Eugenius Philalethes; and all that is of value in his numerical mysticism, geomantic revelations, astromancy, and investigations of spiritual mysteries, is derived from anterior writers. His medical treatises are disfigured by his gross superstition and credulity; but the unheard of experiments and recipes which they occasionally provide make them extremely curious reading. *Très rares, très curieux, et récherchés des amateurs*, his books, one and all, command large prices in the market, and the republication of his marvellous Rosicrucian reveries and romances, is a venture that deserves well at the hands of all students of the byways of occultism.

In John Heydon we find the names Rosicrucian, Rosicrucianism, &c., used in a general sense, and as terms to conjure with. The supposed brethren are confounded with the elder alchemists, theosophists, etc., and an irrational antiquity is gratuitously bestowed on them. The author denies that he is a member of the Fraternity, but he interprets all its secrets, and expounds all its doctrines, in an authoritative manner, and he claims personal acquaintance with various members of the Society, as will appear from the following

Apologue for an Epilogue.

I shall here tell you what Rosie Crucians are, and that Moses was their Father, and he was Θεοῦ παῖς; some say they were of the order of Elias, some say the Disciples of Ezekiel; others define them to be the Officers of the Generalissimo of the World, that are as the eyes and ears of the Great

King, seeing and hearing all things; they are seraphically illuminated, as Moses was, according to this order of the Elements, Earth refined to Water, Water to Air, Air to Fire, so of a man to be one of the Heroes, of a Hero a Daemon, or good Genius, of a Genius a partaker of Divine things, and a companion of the holy company of unbodied Soules and immortal Angels, and according to their vehicles, a versatile, life, turning themselves, Proteus-like, into any shape.

But there are yet arguments to procure Mr Walfoord, and T. Williams, Rosie Crucians by election, and that is the miracles that were done by them in my sight; for it should seem Rosie Crucians were not only initiated into the Mosaical Theory, but have arrived also to the power of working miracles, as Moses, Elias, Ezekiel, and the succeeding Prophets did, being transported where they please, and one of these went from me to a friend of mine in Devonshire, and came and brought me an answer to London the same day, which is four dayes journey; they taught me excellent predictions of Astrology and Earthquakes; they slack the Plague in Cities; they silence the violent Winds and Tempests; they calm the rage of the Sea and Rivers; they walk in the Air; they frustrate the malicious aspect of Witches; they cure all Diseases. I desired one of these to tell me whether my Complexion were capable of the society of my good Genius? When I see you again, said he, I will tell you, which is when he pleases to come to me, for I know not where to go to him. When I saw him again, then he said, Ye should pray to God; for a good and holy man can offer no more acceptable sacrifice to God than the oblation of himself, his soul. He said also, that the good Genii are as the benigne eyes of God, running to and fro in the world, with love and pity beholding the innocent endeavours of harmless and single-hearted men, ever ready to do them good, and to help them; at his going away he bid me beware of my seeming friends, who would do me all the hurt they could, and cause the Governours of the Nations to be angry with me, and set bounds to my liberty: which truly happened to me. Many things more he told me before we parted, hut I shall not name them here.

This Rosie Crucian Physick or Medecines, I happily and unexpectedly light upon in Arabia, which will prove a restauration of health to all that are afflicted with sickness which we ordinarily call natural, and all other diseases. These men have no small insight into the body; Walford, Williams, and others of the Fraternity now living, may bear up in the same likely equipage with those noble Divine Spirits their Predecessors; though the unskilfulness in men commonly acknowledges more of supernatural assistance in hot, unsettled fancies, and perplexed melancholy, than in the calm and distinct use of reason; yet for mine own part, I look upon these Rosie Crucians above all men truly inspired, and more than any that professed themselves so this sixteen hundred years, and I am ravished with admiration of their miracles and transcendant mechanical inventions, for the salving the Phænomena of the world; I may without offence, therefore, compare them with Bezaliel and Aholiab, those skilful workers of the Tabernacle, who, as Moses testifies, were filled with the Spirit of God, and therefore were of an excellent understanding to find out all manner of curious work.

Nor is it any more argument that those Rosie Crucians were not inspired, because they do not say they are, then that others are inspired, because they say they are; the suppression of what so happened would argue sobriety and modesty, when as the profession of it with sober men would be suspected of some piece of melancholy and distraction, especially in these things, where the grand pleasure is the evidence and exercise of reason, not a bare belief, or an ineffable sense of life, in respect whereof there is no true Christian but he is inspired. If any more zealous pretender to prudence and righteousness, wanting either leisure or ability to examine these Rosie Crucian Medecines to the bottome, shall notwithstanding either condemn them or admire them, he hath unbecoming ventured out of his sphere, and I cannot acquit him of injustice or folly. Nor am I a Rosie Crucian, nor do I speak of spite, or hope of gain, or for any such matter; there is no cause, God knows; I envie no man, be he what he will be; I am no Physitian never was, nor never mean to be: what I am it makes no matter as to my profession.

Lastly, these holy and good. men would have me know that the greatest sweet and perfection of a vertuous soul is the kindly accomplishment of her own nature, in true wisdome and divine love; and these miraculous things that are done by them are performed in order that the worth and knowledge within them may be taken notice of, and that God thereby may be glorified, whose witnesses they are; but no other happiness accrues to them, but that hereby they may be in a better capacity of making others happy.

This "Apologue" forms a sort of preface to the sixth book of "The Holy Guide," which is thus entitled—

The Rosie Cross Uncovered, and the Places,
Temples, Holy Houses, Castles, and
Invisible Mountains of the Brethren
discovered and communicated to the
World, for the full satisfaction of
Philosophers, Alchymists, Astromancers,
Geomancers, Physitians, and Astronomers.
By John Heydon, Gent, φιλόνομος, a Servant of God, and
a Secretary of Nature.

This publication is a sort of perverted version of the "Fama Fraternitatis." It represents the Rosicrucians as acknowledging the renewed church in England, and its Christian head Carolus Magnus Secundus, and warning "all learned men to take heed of the 'Aurum Chymicum Britannicum,' published by Elias Ashmole, Esquire." It contains some information on English Rosicrucians, which can hardly be taken seriously even by an enthusiastic believer, but which is worth reprinting on account of the curiosity of its details.

The Rosicrucians in England.

At this day the Rosie Crucians, that have been since Christ, say their fraternity inhabits the west of England, and they have likewise power to renew themselves and wax young again, as those did before the birth of Jesus Christ, as you may read in many books.

Dr F. saith, somewhere there is a castle in the west of England, in the earth and not on the earth, and there the Rosie Crucians dwell, guarded without walls, and possessing nothing they enjoy all things. In this castle are great riches, the halls fair and rich to behold, the chambers made and composed of white marble. At the end of the hall there is a chimney, whereof the two pillars that sustain the mantle tree are of fine jasper, the mantle is of rich calcedony and the lintel is made of fine emeralds trailed with a wing of fine gold, the grapes of fine silver. All the pillars in the hall are of red calcedoine, and the pavement is of fine amber.

The chambers are hanged with rich clothes, and the benches and bedsteads are all of white ivory, richly garnished with pretious stones; the beds are richly covered; there are ivory presses, whereon are all manner of birds cunningly wrought; and in these presses are gowns and robes of most fine gold, most rich mantles furred with sables, and all manner of costly garments.

And there is a vault, but it is bigger then that in Germany, which is as clear as though the sun in the midst of the day had entred in at ten windows, yet it is sevenscore steps underground. And there are ten servants of the Rosie Crucians, fair young men. C. B. reports this:--"When I first came to the Society, I saw a great oven with two mouths, which did cast out great clearness, by which four young men made paste for bread, and two delivered the loaves to other two, and they sit them down upon a rich cloath of silk. Then the other two men took the loaves and delivered them unto one man by two loaves at once, and he did set them into the oven to bake. At the other mouth of the oven there was a man that drew out the white loaves and pasts, and before him was another young man that received them, and put them into baskets which were richly painted."

C. B. went into another chamber, eighty-one cubits from this, and the Rosie Crucians welcomed him. He found a table ready set and the cloth laid; there stood pots of silver and vessels of gold., bordered with precious stones and pearle, and basons and ewers of gold to wash their hands. Then we went to dinner. Of all manner of flesh, fowl, and fish, of all manner of meat in the world, there they had plenty, and pots of gold, garnished with precious stones, full of wine. This chamber was made of chrystal, and painted richly with gold and azure; upon the walls were written and engraven all things past, prevent, and to come, and all manner of golden medecines for the diseased. Upon the pavement was spread abroad roses, flowers, and herbs, sweet smelling above all savours in the world; and in this chamber were divers birds flying about and singing marvellous sweetly.

In this place have I a desire to live, if it were for no other reason but what the sophist sometimes applied to the mountains--*Hos primum sol salutat, ultimosque deserit. Quis locum non amet, dies longiores habentem.* But of this place I will not speak any more, lest readers should mistake me, so as to entertain a suspition that I am of this Order. The medical and other recipes which are given on the authority of the Fraternity may be judged from the following specimens:--

The Rosie Crucians say pearl helpeth swoundings, and withstands the plague of poysons; and smarge and jacinth help the plague, and heale the wounds of venomous stings. The water of Nile makes the women of Egypt quick of conceite and fruitful: sometimes they bear seven children at a birth, and this is salt-peter-water. There is a wonderful vertue in the oyl of tobacco, in the tincture of saffron, in the flower of brimston, in quicksilver, in common salt; and coppress, molten and made a water, kills the poyson of the toadstool. Juyce of poppy and amber, which is no stone but a hard, clammy juyce, called bitumen, easeth the labour of women and the falling-sickness in children.

Now for mettals, if it be true, which all men grant, that precious stones show such power and vertue of healing, what shall the mixtures of all these mettals under a fortunate constellation, made in the conversion of their own planets, do. This mixture they call electrum, sigil, telesme, saying it will cure the cramp, benumming, palsie, falling-sickness, gout, leprosie, dropsie, if it be worn on the heart-finger. Others they make to cause beauty in ladies, &c.

A perfume of R. C. is compounded of the saphirick earth and the æther. If it be brought to its full exaltation, it will shine like the day-star in her fresh eastern glories. It hath a fascinating, attractive quality, for if you expose it to the open air, it will draw to it birds and beasts, and drive away evil spirits. *Astrum Solis*, or the R. C. mineral sun, is compounded of the æther, and a bloody, fiery-spirited earth; it appears in a gummy consistency, but with a fiery, hot, glowing complexion. It is substantially a certain purple, animated, divine salt, and cureth all manner of venereal distempers, consumptions, and diseases of the mind.

We give another medecine, which is an azure or skie-coloured water, the tincture of it is light and bright, it reflects a most beautiful rainbow, and two drops of this water keeps a man healthy. In it lies a blood-red earth of great vertue.

In the pages that immediately follow, I shall reprint the stories, and allegories which are to be found in the works of John Heydon, and which have reference to the Rosicrucian Order. They may be permitted to speak for themselves. It is obvious that they are devoid of historical value, but they are all excessively curious, and the piece which I have entitled, "Voyage to the Land of the Rosicrucians," and which forms the general preface to "The Holy Guide," is an interesting romantic fiction.

A very true Narrative of a Gentleman R. C., who hath the continual society of a Guardian Genius.Oblation of itself was such a sacrifice to God, that a good and holy man could offer no greater, as appears by the acceptance of a gentleman by descent from the lynes of the Plantaginets, who was in Egypt, Italy, and Arabia, and there frequented the society of the inspired Christians, with whom he became acquainted after this manner. In England, being at a tavern in Cheap-side more to hear and better his judgment of the reputed wise than to drink wine, their discourse being of the nature and dignity of Angels, which was interrupted by a gentleman, for so he appeared, that said to another in the company--"Sir, you are not far from the Kingdome of God." At this many were silent, yet several thoughts arose; some desired this strange gentleman to stay, but he refused, and being pressed, he gave the gentleman a paper of white and yellow powder, bade him read the chapter that lay open in the Bible in his chamber, and sing such psalms; then the window flew open and the gentleman vanished.

He burnt the pouder as he was bid, and there appeared a shining flye upon the Bible which he had in his hand. This vanished whilest he slept, which was then about eight in the morning, Gemini being the ascendant, and Mercury in Virgo. The gentleman conceived that this spirit had been with him all his life-time, as he gathered from certain monitory dreams and visions, whereby he was forwarned as well of several dangers as vices.

Mr Waters and two gentlemen more were at his house, and desired him to go along with them to the Exchange, and dine with them and some other merchants, which he did, and going along, one of them espied a ball of gold upon his breast shining so gloriously that it dazled the eyes of them all, and this continued all the rising of Mercury, who was then in Vergo. This spirit discovered himself to him after he had for a whole year together earnestly prayed to God to send a good angel to him, to be a guide of his life and action; also he prayed for a token that this was the will and pleasure of God, which was granted, for in a bright shining day, no cloud appearing, there fell

195

a drop of water upon his hat, which to this day is not dry, and, I think, never will be, although it be worne in this hot weather.

He prayes God to defend him and guide him in the true religion, reading two or three hours in the Holy Bible.

After this, amongst many other divine dreams and visions, he once in his sleep seemed to hear the voice of God, saying to him, "I will save thy soul; I am He that before appeared unto thee." Since doth the spirit every day knock at his doore about three or four o'clock in the morning. He rising, there appeareth a child of faire stature, very comely, who gave him a book which he keepeth very well, yet letteth many see it that can prevaile with him; this book is full of divine things, such as I never red or heard of. Another time his candle did fall down upon the ground and went out, and there appeared before him something about the bignesse of a nut, round and shining, and made a noyse; he strived to take it up, but it turned like quicksilver, so that he could not handle it.

Many gentlemen have been in his company when he hath been pulled by the coat, as they have seen but could not perceive who did it; sometimes his gloves, lying at one end of the table, have been brought and given him, but they see the gloves, as they thought, come of themselves.

Another time, being with some merchants at dinner that were strangers to this spirit, and were abashed when they heard the noise but saw nothing, presently a paper was given to the gentleman, who read it, and so did the others. It said that he should serve God and fear nothing, for the enemies of his father which hated him should all surely die, and so should all that sought to do him hurt, and to be assured he named such a man, and said he shall die such a day, and he died. The merchants were strucken with fear, but he bid them be of good courage, for there was no hurt towards them, and, the better to assure them of it, he told the truth of the whole matter.

Ever since this spirit hath been alwaies with him, and by some sensible signe did ever advertise him of things, as by striking his right eare, if he did not well, if otherwise, his left; if any danger threatened, he was foretold of it. When he began to praise God in psalms, he was presently raised and strengthened with a spiritual and supernatural power. He daily begged of God that He would teach him His will, His law, and His truth; he set one day of the week apart for reading the Scripture and meditation, with singing of Psalms all the day in his house, but in his ordinary conversation he is sufficiently merry, if he like his company and be of a cheerful minde; if he talk of any vain thing, or indiscreetly, or offer to discover any secret he is forbidden, or if he at any time would discover any inspired secret, he is forthwith admonished thereof in his eare. Every morning he is called to prayer. He often goes to meet the Holy Company at certain times, and they make resolution of all their actions.

He gives almes secretly, and the more he bestows the more prosperous he is; he dares not commit any known fault, and hath by Providence of God been directed through many eminent dangers; even those that sought his life died.

At another time, when he was in very great danger, upon the ascendant coming to the body of the Sun, and the conjunction of Saturn and Jupiter opposing his ascendant, he being newly gone to bed, he said that the spirit would not let him alone till he had raised him again and told him he was falsely accused, wherefore he watched and prayed all that night. The day after he escaped the hands of his persecutors in a wonderful manner--one died and the other is very sick. Then came a voice to him, saying, "Sing *Qui sedit in Latibulo Altissimi.*"

Many other passages happen to this party daily, as a hundred will testifie; but it is an endless labour to recite them all. The man is now alive, in good health, and well known among all men to be a friend to all and desirous to do good.

John Heydon encounters the Spirit Euterpe.

Walking upon the plains of Bulverton Hill to study numbers and the nature of things one evening, I could see, between me and the light, a most exquisite divine beauty, her frame neither long nor short, but a main decent stature; attired she was in thin loose silks, but so green that I never saw the like, for the colour was not earthly; in some places it was fancied with gold and silver ribbands, which looked like the sun and lyllies in the field of grass. Her head was overcast with a thin floating tiffany, which she held up with one of her hands, and looked, as it were, from under it. Her eyes were quick, fresh, and celestial, but had something of a start, as if she had been puzzled with a suddain occurrence. From her vaile did leer locks break out, like sun beams from a mist; they ran disheveld to her brest, and then returned to her cheeks in curls and rings of gold. Her hair behind her was rowled to a curious globe, with a small short spire flowered with purple and skie-colour knots. Her rings were pure intire emeralds, for she valued no metal,. and her pendants of burning carbuncles. In brief, her whole habit was youthful and flowery; it smelt like the East, and was thoroughly ayrd with rich Arabian diapasms.

Whilst I admired her perfections, and prepared to make my addresses, she prevents me with a voluntary approach. Here, indeed, I expected some discourse from her, but she, looking very seriously and silently in my face, takes me by the hand and softly whispers: "My love I freely give you, and with it these tokens--mystery and signet; the one opens, the other shuts; be sure to use both with discretion. As for the mysteries of the Rosie Cross, you have my Library to peruse them all. There is not anything here but I

197

will gladly reveal it unto you; I will teach you the virtues of numbers, of names, of angels, and genii of men. I have one precept to commend to you--you must be silent. You shall not in your writings exceed my allowance; remember that I am your love, and you will not make me a prostitute. But because I wish you serviceable to those of your own disposition, I give you an emblematical type of my sanctuary, namely, the Axiomata of the R. C., the secrets of numbers, with a full priviledge to publish it. And now I am going to the invisible region, amongst the ethereal goddesses. Let not that proverb take place with you, Out of sight, out of mind. Remember me and be happy."

I asked her if she would favour me with her name. To this she replyed very familiarly, as if she had known me long before:--"My dear friend H., I have many names, but my best beloved is Euterpe. Observe in your R. C. Axiomata that the genuine time of impression of characters, names, angels, numbers, and genii of men, is when the principles are Spermade and Callado; but being once coagulated to a perfect body, the time of stellification is past. Now the R. C. in old time used strange astrological lamps, images, rings, and plates, with the numbers and names engraven, which at certain hours would produce incredible extraordinary effects. The common astrologer he takes a piece of metalls, another whining associate he helps him with a chrystal stone, and these they figure with ridiculous characters, and then expose them to the planets, not in an Alkemust, but as they dream they know not what. When this is done, all is to no purpose, but though they faile in their practice, they yet believe they understand the Axiomata of numbers well enough. Now, my beloved J. H., that you may know what to do, I will teach you by example:--Take a ripe grain of corn that is hard and drye; expose it to the sun beams in a glass or other vessell, and it will be a dry grain for ever; but if you do bury it in the earth, that the nitrous saltish moysture of the element may dissolve it, then the sun will work upon it and make it sprout to a new body. It is just thus with the common astrologer; he exposeth to the planets a perfect compacted body, and by this meanes thinkes to perform the Rosie Crucian Gamacea, and marry the inferiour and superiour worlds.

"It must be a body reduced into sperme, that the heavenly feminine moisture, which receives and retains the impress of the Astrall Agent; may be at liberty, and immediately exposed to the masculine fire of Nature. This is the ground of the Beril, but you must remember that nothing can be stellified without the joynt magnetism of three heavens--what they are you know already."

When she had thus said, she took out of her bosom two miraculous medalls with numbers and names on them; they were not metalline, but such as I had never seen, neither did I conceive there was in Nature such pure and glorious substances. In my judgment, they were two magical

Telesms, but she called them Saphiricks of the sun and moon. These miracles Euterpe commended to my perusal, and stopt in a mute ceremony. She lookt upon me in silent smiles, mixt with a pretty kind of sadness, for we were unwilling to part, but her hour of translation was come, and, taking, as I thought, her last leave, she past before my eyes into the ether of Nature, excusing herself as being sleepy--otherwise she had expounded them to me. I lookt, admired, and wearied myself in that contemplation; their complexion was so heavenly, their continuance so mysterious, I did not well know what to make of them. I turned aside to see if she was still asleep, but she was gone, and this did not a little trouble me. I expected her return till the day was quite spent, but she did not appear. At last, fixing my eyes on that place where she sometimes rested, I discovered certain pieces of gold, full of numbers and names, which she had left behinde her, and hard by a paper folded like a letter. These I took up, and now the night approaching, the evening star tinned in the West, when taking my last survey of her flowery pillow, I parted from it in these verses—

"Pretty green bank, farewel, and mayst thou wear
Sun-beams, and rose, and lillies all the year;
She slept on thee, but needed not to shed
Her gold, 'twas joy enough to be her bed.
Thy flowers are favourites, for this loved day
They were my rivals, and with her did play;
They found their heaven at hand, and in her eyes
Enjoy'd a copy of their absent skies.
Their weaker paint did with true glories trade,
And mingl'd with her cheeks one posy made;
And did not her soft skin confine their pride,
And with a skreen of silk her flowers divide,
They had suck'd life from thence, and from her heat
Borrow'd a soul to make themselves compleat.
O happy pillow! though thou art laid even
With dust, she made thee up almost a heaven;
Her breath rain'd spices, and each amber ring
Of her bright locks strew'd bracelets o'er thy spring.
That earth's not poor, did such a treasure hold,
But thrice inrich'd with amber, spice, and gold."

Thus much at this time and no more am I allowed by my mistress Euterpe to publish. Be, therefore, gentle reader, admonished, that with me you do earnestly pray to God, that it please Him to open the hearts and ears of all ill-hearing people, and to grant unto them His blessing, that they may be able to know Him in His omnipotency, with admiring contemplation of

Nature, to His honour and praise, and to the love, help, comfort, and strengthening of our neighbours, and to the restoring of all the diseased by the medecines above taught.

I had given you a more large account of the mysteries of Nature and the Rosie Cross, but whilst I studied medecines to cure others, my deare sister Anne Heydon dyed, and I never heard she was sick (for she was one hundred miles from mee), which puts an end to my writings, and thus I take my leave of the world. I shall write no more; you know my books by name, and this I write that none may abuse me by printing books in my name, as Cole does Culpeper's. I return to my first happy solitudes.

Voyage to the Land of the Rosicrucians.

We travelled from Sydmouth for London and Spain by the south sea, taking with us victuals for twelve moneths, and had good winds from the East, though soft and weake, for five moneths' space and more. But then the winds came about into the West, so as we could make little way, and were sometimes in purpose to turn back. Then again there arose strong and great winds from the South, with a point East, which carried us up towards the North, by which time our victuals failed us, and we gave ourselves for lost men, and prepared for death. We did lift up our hearts and voices to God, beseeching Him of His mercy that He would discover land to us, that we might not perish. The next day about evening we saw before us, towards the North, as it were thick clouds, which did put us in hope of land, knowing that part of the south sea was utterly unknown, and might have islands or continents hitherto not come to light. We bent our course thither all that evening, and in the dawning of the next day discerned a land flat and full of boscage. After an houre and a half's sayling, we entred into a good haven, the port of a faire city, not great indeed, but well built, and that gave a pleasant view from sea. We came close to shore, and offered to land, but straightwayes we saw divers people with bastons in their hands forbidding us, yet without any cryes or fierceness, but onely warning us off by signes that they made, whereupon, being not a little discomfitted, we were advising with ourselves what we should do, during which there made forth to us a small boat, with about eight persons in it, whereof one had in his hand a tipstaff of yellow cane, tipped at both ends with green, who came aboard without any shew of distrust, and drew forth a little scroule of parchment, somewhat yellower than our parchment, and shining like the leaves of writing tables, but otherwise soft and flexible, and delivered it to our foremost man. In this scroule were written in antient Hebrew, antient Greeke, good Latine of the School, and in Spanish, these words:--"Land ye not, none of you, and provide to be gone from this coast within sixteen dayes, except you have further time given you. Mean while, if you want fresh water, victual, or help for your sick, or that your ship needeth repaire, write down your wants, and you shall have that which belongeth to mercy." This scroule was signed with a stamp of cherubin's wings, not spread but hanging downwards, and by them a crosse. This being delivered, the officer returned, and left onely a servant to receive our answer. Consulting amongst ourselves, the denial of landing, and hasty warning us away, troubled us much; on the other side, to finde the people had languages, and were full of humanity, did comfort us; above all, the signe of the crosse was to us a great rejoycing and a certain presage of good. Our answer was in the Spanish tongue--that our ship was well, our sick many, and in very ill case, so that if they were not permitted to land, they ran in danger of their lives. Our other wants we set down in particular, adding that we had some little merchandize, which, if it pleased them to deale for, might supply our wants without being chargable unto them. We offered some reward in pistolet unto the servant, and a piece of crimson velvet for the officer, but he took them not, nor would scarce look upon them, and so left us in another boat which was sent for him.

About three hours after there came towards us a person of place. He had a gown with wide sleaves of a kinde of water chamolot, of an excellent green colour, farre more glossie than ours. His under apparel was green azure, and so was his hat, being in the form of a turban, daintily made and not so large as Turkish turbans. The locks of his haire came below the brims of it. A reverend man was he to behold. He came in a boat partly gilt, with foure persons more, and was followed by another boat, wherein were some twenty. When he was within a flight-shot of our ship, signes were made that we should send some to meet him, which we presently did in our ship boat, sending the principall man amongst us, save one, and foure of our number with him. When we were come within six yards of their boat, they called to us to stay, and thereupon the man whom I before described stood up, and with a loud voice, in Spanish, asked, "Are ye Christians?" We answered that we were, at which he lift up his right hand towards Heaven, and drew it softly to his mouth (which is the gesture they use when they thank God), and then said, "If ye will swear by the merit of the Saviour that ye are no pirates, nor have shed blood, lawfully or unlawfully, within forty dayes past, you may have license to land." We said that we were all ready to take that oath, whereupon one of those with him, being, as it seemed, a notarie, made an entrie of this act, which done, another, after his lord had spoken a little to him, said:--"My lord would have you know that it is not of pride that he commeth not aboard your ship, but for that you declare that you have many sick amongst you, he was warned by the conservation of health that he should keep a distance." We were his humble servants, and accounted for great honour and singular humanity towards us that which had been already done, but hoped that the nature of the sickness was not

201

infectious. So he returned, and a while after came the notary aboard, holding a fruit like an orange, but of colour between orange-tawney and scarlet, which cast a most excellent odour. He used it for a preservative against infection. He gave us our oath, "by the name of Jesus and His merits," and told us that next day, by six in the morning, we should be sent to and brought to the strangers' house, where we should be accommodated both for our whole and our sick. When we offered him some pistolets, he smiling said he must not be twice paid for one labour.

The next morning there came the same officer that came to us at first with his cane, to conduct us to the strangers' house. "If you will follow my advice," said he, "some few will first go with me and see the place, and how it may be made convenient for you; then you may send for your sick and the rest of your number." We thanked him, and said that this care which he took of desolate strangers God would reward, and six of us went ashore with him. He led us thorow three faire streets, and all the way there were gathered some people on both sides in a row, but in so civill a fashion as if it had been not to wonder at us, but to welcome us. Divers of them as we passed put their arms a little abroad, which is their gesture when they bid any welcome. The strangers' house is faire and spacious, built of brick, and with handsome windows, some of glass, some of a kind of cambrick oyled. He brought us into a faire parlour above staires, and then asked what number of persons we were, and how many sick? We answered that we were in all 250, whereof our sick were seventeen. He desired us to stay till he came back, which was about an houre after, and then he led us to see the chambers provided for us, being in number 250. They cast it that foure of those chambers, which were better than the rest, might receive foure of our principal men; the rest were to lodge us. The chambers were handsome, cheerful, and furnished civilly. Then he led us to a long gallery, where he showed us along one side seventeen cells, having partitions of cedar, which gallery and cells, being in all 900, were instituted as an infirmary. He told us withall that as any one sick waxed well he might be removed to a chamber, for which purpose there were set forth ten spare chambers. This done, he brought us back to the parlour, and lifting up his cane a little, as they doe when they give any command, said to us:--"Ye are to know that the custom of the land requireth that, after this day and to-morrow, which we give you for removing your people from your ship, you are to keep within doores for three dayes; do not think yourselves restrained, but rather left to your rest. You shall want nothing; there are six of our people appointed to attend you for any business you may have abroad." We gave him thanks with all affection and respects, and said:--"God surely is manifested in this land." We offered him also twenty pistolets, but he smiled, and said:--"What! twice paid!" and so left us. Soon after our dinner was served in, which was right good viands both for bread, meat, wine, &c., better than any diet that I have known in Europe. We had drink of three sorts, ale, beer, syder, all wholesome; wine of the grape, and another drink of grain, like our mum but more clear, and a kinde of perry, like the peare juice, made of a fruit of that countrey, a wonderfull pleasing and refreshing drink. Besides, there were brought in great store of those scarlet oranges for our sick, which were an assured remedy for sicknesse taken at sea. There was given us also a box of small grey pills which they wished our sick should take, one every night before sleeping, to hasten their recovery. The next day, after that our trouble of carriage of our men and goods out of our ship was somewhat settled, I thought good to call our company together, and said unto them;-- "My dear friends, let us know ourselves, and how it standeth with us. We are cast on land, as Jonas was out of the whale's belly, when we were as buried in the deep, and now we are on land, we are but between death and life, for we are beyond both the old world and the new. Whether ever we shall see Europe God onely knoweth. A kinde of miracle hath brought us hither, and it must be little lesse that shall take us hence. Therefore in regard of our deliverance past, and danger present, let us look to God and every man reform his own wayes. We are come amongst a Christian people, full of piety and humanity. Let us not bring confusion of face upon ourselves by shewing our vices or unworthinesse, They have cloistered us for three daies; who knoweth whether it be not to take some taste of our manners and conditions, and if they find them bad to banish us straight wayes, if good to give us further time? For God's love let us so behave ourselves as we may be at peace with God and may finde grace in the eyes of this people." Our company with one voice thanked me for my good admonition, and promised to live soberly and civilly, without giving the least occasion of offence. We spent our three dayes joyfully, during which time we had every houre joy of the amendment of our sick.

The morrow after our three dayes, there came to us a new man, cloathed in azure, save that his turban was white with a small red crosse at the top. He had also a tippet of fine linnen. He did bend to us a little, and put his arms broad; we saluting him in a very lowly manner. He desired to speak with some few of us, whereupon six onely stayed, and the rest avoided the room. He said: I am by office governour of this house of strangers, and by vocation a Christian priest of the Order of the Rosie Crosse, and am come to offer you my service, as strangers and chiefly as Christians. The State hath given you licence to stay on land for the space of six weeks, and let it not trouble you if your occasions ask further time, for the law in this point is not precise. Ye shall also understand that the strangers' house is at this time rich and much afore-hand, for it hath laid up revenue these 36000 years--so long it is since any stranger arrived in this part. Therefore take ye no care; the State will defray you all the time you stay. As for any merchandize ye have brought, ye shall be well used, and have your return either in merchandize or gold and silver, for to us it is all one. If you have any other request to make, hide it not, onely this I must tell you that none of you must go above a juld, or karan (that is with them a mile and an half), from the walls of the city without especiall leave." We answered, admiring this gracious and parent-like usage, that we could not tell what to say to expresse our thanks, and his noble free offers left us nothing to ask. It seemed that we had before us a picture of our salvation in Heaven, for we that were awhile since in the jaws of death were now brought into a place where we found nothing but consolations. For the commandement laid on us, we would not faile to obey it, though it was impossible but our hearts should be enflamed to tred further upon this happy and holy ground. Our tongues should cleave to the roof of our mouth ere we should forget either his reverend person or this whole nation in our prayers. We also humbly besought him to accept us as his true servants, presenting both our persons and all we had at his feet. He said he was a priest and looked for a priest's reward, which was our brotherly love, and the good of our souls and bodies. So he went from us, not without tears of tendernesse in his eyes, and left us confused with joy and kindness, saying amongst ourselves that we were come into a land of angels.

The next day, about ten of the clock, the governour came to us again, and, after salutation, said familiarly that he was come to visit us, called for a chair, and sat him down. We, being some ten of us (the rest were of the meaner sort, or else gone abroad), sat down with him, when he began thus:--"We of this island of Apanua or Chrisse in Arabia (for so they call it in their language), by means of our solitary situation, the laws of secresy which we have for our travellers, and our rare admission of strangers, know well most part of the habitable world and are ourselves unknown. Therefore, because he that knoweth least is fittest to ask questions, it is more reason, for the entertainment of the time, that ye ask me questions than that I ask you." We humbly thanked him, and answered that we conceived, by the taste we had already, that there was no worldly thing more worthy to be known than the state of that happy land, but since we were met from the several ends of the world, and hoped assuredly that we should meet one day in the Kingdome of Heaven, we desired to know (in respect that land was so remote, divided by vast, unknown seas from where our Saviour walked on earth) who was the apostle of that nation, and how it was converted to the faith. It appeared in his face that he took great contentment in this question in the first place, "for (said he) it sheweth that you first seek the Kingdome of Heaven.

"About 20 years after the Ascension of our Saviour, it came to passe that there was seen by the people of Damcar, on the eastern coast of our island, within night, as it might be some mile into the sea, a great pillar of light, in form of a column or cylinder rising from the sea a great way towards Heaven. On the top was a large crosse of light, more resplendent than the body of the pillar, upon which so strange a spectacle the people of the city gathered upon the sands to wonder, and after put into a number of small boats to go neerer this marvellous sight. But when the boats were come within about 60 yards of the pillar they found themselves bound and could go no further. They stood all as in a theatre, beholding this light as an heavenly signe. There was in one of the boats one of the wise men of the Society of the Rosie Crucians, whose house or colledge is the very eye of this Kingdome, who, having awhile devoutly contemplated this pillar and crosse, fell down upon his face, then raised himself upon his knees, and, lifting up his hands to Heaven, made his prayers in this manner:

"'Lord God of Heaven and earth, Thou hast vouchsafed of Thy grace to those of our order to know Thy works of creation and the secrets of them, and to discern (as far as appertaineth to the generation of men) between divine miracles, works of Nature, works of art, and impostures and illusions of all sorts. I do here acknowledge and testifie before this people, that the thing which we now see is Thy finger and a true miracle. And for as much as we learn in our books that Thou never workest miracles but to a divine and excellent end (for the laws of Nature are Thine own laws, and Thou exceedest them not but upon great cause), we most humbly beseech Thee to prosper this great signe, and to give us the interpretation and use of it in mercy, which Thou doest in some part promise by sending it unto us.'

"When he had made his prayer, he presently found the boat he was in unbound, whereas the rest remained still fast. Taking that for leave to approach, he caused the boat to be softly rowed towards the pillar, but ere he came near the pillar and crosse of light brake up, and cast itself abroad into a firmament of many stars, which also soon vanished, and there was nothing left but a small ark of cedar, not wet at all with water, though it swam. In the fore-end of it grew a small green branch of palme, and when the Rosie Crucian had taken it with all reverence into his boat, it opened of itself, and there were found a book and letter, both written in fine parchment, and wrapped in suidons of linnen, the book containing all the canonical books of the Old and New Testament, according as you have them, while the Apocalypse itself, and some other books of the New Testament, not at that time written, were, nevertheless, therein. And for the letter, it was in these words:--

"'I John, a servant of the Highest and Apostle of Jesus Christ, was warned by an angell, that appeared to me in a vision of glory, that I should commit this ark to the floods of the sea. Therefore I do testifie and declare unto that people where God shall ordain this ark to come to land, that in the same day is come unto them salvation and peace and goodwill from the Father and from the Lord Jesus.'

"There was also as well in the book as the letter a great miracle wrought, conform to that of the apostles in the originall gift of tongues, for there being at that time in this land Hebrews, Persians, and Indians, besides the natives, every one read upon the book and the letter as if they had been written in his own language. Thus was this land saved from infidelity through the apostolicall and miraculous evangelism of S. John."

Here he paused, and a messenger called him from us, so this was all that passed in that conference. The next day the same Governour came again to us immediately after dinner, and after we were set, he said:--"Well, the questions are on your part." One of our number said, after a little pause, that there was a matter we were no less desirous to know than fearful to ask, but encouraged by his rare humanity towards us, we would take the hardiness to propound it. We well observed those his former words, that this happy island was known to few, and yet knew most of the nations of the world, which we found to be true, considering they had the languages of Europe, and knew much of our state and business, yet we, notwithstanding the remote discoveries of this last age, never heard the least inkling of this island; we never heard tell of any ship of theirs that had been seen to arrive upon any shore of Europe. And yet the marvell rested not in this, for its scituation in the secret conclave of such a vast sea mought cause it, but that they should have knowledge of the languages, books, affaires of those that lye such a distance from them, was a thing we could not tell what to make of, for it seemed a propriety of divine powers and beings to be hidden to others, and yet to have others open as in a light to them. At this speech the Governour gave a gratious smile, and said that we did well to ask pardon for a question which imported as if we thought this a land of magicians, that sent forth spirits of the aire into all parts to bring them intelligence of other countries. It was answered by us in all possible humblenesse, but yet with a countenance takeing knowledge that he spake it but merrily, that we were apt enough to think there was something supernaturall in this island, but rather as angelicall than magicall; but to let his lordship know truly what made us doubtful to ask this question, was because we remembred he had given a touch in his former speech that this land had laws of secresy touching strangers. To this he said:--"You remember aright, and in that I shall say I must reserve particulars which it is not lawful to reveal, but there will be enough left to give you satisfaction. You shall understand that about three thousand years agoe, the navigation of the world (specially for remote voyages) was greater than it is now. Whether it was that the example of the Ark that saved the remnant of men front the universall deluge, gave confidence to adventure, or what it was; but such is the truth. The Phoenicians and Tyrians had great fleets, so had the Carthaginians, their colony. To ward the East the shipping of Ægypt and Palestina was likewise great. China also and America abounded in tall ships. This island had fifteen

206

hundred of great content. At that time this land was known and frequented by ships and vessels of all the nations before named, and they had many times men of other countries that were no saylers, that came with them--as Persians, Chaldeans, Egyptians, and Grecians, so as almost all nations resorted hither, of whom we have some stirps with us at this day. Our own ships went sundry voyages.

"At the same time, the inhabitants of the Holy Land did flourish. For though the narration and discription made by a great man with you, that the descendants of Neptune planted there, and of the magnificent temple, palace, city, and hill (see my *Rosie Crucian Infallible Axiometa*), and the manifold navigable rivers (which as so many chains environed the site and temple), and the severall degrees of ascent whereby men did climb up to the same as if it had been a *Scala Cœli*, be all poeticall and fabulous, yet so much is true that the said country of Judea, as well as Peru, then called Coya--Mexico, then named Tyrambel--were mighty, proud kingdomes in arms, shipping, and riches., At one time both made two great expeditions, they of Tyrambel through Judea to the Mediterrane sea, and they of Coya through the South Sea upon this our island. For the former of these, which was into Europe, the same author amongst you had some relations from his Beata (see the "Harmony of the World," lib. i., the Preface). Assuredly such a thing there was, but whether the ancient Athenians had the glory of the repulse of those forces I can say nothing; but certain it is there never came back either ship or man from that voyage. Neither had those of Coya had better fortune if they had not met with enemies of great clemency. The King of this island, by name Phroates, who was raised three times from death to life, a wise man and great warrior, knowing his own strength and that of his enemies, handled the matter so as he cut off their landforces from their ships, and entoyled both their navy and camp with a greater power than theirs, compelling them to render themselves without striking stroke. After they were at his mercy, contenting himself only with their oath that they should no more beare armes against him, he dismissed them in all safety; but the Divine revenge overtook, not long after, these proud enterprises, for within less than the space of one hundred years the island was utterly destroyed by a particular deluge or inundation, these continents then having far greater rivers and far higher mountaines to pour down waters than any part of the Old World. The inundation was not past forty foot deep in most places, so that, although it destroyed man and beast generally, yet some few wilde inhabitants of the wood escaped. Birds also escaped by flying to the high trees and woods. As for men, although they had buildings in many places higher than the waters, yet that inundation had a long continuance, whereby they of the vaile that were not drowned perished for want of food. So marvel you not at the thin population of America, nor at the rudeness of the people, younger a thousand years, at the least, then the rest of the world, for there was so much time between the universal flood and their particular inundation. The poor remnant of humane seed which remained in their mountaines peopled the country again slowly, and, being simple and savage, were not able to leave letters, arts, and civility to their posterity. Having likewise in their mountainous habitations been used (in respect of the extream cold) to cloathe themselves with skins of tygers, bears, and great hairy goates, when they came down into the valley and found the intolerable heats which are there, they were forced to begin the custome of going naked, which continueth at this day, onely they take great pride in the feathers of birds. . . . By this main accident of time we lost our traffique with the Americans, with whom, in regard they lay nearest to us, we had most commerce. As for other parts of the world, navigation did everywhere greatly decay, so that part of entercourse which could be from other nations to sayle to us hath long since ceased.

But now of the cessation of intercourse which mought be by our sayling to other nations, I cannot say but our shipping for number, strength, marriners, pilots, and all things is as great as ever; and, therefore, why we should set at home I shall now give you au account by itself. There raigned in this island, about nineteen hundred years agoe, a King whose memory of all others we most adore, not superstitiously, but as a divine instrument, though a mortall man. His name was Eugenius Theodidactus (you may read this at large in our "Idea of the Law"), and we esteem him as the lawgiver of our nation. This King had a large heart, inscrutable for good, and was wholly bent to make his kingdome and people happy. He, therefore, takeing into consideration how sufficient this land was to maintain itself without any aid of the forrainer, being 5600 miles in circuit and of rare fertility in the greatest part thereof; finding also the shipping might be plentifully set on worke by fishing and by transportation from port to port, and likewise by sayling unto some small islands not farr from us, and under the Crown and laws of this State; recalling the flourishing estate wherein this land then was, though nothing wanted to this noble and heroicall intention but to give perpetuity to that which was so happily established. Amongst other fundamentall) laws of this kingdome, he did ordaine the interdicts and prohibitions which we have touching entrance of strangers, doubting novelties and commixture of manners. Nevertheless, he preserved all points of humanity in making provision for the relief of strangers distressed, whereof you have tasted," at which speech we all rose up and bowed ourselves.

He went on:--"That King also still desiring to joyn humanity and policy, and thinking it against humanity to detaine strangers against their will, and against policy that they should return to discover their knowledge of this state, did ordain that of the strangers permitted to land, as many at all times mought depart as would, but as many as would stay should have very good conditions, wherein he saw so farr that in so many ages since the prohibition, we have memory not of one ship that ever returned, and but of thirteen persons, at severall times, that chose to return in our bottoms. What those few may have reported abroad, I know not, but whatever they said could be taken but for a dream. For our travelling hence, our law-giver thought fit altogether to restrain it, but this restraint hath one admirable exception, preserving the good which commeth by communication with strangers, and avoiding the hurt. Ye shall understand that among the excellent acts of that King one hath the pre-eminence--the erection and institution of an Order, or Society, which we call the Temple of the Rosie Crosse, the noblest foundation that ever was upon earth, and the lanthorne of this Kingdome. It is dedicated to the study of the works and creatures of God. Some think it beareth the founder's name a little corrupted, as if it should be F. H. R. C. his house, but the records write it as it is spoken. I take it to be denominate of the King of the Hebrews, which is famous with you, and no stranger to us, for we have some parts of his works which you have lost, namely, that Rosie Crucian M which he wrote of all things past, present, or to come, and of all things that have life and motion. This maketh me think that our King finding himself to symbolize with that King of the Hebrews, honoured him with The Title of this Foundation, and I finde in ancient records this Order or Society of the Rosie Crosse is sometimes called the Holy House, and sometimes the Colledge of the Six Days' Works, whereby I am satisfied that our excellent King had learned from the Hebrews that God had created the world and all therein within six days, and therefore he instituting that House for the finding out of the one nature of things did give it also that second name. When the King had forbidden to all his people navigation into any part not under his crown, he had, nevertheless, this ordinance, that every twelve years there should be set forth two ships appointed to severall voyages; that in either of these ships there should be a mission of three of the Fellows or Brethren of the Holy House, whose errand was to give us knowledge of the affaires and state of those countries to which they were designed, and especially of the sciences, arts, manufactures, and inventions of all the world, and withall to bring unto us books, instruments, and patterns in every kinde; that the ships after they had landed the Brethren of the Rosie Crosse should return, and that the Brethren R. C. should stay abroad till the new mission. These ships were not otherwise fraught than with store of victualls, and treasure to remaine with the Brethren for buying such things and rewarding such persons as they should think fit. Now for me to tell you how the vulgar sort of marriners are contained from being discovered at land, and how they that must be put on shore colour themselves under the name of other nations, and to what places these voyages have been designed, and what rendezvous are appointed for the new missions, and the like circumstances,

I may not do it, but thus, you see, we maintain a trade, not for gold, silver, or jewels, nor any commodity of matter, but onely for God's first creature, which was light, to have light, I say, of the growth of all parts of the world."

When he had said this he was silent, and so were we all, for we were astonished to hear so strange things so probably told. He perceiving that we were willing to say somewhat, but had it not ready, descended to aske us questions of our voyage and fortunes, and in the end concluded that we mought do well to think what time of stay we would demand of the State, for he would procure such time as we desired. Whereupon we all rose up and presented ourselves to kisse the skirt of his tippet, but he would not suffer us, and so took his leave. When it came once amongst our people that the State used to offer conditions to strangers that would stay, we had worke enough to get any of our men to look to our ship, and to keep them from going to the Government to crave conditions.

We took ourselves now for freemen, and lived most joyfully, going abroad and seeing what was to be seen in the city and places adjacent, obtaining acquaintance with many in the city, at whose hands we found such humanity as was enough to make us forget all that was dear to us in our own countries. Continually we met with things right worthy of observation and relation, as indeed if there be a mirrour in the world worthy to hold men's eyes, it is that countrey. One day there were two of our company bidden to a feast of the fraternity, as they call it, and a most naturall, pious, and reverend custome it is, shewing that nation to be compounded of all goodnesse. It is granted to any man who shall live to see thirty persons descended of his body alive together, and all above three years old, to make this feast, which is done at the cost of the State. The Father of the fraternity, whom they call the R. C., two days before the feast taketh to him three of such friends as he liketh to chuse, and is assisted also by the governour of the city where the feast is celebrated, and all the persons of the family, of both sexes, are summoned to attend upon him. Then, if there be any discords or suits, they are compounded and appeased. Then, if any of the family be distressed or decayed, order is taken for their relief and competent means to live. Then, if any be subject to vice, they are reproved and censured. So, likewise, direction is given touching marriage and the courses of life. The governour assisteth to put in execution the decrees of the Tirsan if they should be disobeyed, though that seldome needeth, such reverence they give to the order of Nature. The Tirsan doth also then chuse one man from amongst his sons to live in house with him, who is called ever after the Sonne of the Vine. On the feast day the father, or Tirsan, commeth forth after Divine Service in to a large room, where the feast is celebrated, which room hath an half-pace at the upper end. Against the wall, in the middle of the half-pace, is a chaire placed for him, with a table and carpet before it. Over the chaire is a slate, made round or ovall, and it is of an ivie somewhat whiter than ours, like the leaf of a silver aspe, but more shining, for it is green all winter. The slate is curiously wrought of silver and silk of divers colours, broyding or binding in the ivie. It is the work of some of the daughters of the family, and is vailed over at the top with a fine net of silk and silver, but the substance of it is true ivie, whereof, after it is taken down, the friends of the family are desirous to have some leaf to keep. The Tirsan commeth forth with all his generation or linage, the males before him and the females following him, and if there be a mother from whose body the whole linage is descended, there is a traverse placed in a loft above, on the right hand of the chaire, with a privie doore and a carved window of glass, leaded with gold and blew, where she sitteth but is not seen. When the Tirsan is come forth, he sitteth down in the chaire, and all the linage place themselves against the wall, both at his back and upon the return of the hall, in order of their yeares, without difference of sex, and stand upon their feet. When he is set, the roome being alwayes full of company, but without disorder, after some pause there commeth in from the lower end of the room a Taratan, or herald, and on either side of him two young lads, whereof one carrieth a scrowle of their shining yellow parchment, and the other a cluster of grapes of gold, with a long foot or stalke. The heralds and children are cloathed with mantles of sea-water green sattin, but the herald's mantle is streamed with gold and hath a traine. Then the herald with three curtsies, or rather inclinations, commeth up as far as the half-pace, and taketh into his hand the scrowle. This is the King's charter, containing gifts of revenue and many priviledges, exemptions, and points of honour, granted to the father of the fraternity; it is stiled and directed, "To *such an one*, our well beloved friend and Creditour," which is a title proper only to this case, for they say the King is debtor to no man but for propagation of his subjects. The seal set to the King's charter is R. C., and the King's image embossed or mouled in gold. This charter the herald readeth aloud, the father, or Rosie Crucian, standing up, supported by two of his sons. Then the herald mounteth the half-pace and delivereth the charter into his hands, and with that there is an acclamation--"Happy are the people of Apanua!" Then the herald taketh into his hand, from the other childe, the cluster of grapes, which are daintily enamelled. If the males of the Holy Island are the greater number, the grapes are enamelled purple, with a sun set on the top. If the females prevaile, they are enamelled into a greenish yellow, with a crescent on the top. The grapes are in number as many as the descendants of the fraternity. This golden cluster the herald delivereth also to the Rosie Crucian, who presently delivereth it to that sonne formerly chosen to be in his house with him, who beareth it before his father as an ensign of honour when he goeth in publick ever after. After this ceremony, the father, or Rosie Crucian, retireth, and after some time commeth forth again to dinner, where he sitteth alone under the slate--none of his descendants sit with him, except he happ to be of the Holy House. He is served only by his own male children upon the knee; the women stand about him, leaning against the wall. The room below the half-pace hath tables on the sides for the ghests, who are served with great and comely order. Towards the end of dinner (which in their greatest feasts never lasteth above an hour and an half) there is an hymne sung, varied according to the invention of him that composeth it (for they have an excellent poesie), but the subject is alwayes the praise of Adam, Noah, and Abraham, whereof the two former peopled the world, and the last was the father of the faithfull, concluding with a thanksgiving for the nativity of our Saviour Jesus Christ, in whose birth only the births of all are blessed. Dinner being done, the R. Crucian, having withdrawne himself into a place where he maketh some private prayers, commeth forth the third time to give the blessing with all his descendants, who stand about him as at first. He calls them forth by one and by one as he pleaseth, though seldome the order of age be inverted. The person called (the table being before removed) kneeleth down before the chaire, and the father layeth his hand upon his or her head, and giveth the blessing in these words:--"Son (or daughter) of the Holy Island, thy father saith it; the man by whom thou hast breath and life speaketh the words; the blessing of the Everlasting Father, the Prince of Peace, and the Holy Spirit be upon thee, and make the dayes of thy pilgrimage good and many." If there be any of his sons of eminent merit and vertue (so they be not above two), he calleth for them again, and saith, laying his arm over their shoulders, they standing; "Sons, it is well ye are borne; give God the praise, and persevere to the end!" withall delivering to either a jewel made in the figure of an Bare of wheat, which they ever after doe wear in the front of their turban, or hat. This done, they fall to musick and dances, and other recreations. This is the full order of that Feast of the Rosie Cross.

By that time six or seven dayes were spent, and I was fallen into a straight acquaintance with a merchant of that city, whose name was Nicholas Walford, and his man, Sede John Booker. He was a Jew and circumcised, for they have some few stirps of Jews yet among them, whom they leave to their own religion, which they may the better doe, because they are of a farr differing disposition from the Jews in other parts, giving unto our Saviour many high attributes, and loving the nation of Chassalonia extreamly. This man of whom I speak would ever acknowledge that Christ was born of a Virgin, and was more than man; he would tell how God made Him ruler of the Seraphims which guard His throne (read the "Harmony of the World"). They call Him also the milken way Emepht, and the Eliah of the Messiah, and many other high names, which, though they be inferior to His Divine Majesty, are farr from the language of other Jews. For the country of Apamia, the Holy Island, or Chassalonia, for it is all one place, this man would make no end of commending it, being desirous, by tradition amongst the Jews there, to have it believed that the people were of the generations of Abraham by another son, whom they call Nachoran, and that Moses by a secret Cabala (read the "Temple of Wisdome," lib. 4) ordained the Laws of Jerusalem which they now use, and that when Messiah should come and sit in His throne at Hierusalem, the King of Chassalonia should sit at his feet, whereas other kings should keep a great distance. Setting aside the Jewish dreamer, the man was wise and learned, excellently seen in the laws and customs of that nation. Amongst other discourses I told him I was much affected with the relation from some of the company of their Feast of the Fraternity, and because propagation of families proceeded from nuptial copulation, I desired to know what laws they had concerning marriage, and whether they were tyed to one wife. To this he said:--"You have reason to commend that excellent institution of the Feast of the Family. Those families that are partakers of its blessing flourish ever after in an extraordinary manner. You shall understand that there is not under the Heavens so chast a nation as this of Apamia. It is the virgin of the world. I have read in one of your books of an holy hermit that desired to see the spirit of fornication, and there appeared to him a little foule ugly æthiope. But if he had desired to see the spirit of chastitie of the Holy Island, it would have appeared in the likenesse of a faire beautiful cherubin, for there is nothing amongst mortall men more admirable than the chaste mindes of this people. There are no stewes, no dissolute houses, no curtisans. They wonder with detestation at you in Europe which permit such things; they say ye have put marriage out of office, for marriage is a remedy for unlawfull concupiscence, and naturall concupiscence seemeth as a spur to marriage; but when men have at hand a remedy more agreeable to their corrupt will, marriage is almost expulsed. And therefore there are seen with you infinite men that marry not, but choose a libertine and impure single life; and many that do marry, marry late, when the prime and strength of their years is past. When they do marry, what is marriage to them but a very bargain, wherein is sought alliance, or portion, or reputation, with some indifferent desire of issue, and not the faithfull nuptial union of man and wife that was first instituted? Neither is it possible that those who have cast away so basely so much of their strength should greatly esteeme children (being of the same matter) as chaste men doe. So likewise during marriage is the case much amended, as it ought to be, if those things were tolerated only for necessity? The haunting of dissolute places, or resort to curtizans, are no more punished in married men than in batchelors; the depraved custome of change and the delight in meretricious embracements (where sin is turned into art), make marriage a dull thing, and a kinde of imposition, or tax. They hear you defend these things as done to avoid greater evils, as advoutries, deflowering of virgins, unnaturall lust, and the like, but these vices and appetites do still remain and abound, unlawfull lusts being like a furnace; if you stopp the flames altogether, it will quench; but if you give it any vent, it will rage. As for masculine love, they have no touch of it, and yet there are not so faithfull and inviolate friendships in the world as are there. Their usual saying is, that whosever is unchaste cannot reverence himself, and that the reverence of a man's self is, next religion, the chiefest bridle of all vice."

I confessed the righteousnesse of Aquanna was greater than the righteousnesse of Europe, at which he bowed his head, and went on in this manner. "They have also many wise and excellent laws touching marriage. They allow no polygamie. They have ordained that none doe intermarrie or contract until a month be past from their first interview. Marriage without consent of parents they do not make void, but they mulct it in the inheritours, for the children of such marriages are not admitted to inherit above a third their parents' inheritance. I have read, in a book of one of your men, of a faired commonwealth, where the married couple are permitted before the contract to see one another naked. This they dislike, for they think it a scorn to give a refusall after so familiar knowledge; but because of many hidden defects in men and women's bodies, they have neare every towne a couple of pooles (which they call Adam and Eve's pooles), where it is permitted to one of the friends of the man and one of the woman to see them severally bathe naked."

As we were thus in conference, there came one that seemed to be a messenger, in a rich nuke, that spake with the Jew, whereupon he turned to me and said, "You will pardon me, for I am commanded away in haste." The next morning he came to me joyfully, and said--"There is word come to the Governour of the city that one of the Fathers of the Temple of the Rosie Crosse, or Holy House, will be here this day seven-night. We have seen none of them this dozen years. His comming is in state, but the cause is secret. I will provide you and your fellows of a good standing to see his entry." I thanked him and said I was most glad of the news. The day being come, he made his entry. He was a man of middle stature and age, comely of person, and had an aspect as if he pittied men. He was cloathed in a robe of fine black cloth, with wide sleeves and a cape. His under garment was of excellent white linnen, down to the foot, with a girdle of the same, and a sindon or tippet of the same about his neck. He had gloves that were curious and set with stones, and shoes of peach-coloured velvet. His neck was bare to the shoulders; his hat was like a helmet, or Spanish *montera*, and his locks, of brown colour, curled below it decently. His beard was cut round and of the same colour with his haire, somewhat lighter. He was carried in a rich chariot, without wheels, litter-wise, with two horses at either end, richly trapped in blew velvet embroydered, and two footmen on each side in the like attire. The chariot was of cedar, gilt and adorned with chrystall, save that the fore-end had pannells of sapphire, set in borders of gold, and the hinder-end the like of emerauds of the Peru colour. There was also a sun of gold radiant upon the top in the midst, and on the top before a small cherub of gold with wings displayed. The chariot was covered with dotts of gold tissued upon blew. He had before him fifty attendants, young men, all in white satten loose coats to the mid legg, stockings of white silk, shoes of blew velvet, and hats of the same, with fine plumes of divers colours set round like hat-bands. Next before the chariot went two men bare-headed, in linnen garments down to the foot, girt, and shoes of blew velvet, who carried the one a crosier, the other a pastorall staff like a sheep-hooke, the crosier being of palme-wood, the pastorall staff of cedar. Horsemen he had none, as it seemed, to avoid all tumult and trouble. Behinde his chariot went all the officers and principals of the companies of the city. He sat alone upon cushions, of a kinde of excellent blew plush, and under his feet curious carpets of silk of divers colours, like the Persian but farr finer. He held up his bare hand, blessing the people in silence. The street was wonderfully well kept; the windows likewise were not crouded, but everyone stood in them as if they had been placed. When the shew was past, the Jew said to me--"I shall not be able to attend you as I would, in regard of some charge the city hath layd upon me for the entertainment of this Rosie Crucian." Three days after he came to me again, and said--"Ye are a happy man; the Father of the Temple of the Rosie Cross taketh notice of your being here, and commands me to tell you that he will admit all your company to his presence, and have private conference with one of you that ye shall choose, and for this hath appointed the day after to-morrow. And because he meaneth to give you his blessing, he hath appointed it in the forenoon." We came at our day, and I was chosen for the private accesse. We found him in a faire chamber, richly hanged, and carpeted underfoot, without any degrees to the state. He was set upon a low throne, richly adorned, and a rich cloth of state over his head, of blew sattin embroydered. He had two pages of honour, on either hand one, finely attired in white. His under garments were like that he wore in the chariot, but, instead of his gown, he had on him a mantle with a cape, of the same fine black, fastned about him. We bowed low at our entrance, and when we were come neare his chair, he stood up, holding forth his hand ungloved, in posture of blessing, and every one of us stooped down and kissed the hem of his tippet. That done, the rest departed, and I remained. Then he warned the pages forth of the roome, caused me to sit down beside him, and spake thus in the Spanish tongue:--

"God bless thee, my son; I will give thee the greatest jewel I have; I will impart unto thee, for the love of God and men, a relation of the true state of the Rosie Crosse. First, I will set forth the end of our foundation; secondly, the preparations and instruments we have for our workes; thirdly,

215

the several functions whereto our fellows are assigned; and fourthly, the ordinances and rights which we observe. The end of our foundation is the knowledge of causes and secret motions of things, and the enlarging of the bounds of Kingdomes to the effecting of all things possible. The preparations and instruments are these. We have large caves of several depths, the deepest sunke 36,000 feet. Some are digged under great hills and mountaines, so that, if you reckon together the depths of the hill and of the cave, some are above seven miles deep. These caves we call the lower region, and we use them for all coagulations, indurations, refrigerations, and conservations of bodies. We use them likewise for the imitation of natural mines, and the production of new artificial mettalls by compositions and materials which we lay there for many years. We use them also sometimes for cureing some diseases, and for prolongation of life in hermits that choose to live there, well accomodated of all things necessary, by whom also we learn many things (read our 'Temple of Wisdome'). We have burialls in several earths, where we put diverse cements, as the Chineses do their borcellane; but we have them in greater variety, and some of them more fine. We have also great variety of composts and soyles for the making of the earth fruitfull. We have towers, the highest about half a mile in height, and some of them set upon high mountaines, so that the vantage of the hill with the tower is, in the highest of them, three miles at least. These places we call the upper region, accounting the aire between the highest places and lowest as a middle region. We use these towers, according to their severall heights and situations, for insolation, refrigeration, conservation, and the view of divers meteors--as winds, rain, snow, haile, and some of the fiery meteors also. Upon them, in some places, are dwellings of hermits, whom we visit sometimes, and instruct what to observe (Read our 'Harmony of the World'). We have great lakes, both salt and fresh, whereof we have use for the fish and fowle. We use them also for burials of some naturall bodies, for we find a difference in things buried in earth, or in aire below the earth, and things buryed in the water. We have also pooles, of which some do straine fresh water out of salt, and others by arts do turne fresh water into salt. We have also some rocks in the midst of the seas, and some bayes upon the shore, for works wherein are required the aire and vapour of the sea. We have likewise violent streams and cataracts which serve us for many motions, and engines for multiplying and enforcing winds to set on going divers other motions.

"We have a number of artificiall wells and fountaines, in imitation of the natural sources; also baths tincted upon vitrioll, sulphur, steell, brasse, lead, nitre, and other minerals. Again, we have little wells for infusion of many things, where the waters take the vertue quicker and better than in vessels or basines; and amongst them we have water which we call water of

Paradise, being, by that we do to it, made very soveraign for health and prolongation of life.

"We have also great and spacious houses, where we imitate and demonstrate meteors--as snow, hail, raine, some artificiall raines of bodies and not of water, thunders, lightnings; also generation of bodies in the aire-- as frogs, flies, and divers others.

"We have certain chambers, which we call Chambers of Health, where we qualify the aire as we think good and proper for the cure of divers diseases and preservation of health.

"We have also faire and large baths, of severall mixtures, for the cure of diseases and the restoring of man's body from arefaction, and others for the confirming of it in strength of sinews, vitall parts, and the very juyce and substance of the body.

"We have also large and various orchards (see the epistle to the 'Harmony of the World') and gardens (wherein we do not so much respect beauty as variety of ground and soyle, proper for diverse trees and herbs), some very spacious, where trees and berries are set, whereof we make divers kindes of drinks, besides the vineyards. In these we practise likewise all conclusions of grafting and inoculating, as well of wild trees as fruit trees, which produce many effects. We make by art, in the same orchards and gardens, trees or flowers to come earlier or later than their seasons, and to beare more speedily than by their naturall course they do. We make them also by art much greater than their nature, and their fruit greater, sweeter, and of differing taste, smell, colour, and figure from their nature. Many of them we so order as they become of medicinall use.

"We have also means to make divers plants rise by mixtures of earths without seeds, and to make divers plants differing from the vulgar, and to make one tree or plant turn into another.

"We have also parks and enclosures of all sorts of beasts and birds, which we use not only for view or rarenesse, but likewise for dissections and tryalls, that thereby we may take light what may be wrought upon the body of man. Herein we finde many strange effects as the continuing life in them though divers parts, which you account vitall, be perished and taken forth--resuscitation of some that seem dead in appearance--and the like. We try also all poysons and other medecines upon them. By art, likewise, we make them greater or smaller than their kinde is. We make them more fruitfull, and, contrary-wise, more barren than their kinde is. We make them differ in colour, shape, activity. We have commixtures and copulations of divers kindes, which have produced many new kinds, and them not barren as the generall opinion is. We make a number of kindes of serpents, worms, flies, fishes, of putrefaction, whereof some are advanced (in effects) to perfect creatures, and have sexes and propagate. Neither do we this by chance, but know beforehand of what matter and commixture what kinde

217

of creatures will arise. We have also particular pooles where we make trialls upon fishes.

"We have also places for breed and generation of those kinds of worms and flies which are of speciall use, such as are with you your silkworms and bees.

"I will not hold you long with recounting of our brew-houses, bake-houses, and kitchins, where are made divers drinks, breads, and meats, rare and of speciall effects. Wines we have of grapes, and drinks of other juyces of fruits, graines, and roots; also of mixtures with honey, sugar, manna, and fruits dryed and decocted; also of the teases or wounding of trees, and of the pulp of canes. These drinks are of several ages, some to the age or last of forty yeares. We have drinkes also brewed with severall herbs, roots, and spices, yea, with severall fleshes and white meats; some of the drinks are in effect meat and drink both, so that divers, especially in age, do desire to live with them, with little or no meat or bread. Above all we strive to have drinks of extream thin parts, to insinuate into the body without biting sharpnesse, or fretting, insomuch as some of them put upon the back of your hand, will, with a little stay, passe through to the palm and yet taste milde to the mouth. We have waters which we ripen in that fashion as they become nourishing. Breads we have of severall grains, roots, and kernels, some of flesh and fish dried with divers kindes of leavenings and seasonings so that some doe extreamly more appetite, some nourish so as divers doe live of them very long without any other meat. For meats, we have some of them so beaten, made tender, and mortified, yet without corrupting, as a weake heat of the stomach will turn them into good chylus. We have some meats also, bread and drinks, which taken by men, enable them to fast long after, and some others that make the very flesh of men's bodies sensibly more hard and tough, and their strength far more great than otherwise it would be.

"We have dispensatories, or shops of medicines, wherein you may easily thinke if we have such variety of plants and living creatures, more than you have in Europe, the simples, drugs, and ingredients of medecines, must likewise be in so much the greater variety. We have them of divers ages and long fermentations; for these preparations we have not only all manner of exquisite distillations and separations, especially of gentle heats and percolations through divers strainers, but also exact formes of compositions, whereby they incorporate almost as they were naturall simples.

"We have also divers mechanicall arts which you have not, and stuffs made by them, as papers, linnen, silks, tissues, dainty works of feathers of wonderfull lusture, excellent dies, and many others--shops likewise, as well for such as are not brought into vulgar use amongst us as for those that are, for you must know that of the things fore-cited many of them are grown into use throughout the kingdome, but yet if they did flow from our invention, we have of them also for paterns and principals.

"We have furnaces of great diversities, fierce and quick, strong and constant, soft and milde, blowne quite dry, moist, and the like. Above all we have heats in imitation of the sun's and heavenly bodies' heats, that pass divers inequalities, and, as it were arts, progresses and returns, whereby we produce admirable effects. Besides we have heats of dungs, and of bellies and maws of living creatures, of their bloods and bodies, of hayes and herbs layed up moist, of brine unquenched, and such like--instruments also which generate heat only by motion, places for strong insolations, places under the earth which by nature or art yeeld heat.

"We have also perspective-houses where we make demonstrations of all lights and radiations, and of all colours; out of things uncoloured and transparent we can represent unto you severall colours, not in rain-bows, as it is in gemms and prismes, but of themselves single. We respect also all multiplications of light, which we carry to great distances, and make so sharpe as to discern small points and lines, all colourations of light, all delusions and deceits of the sight in figures, magnitudes, motions, colours, all demonstrations of shadows. We finde also divers means, yet unknown to you, of producing light originally from divers bodies. We procure means of seeing bodies afar off; as in the heaven, and represent things near as farr off, and things afarr off as near. We have also helps for the sight farr above spectacles and glasses, and means to see minute bodies distinctly, as the shapes and colour of small flies and wormes, observation in urine and bloods. We make artificial Rainbowes, halos, and circles about light. We represent also all manner of reflections, refractions, and multiplications of visuall beams of objects.

"We have also pretious stones of all kinds, many of great beauty, and to you unknown, crystals likewise and glasses of divers kinds, amongst them some of mettals vitrificated, and other materials besides those of which you make glasse; also a number of fossiles and imperfect minerals which you have not, likewise loadstones of prodigious vertue, and other rare stones, both naturall and artificiall. We have sound-houses, where we practise and demonstrate all sounds and their generation. We have harmonies (read the 'Harmony of the World') which you have not, of quarter and lesser kindes of sounds--divers instruments of musick to you unknown, some sweeter than any you have, together with bells and rings that are dainty and sweet. (See my book of 'Geomancy and Telesmes.') We represent small sounds as great and deep, great sounds as extenuate and sharpe; we make divers tremblings and warblings of sounds which in their originall are entire. We represent and imitate all articulate sounds and letters (read my 'Cabbala, or Art, by which Moses shewed so many signs in Ægypt'), and the voices and notes of many beasts and birds. We have certain helps which, set to the ear, do further the hearing greatly. We have strange and artificiall ecchos, reflecting the voice many times, and, as it were, to sing it, some that give back the voice louder than it came, some shriller, some deeper, some rendring the voice differing in the letters, or articular sound, from that they receive. We have also means to convey sounds in trunks and pipes, in strange lines and distances.

"We have also perfume houses, wherewith we joyne all practices of taste. We multiply smells which may seem strange. We imitate smells, making them breathe out other mixtures than those that give them. We make divers imitations of taste, so that they will deceive any man's tastes; and in this Temple of the Rosie Crosse we contain also a confiture-house, where we make all sweet-meats, dry and moist, and pleasant wines, milks, broaths, and sallets, in farr greater variety than you have.

"We have also engine-houses, where are prepared engines and instruments for all sorts of motions. There we imitate and practise swifter motions than any you have, and make and multiply them more easily and with small force, by wheels and other means. We make them stronger than yours are, exceeding your cannons and basilisks. We represent also ordinance, instruments of warr, and engines of all kinds, likewise new mixtures and compositions of gunpouder, wild-fire burning in water and unquenchable, also fire-works of all variety, both for pleasure and use. We imitate also flights of birds; we have some degrees of flying in the aire (read the 'Familiar Spirit'). We have ships and boats for going under water, also swimming girdles and supporters. We have curious clocks and other like motions of returne, and some perpetuall motions We imitate also motions of living creatures, by images of men, beasts, birds, fishes, and serpents. We have also a great number of other various motions, strange for equality, finenesse, and subtility.

"We have also a mathematicall pallace, where are represented all instruments, as well of geometry, as astronomy, geomancy, and telesmes.

"We have also houses of deceits of the senses, where we represent all manner of feats of jugling, false apparitions, impostures, illusions, and their fallacies; and surely you will easily believe that we, that have so many things truly naturall which induce admiration, could in a world of particulars deceive the senses, if we would disguise those things and labour to make them seem more miraculous. But we do hate all impostures and lyes, insomuch as we have severaly forbidden it to all our brethren, under pain of ignominy and fines, that they do not show any naturall worke or thing adorned or swelling, but only pure as it is, and without all affectation or strangenesse.

"These are, my son, the riches of the Rosie Crucians (read our 'Temple of Wisdome'). For the several employments and offices of our fellowes, we have twelve that sayle into forrain countries under the names of other nations, for our own we conceal; but our seal is R. C., and we meet upon a day altogether. These bring us the books, abstracts, and patterns of experiments of all other parts. These we call merchants of light.

"We have three that collect the experiments in all books. These we call depredatours. We have three that collect the experiments of all mechanicall arts, liberall sciences, and practices which are not brought into arts. These we call mystery men. We have three that try new experiments, such as themselves think good. These we call pioners or miners. We have three that draw the experiments of the former foure [divisions] into titles and tables, to give the better light for the drawing of observations and of axioms out of them. These we call compliers. We have three that band themselves, looking into the experiments of their fellowes, and cast about how to draw of them things useful for man's life and knowledge, as well for works as for strange demonstration of causes, means of natural divinations, and the easie and cleare discovery of the vertues and parts of bodies. These we call dowry men or benefactors. Then, after diverse meetings and consults of our whole number, to consider of the former labours and collections, we have three that take care out of them to direct new experiments of a higher light, more penetrating into Nature than the former. These we call lamps. We have three others that doe execute the experiments so directed and report them. These we call inoculators. Lastly, we have three that raise the former discoveries by experiments into greater observations, axiomes, and aphorismes. These we call interpreters of. Nature. "We have also novices and apprentices, that the succession of the former employed men of our fraternity of the Rosie Crosse do not faile; also great numbers of servants and attendants, men and women. We have consultations which of the inventions and experiences shall be published and which not. We take all an oath of secrecy for the concealing of those which we think fit to keep secret, though some of those we doe reveale sometimes to the State. (Read our 'Temple of Wisdom.')

"For our ordinances and rites we have two very long and faire galleries in the Temple of the Rosie Crosse. In one of these we place patterns and samples of all manner of the more rare and excellent inventions; in the other we place the statues of all principal inventours. There we have the statues of the discoverer of the West Indies, also the invention of ships, and the monk that was the inventour of ordinance and gunpowder; the inventours of musick, letters, printing; observations of astronomy, astromancy, and geomancy; the invention of works in mettal, of glasse, of silke of the worme; of wine, corn, and bread; the inventour of sugars, and all these by more certain tradition than you have. Then have we divers inventours of our own. Upon every invention of value we erect a statue to the inventour, and give him a liberal and honourable reward. These statues are some of brasse, some of marble and touchstone, some of cedar and other speciall woods gilt and adorned, some of iron, some of silver, some of gold, telesmatically made.

"We have certain hymnes and services, which we say daily, of laud and thanks to God for His marvellous works; also formes of prayers imploring His ayde and blessing for the illumination of our labours, and the turning of them into good and holy uses. "Lastly, we have circuits or visits of divers principal cities of the kingdome, where we doe publish such news, profitable inventions, as we think good, and we doe also declare natural divinations of diseases, plagues, swarms of hurtfull creatures, scarcity, tempests, earthquakes, great inundations, comets, temperature of the year, and divers other things, and we give counsel thereupon for the prevention and remedy of them."

When he had said this, he desired me to give him an account of my life, that he might report it to the Brethren of the Rosie Crosse, after which he stood up; I kneeled down, and he laid his right hand upon my head, saying, "God blesse thee, my son, and God blesse these relations which we have made! I give thee leave to publish them for the good of other nations, for we are here in God's bosome, a land unknown."

And so he left me, having assigned a value of about two thousand pounds in gold for a bounty to me and my fellows, for they give great largesses where they come upon all occasions.

CHAPTER XIV. ROSICRUCIANISM IN FRANCE.

WHEN the documents of the Fraternity were first published, Professor Buhle tells us that France "had greatly the start of Germany and England" in general illumination, that she was consequently protected against the delusion of her neighbours, and that Rosicrucianism "never had even a momentary success" therein. On the other hand, Gabriel Naudé published in 1623 his "Instruction à la France sur la vérité de l'Histoire des Frères de la Roze-Croix," which opens by asserting, without apology of any kind, that the French by their disposition are quick to embrace and to follow every species of novel and ridiculous opinion. They are accused of excessive credulity, and are the laughing-stock of more sober nations. They have credited every absurdity from Postel the resuscitated and *mère Jeanne* to the rejuvenating Fountain of Borico and the immortality and return of Paracelsus. The history of the Brethren R. C. is declared to be the most outrageous of all; their books are useless and completely incomprehensible, even when stripped of their enigmas. None but impostors have claimed to be initiated members, and the false reports spread abroad by the society are prejudicial to all kingdoms, and all forms of government.

This book, though dull and verbose, was undoubtedly instrumental in preventing the spread of the new doctrines. De Quincey affirms that France was never wanting in the "ignobler elements of credulity," but that she has always lacked its nobler or imaginative part. "On this account the French have always been an irreligious people. And the scheme of Father Rosycross was too much connected with religious feelings, and moved too much under a religious impulse, to recommend itself to the French."

The first appearance of Rosicrucianism in France was in the year 1623, when the following mysterious placard was affixed to the walls of Paris:-- "We, the deputies of our chief college of the Brethren of the Rosy Cross, now sojourning, visible and invisible, in this town, do teach, in the name of the Most High, towards whom the hearts of the Sages turn, every science, without either books, symbols, or signs, and we speak the language of the country in which we tarry, that we may extricate our fellow-men from error and destruction."

There are at least four different versions of this manifesto. Gabriel Naudé reads--"By the grace of the Most High . . . we teach, without the assistance of books or signs, how to speak the language of every country where we elect to stay, in order that we may rescue our fellowmen from the error of death." A French brochure, published in 1623, and entitled "Effroyables pactions faites entre le diable et les prétendus invisibles, avec leur damnables instructions, perte déplorable de leurs escoliers, et leur misérable fin," presents still more important variations. "We, the deputies of the College of the Rosie-Cross, advise all those who seek entrance into our society and congregation, to become initiated into the knowledge of the Most High, in whose cause we are at this day assembled, and we will transform them from visible beings into invisible, and from invisible into visible, and they shall be transported into every foreign country to which their desire may lead them. But, to arrive at the knowledge of these marvels, we warn the reader that we can divine his thoughts, that if mere curiosity should prompt the wish to see us, he will never communicate with us, but if an earnest determination to inscribe himself on the register of our confraternity should actuate him, we will make manifest to such an one the truth of our promises, so that we by no means expose the place of our abode, since simple thought, joined to the determined will of the reader, will be sufficient to make us known to him, and reveal him to us."

To this proclamation, in his "Histoire de la Magie," Eliphas Lévi adds: "Public opinion concerned itself about this mysterious manifestation, and if any demanded openly who were the Rose-Cross brethren, an unknown personage frequently took the inquirer apart, and said to him gravely:--

"Predestined to the reformation which must soon be accomplished in the whole universe, the Rosicrucians are the depositaries of supernatural wisdom, and undisturbed possessors of all Nature's gifts, they can dispense them at pleasure.

"In whatsoever place they may be, they know all things which are going on in the rest of the world better than if they were present; they are not subject to hunger or thirst, and have neither age nor disease to fear.

"They can command the most powerful spirits and genii.

"God has covered them with a cloud to defend them from their enemies, and they cannot be beheld except by their own consent, had any one eyes more piercing than are the eagle's. "Their general assemblies are held in the pyramids of Egypt; but, like the rock whence the spring of Moses issued, these pyramids proceed with them into the desert, and follow them into the 'Land of Promise.'"

No authority is given for this statement, and it is in all probability one of those romantic falsifications with which Eliphas Lévi took pleasure in mystifying his readers, and which make him absolutely worthless as a sober historian.

This manifesto, whatever its original form, attracted general and chiefly hostile attention, and it was accounted for in various ways by the pamphleteers of the period. Naudé considers it a hoax. "If we seek for the precise origin of this squall of wind which now whistles over our country, we shall find that the report of this fraternity having been spread abroad some short time since in Germany, certain professors, doctors, and students of this city were moved by curiosity to investigate the matter by means of the new books which were made known to them by publishers after their return from the Frankfort fair; but discovering nothing except chimeras and rodomontade therein, they preferred, while awaiting the farce, to divert themselves by this comedy--

Quam protinus urbi
Pandere, res alta sylva et caligine mersas,

and compromise their reputation by becoming its first denouncers, judging that there were fools enough in Paris to prevent this folly from stagnating. And, in fact, about three months ago one of these individuals, knowing that the King being at Fontainebleau, the realm tranquil, and Mansfield too remote for daily news, there was a scarcity of topics on 'Change, as well as in all circles, concluded to supply you with gossip by placarding the public places with this notice, containing six lines of manuscript."On the other hand, the anonymous author of an "Examination of the unknown and novel Caballa of the Brethren of the Rose-Cross" accepts the manifesto as authentic, and denounces it with terrible earnestness. "Flagrant blasphemies are to be found in these few lines. In the first place, these sacrilegious wretches pretend to have enrolled themselves under the banner of that cross, which their master, the prince of darkness, abhors beyond anything. In the second place, they assert that they can become invisible at pleasure, a quality incommunicable to any natural body which consists of matter and form, and one which can never be acquired by any legitimate science. In the third place, they boast that they can teach every branch of learning in a moment, without books or signs, which evidently transcends the possibilities of the human intellect, for, though the acquisition of the sciences may be certainly facilitated by means of abridgements and epitomes, it can only be accomplished by degrees and with time. In the fourth place, they claim to be acquainted with all dialects and with every variety of language--a prerogative never conferred except on the apostles, whose lives were very different from theirs. It remains to be concluded that such persons are not commissioned by God to save us from error and destruction, but are raised up by Satan to drag into the abyss those souls which are carried away by an overweening curiosity."

The most copious information with regard to the strange manifesto is to be found in the "Frightful Compacts between the Devil and the so-called Invisibles," a pamphlet full of malicious libels, which, however, are so curious that some of them are worth reproducing as briefly as possible. According to this account, the manuscript placard was posted in several parts of Paris, and awakened the curiosity of the learned and illiterate alike. Every one was astounded at the asserted invisibility of the Brethren, and at their gift of tongues. According to some, they must be the messengers of the Holy Ghost, others said that they were persons of eminent sanctity, the rest, that the whole business was one of illusions and of magic. By many the power of discerning the inmost thoughts was admired beyond the other privileges, but that such a faculty was inherent in Deity only, and they were incredulous in this respect. Then it was urged that the devil had knowledge of things both past and present, but that if he had knowledge of things present, thoughts must be included in this class, and that, therefore, the devil might not only know them, but might impart the same knowledge to his emissaries.

A certain lawyer of Paris, says this mendacious chronicle, conceived a violent desire to be enrolled in the new order, on account of the obvious advantages of occasional invisibility, and he had no sooner formed the project than one of the Invisibles appeared before him, and informing him that he could read his thoughts, directed his petrified listener to meet him that evening at eight o'clock opposite a certain market, when he should attain his desire. This said, the mysterious being disappeared as miraculously as he had come thither; and the lawyer, convinced by his own senses that there was some truth in the claims of the placard, did not fail to repair to the appointed place, where the same personage met him, bandaged his eyes, whirled him through a maze of alleys, and brought him to the abode of the Invisibles. There his eyes were uncovered, and he found himself in the presence of five senatorial persons, who gravely informed him that they too were well acquainted with his aspirations, but before they could gratify them he must be prepared to take the oath of fidelity, and to write four words upon a paper, namely, "I renounce my self." The appropriate preliminary to a new faith was to blindfold one's eyes to the teachings of all the old beliefs. The neophyte complied, after which one of then breathed in his ear, and this breathing he believed to be the wind of the Holy Spirit instead of the devil's respiration. They caused him to behold innumerable illusions by the operation of the fiends, instructed him in the magical utterances by which he could become invisible at pleasure, in the imprecations which he must pronounce against the Roman Church, and in the homage which he must pay both morning and evening to their master Satan, in recognition of the marvels he had lavished for the benefit of the men of that time. This finished, they caused the lawyer to strip, the magic ointment was rubbed over his body, and having been enjoined to bathe in the river at daybreak, he sat down with them to a sumptuous repast at his own expense, after which his eyes were again bandaged, and he was led back to the meeting-place of the previous evening. Though partially drunk, he determined to fulfil his duty and plunge at once into the river, wherein he attempted to swim, in order to cleanse himself more thoroughly, but the unfortunate man was drowned, and thus, says the anonymous historian, he was truly changed from a visible into an invisible being, yet not, also, from one invisible into one visible, for to this day hath his body been discovered by none, though sought for with diligent anxiety. "Such are the first fruits of the study of the invisible doctors at the end of last July." Other stories equally credible are told by the same writer to illustrate the tragical consequences of a voluntary connection with the infamous Invisibles. A soldier was commanded by them, on his initiation, to enrol himself among a band of assassins, when he was speedily assassinated. A magistrate of Picardy, in answer to his unexpressed wish, was miraculously visited by one of the mystic six in his own closet, was initiated into the Order, and in two days committed suicide. An Anglo-Frenchman who had entered upon the same unhappy course, wishing to revisit England, was instantaneously translated to Boulogne: and requesting the demon who had brought him to bear him across the Straits to London, he was seized with fury and cast into the sea between Calais and Dover with a frightful noise. This occurred in the presence of two hundred Dutch ships on a voyage from Amsterdam to India.

According to this singular and scurrilous pamphlet, the Rosicrucians or Invisibles, who are identical in the mind of the writer, but whom he distinguishes from the Spanish illuminati, numbered in all thirty-six, and they were divided into six bands. Their general assembly was held at Lyons on June 23, 1623, at 10 P.M., which was two hours before the Grand Sabbath of the Witches. There, by the power of an anthropophagous necromancer, Astaroth, one of the princes of the infernal hordes, appeared in light and splendour, and was represented by the magician as a messenger of the Most High. All prostrated themselves before the demon, who asked what they desired, and was informed by their spokesman that they were a little flock which he had assembled, in the name of the master of Astaroth, to serve him henceforth on such conditions as were laid down in the paper which he now offered to the emissary of the king. It contained the "Articles of Agreement between the Necromancer Respuch and the Deputies for the establishment of the College of the Rosicrucians." The subscribers certified before the most high to have entered into the following compacts, namely, they promised to receive with submission the orders of the supreme sacrificer, Respuch, renouncing baptism, chrism, and unction received in the name of Christ; detesting and abhorring all forms of prayer, confession, sacraments, and all faith in the resurrection of the body; promising to proclaim the teachings imparted to them by Respuch through all quarters of the globe; and pledging their honour and their life, without any hope of pardon, grace, or absolution, to perform all this; in proof of which they had opened each of them a vein in the left arm, and had signed this parchment each with his own blood. The magician, on his part, promised to the deputies, severally and collectively, that he would transport them at any moment from east to west, or from north to south, and cause them to speak naturally every language in the universe. By this agreement he bound himself to enable them to enter and leave all palaces, houses, chambers, and cabinets, through closed and locked doors, to endue them with the most persuasive eloquence, to enable them to cast horoscopes and to read the most secret thoughts, to make them admired by the learned, sought after by the curious, magnified above the prophets of old, and to give each of them, on his signing the parchment, a golden ring enriched by a precious sapphire, under which there should be a demon who would act as their guide. Astaroth, assuming the likeness of a radiant youth, caressed and embraced his victims, who blindly mistook him for the apparition of a powerful deity, and, being promised his continual providence, they solemnly bound themselves never to derogate from the articles to which they had subscribed, whatever might happen, to turn a deaf ear to the Gospel of Christ, and to publish among all the nations to whom they were transported the truth of the mighty dominion whereof he was the emissary, in order that by their preaching they might dissipate the errors of those men who believed in the immortality of the soul. The articles were then ratified, confirmed, and approved by Astaroth on the part of his master, after which the demon vanished to assist at the Sabbath, which was held, from eleven at night to one in the morning, on the vigil of S. John the Baptist, in the vicinity of the labyrinth among the Pyrenees. The necromancer was left alone with the invisibles, who were to receive the powers promised by being breathed on in the following manner:--All stripped naked and prostrated themselves with their faces flat upon the earth; the magician, with a pot of grease and unguents, rubbed each of them, after the ancient fashion of Thessalian sorcery, on the upper part of the neck, the arm pits, the lower portion of the spine, the parts of generation, and the fundament; then he breathed in the right ear of each deputy, saying: "Depart and rejoice in the result of my promises." He gave the demoniacal ring to all of them, and then a sudden blast of wind transported them, at the command of the magician, an hundred leagues, to the great assembly of the sorcerers. Here, as new comers, they received from Satan the mark of magicians; six of them were sent into Spain, six into Italy, six into France, six into Germany, four to Sweden, two into Switzerland, two into Flanders, two into Lorraine, and the remaining two into Burgoyne. Thus they were commissioned only to go into Catholic countries, and not into the lands of the heretic and the infidel, who without the pale of the Church, saith the zealous chronicler, are already in the claws of hell. The six who were despatched to France reached Paris on July 14th, each lodged separately to avoid suspicion, and met daily where the first wish carried them,--sometimes on Parnassus, on the columns of Montfaucon, in the quarries of Montmatre, &c. Recognising the difficulties of evangelising Paris, they spent much time in deliberation; their hotel expenses increased, and the devil already failed in his promise that their purses should always be well supplied. They sold their horses in order to buy furniture and hire lodgings, where they would have more liberty to go in quest of pupils. After the sale, however, they changed their mind, and took two furnished rooms in the Marais du Temple, which is actually mentioned in the "Apologia" of Robert Fludd, as the abode of a Rosicrucian, and it was at this period that the manuscript placard was affixed by them to the walls of Paris.

The "Examination of the unknown and novel Caballa of the Brethren of the Rose-Cross" agrees with the "Frightful Compacts," in asserting that the chief of this "execrable college" is Satan, that its first rule is the denial of God, blasphemy against the most simple and undivided Trinity, trampling on the mysteries of the redemption, spitting in the face of the mother of God and at all the saints. The second is the abhorrence of the name Christian, renunciation of baptism, the intercession of the Church, and the sacraments. By the third they offer sacrifice to the devil, make compacts with him, commit adultery with him, offer innocent children to him, &c. By the fourth they frequent the Sabbaths, cherish toads, make poisonous powders, dance with fiends, raise tempests, ravage fields, destroy orchards, assassinate and torture their neighbours by the infliction of innumerable diseases.

The spirit which prompted these grotesque calumnies, manufactured from the foulest gutters of black magic, is easily discernible. The writers were Catholics incensed by the Protestantism of the Rosicrucian manifestoes, meeting violence by violence, and doctrines of Papal extermination with charges of blasphemy, atheism, and devil-worship. Gabriel Naudé is the most reasonable of all the Franco-Rosicrucian critics, but he is unendurably stupid, and splutters in a seething sea of classical quotations.

In addition to the privileges and powers which are openly claimed by the Rosicrucians, Naudè enumerates the following, some of which are to be found indirectly in their documents, and others he has extracted by a somewhat perverse interpretation:--

"They affirm that the contemplations of their founder surpass everything which has been ever known, discovered, or understood, since the creation of the world, through human study, divine revelation, or the ministration of angels.

"That they are destined to accomplish the approaching restoration of all things to an improved condition before the end arrives.

"That they possess wisdom and piety in a supreme degree, are undisturbed owners of all that is desirable among the bounties of Nature, and can dispense her gifts at will.

"That in whatsoever place they may be they know all that takes place elsewhere better than if they were present.

"That they are subject neither to hunger, thirst, age, illness, or other natural inconvenience. "That they learn by revelation of those persons who are worthy of admission into their society.

"That it is possible for them always to live as if they had existed from the beginning of the world, or would remain till the end of the ages.

"That they possess a book in which they can ascertain all things which are to be found in books now existing, or will be found in the books of the future.

"That they can compel the most mighty spirits and demons into their service, and by the power of their incantations can draw pearls and precious stones towards them.

"That God has enveloped them in a cloud to conceal them from their enemies, unless, at least, they have eyes more penetrating than the eagle's.

"That the first eight Brethren of the Rose-Cross had the gift of healing all diseases to such an extent that they were overwhelmed by the concourse of sufferers, and that one of them, who was an adept in Kabbalistic Mysteries, witness his book called H, cured the young Count of Norfolk of the leprosy when he was in England.

"That God has determined to increase the number of their Fraternity.

"That they have discovered a new language to give expression to the nature of all things.

"That by their means the triple crown of Peter will be ground into the dust.

"That they confess freely and publicly, with no fear of repression, that the pope is Anti-Christ.

"That they denounce the blasphemies of East and West, meaning Mahomet and the Pope, and recognise but two sacraments, with the ceremonies of the early Church, renewed by their congregation. "That they acknowledge the fourth monarchy and the Emperor of the Romans as their Lord, and as the head of all Christendom.

"That they will furnish him with more gold and silver than the Spanish King derives from both the Indies, the more so as their treasures are inexhaustible.

"That their college, which they name the College of the Holy Ghost, can suffer no injury; even should a hundred thousand persons behold and remark it.

"That they possess several mysterious volumes in their library, one of which, that, namely, which they prize next to the Bible, is that which the revered and illuminated father R. C. held in his right hand after death.

"Finally, that they are convinced and certain that the truth of their maxims will abide to the very end of the world."

No voice appears to have been raised in France in defence of the persecuted Order. "It is known upon the contemporary authority of the *Mercure de France*," says a writer in "Chambers' Journal," "that a popular panic"--the natural result of these atrocious calumnies--"was excited by the fear of this mysterious sect, none of whose members had ever been seen. . .

. . The most absurd stories about them were daily reported, and found listeners. An innkeeper asserted that a mysterious stranger entered his inn, regaled himself on his best, and suddenly vanished in a cloud when the bill was presented. Another had been served as scurvy a trick by a similar stranger, who lived upon the choicest fare, and drunk the best wines of his house for a week, and paid him with a handful of new gold coins, which turned into slates on the following morning. It was also said that several persons on awakening in the middle of the night found individuals in their bed chambers, who suddenly became invisible, though still palpable, when the alarm was raised. Such was the consternation in Paris, that every man who could not give a satisfactory account of himself was in danger of being pelted to death; and quiet citizens slept with loaded muskets at their bedsides, to take vengeance upon any Rosicrucian who might violate the sanctity of their chambers."

In two years the excitement died away; no further manifestoes were attempted, and the mysterious Order of the Invisibles of the Rose-Cross, if it had in reality ever visited Paris, migrated to more tolerant climes, and its very existence was shortly afterwards forgotten in the interests of the next ephemeral novelty.

CHAPTER XV. CONNECTION BETWEEN THE ROSICRUCIANS AND FREEMASONS.

PROFESSOR BUHLE affirms as the "main thesis" of his concluding chapter that "Freemasonry is neither more nor less than Rosicrucianism as modified by those who transplanted it into England." His elegant and interesting hypothesis rests on a microscopical foundation of actual fact. A passage in Fludd's rejoinder to the "Exercitatio Epistolæ" of Gassendi states that the *Fratres R. C.* are thenceforth to be called *sapientes* or *sophos*. The German critic's discriminating commentary on this statement is that the old name was abolished, but as yet a new one had not been conferred, and that the immediate hint for the name Masons was derived from the Rosicrucian legend concerning the "House of the Holy Ghost," an allegorical building which typified the secret purpose of the Society. Having fathered Freemasonry on the renowned Kentish Rosicrucian, Professor Buhle enters on a Quixotic quest through the folios of his victim in search of corroborating passages, and discovers in the "Summum Bonum," which Fludd disowned, as we have seen, that Jesus was the *lapis angularis* of the human temple in which men are stones, and that the author calls upon his students to be transformed from dead into living philosophical stones. "Transmutemini, transmutemini, de lapidibus mortuis in lapides vivos philosophicos." On this foundation rests his whole hypothesis concerning the transfiguration of the Rosicrucian Fraternity and its reappearance as the Masonic Brotherhood. It is needless to say that it is slender and unsatisfactory in the extreme.

I do not propose to discuss the origin of Freemasonry. That vexatious question has been perpetually debated with singularly unprofitable results. All I am concerned with proving is that there is no traceable connection between Masonry and Rosicrucianism. The former is defined by its initiates to be "a science of morality, veiled in allegory, and illustrated by symbols," and again as "a system of doctrines taught, in a manner peculiar to itself, by allegories and symbols. . . . Its ceremonies are external additions, which affect not its substance." The two doctrines of the unity of God and the immortality of the soul constitute "the philosophy of Freemasonry." It has never been at any period of its history an association for scientific researches and the experimental investigation of Nature, which was a primary object with the Rosicrucian Brotherhood. It has not only never laid claim to the possession of any transcendental secrets of alchemy and magic, or to any skill in medicine, but has never manifested any interest in these or kindred subjects. Originally an association for the diffusion of natural morality, it is now simply a benefit society. The improvement of mankind and the encouragement of philanthropy were and are its ostensible objects, and these also were the dream of the Rosicrucian, but, on the other hand, it has never aimed at a reformation in the arts and sciences, for it was never at any period a learned society, and a large proportion of its members have been chosen from illiterate classes. It is free alike from the enthusiasm and the errors of the elder Order, for though at one time it appears to have excluded Catholics from its ranks, as at this day the Catholic Church excommunicates and denounces its members, it has been singularly devoid of prejudices and singularly unaffected by the crazes of the time. It has not committed itself to second Advent theories; it does not call the Pope Antichrist; it does not expect a universal cataclysm. It preaches a natural morality, and has so little interest in mysticism that it daily misinterprets and practically despises its own mystical symbols.

Those who believe in the hypothesis of Professor Buhle cannot shew that Fludd was either a Rosicrucian or a Freemason. There is some reason to believe that the former Brotherhood did split up subsequently into different sections, but there is no tittle of evidence to prove that they developed into Freemasons. Mackey says that they protracted their existence till the middle of the eighteenth century, and then ceased to meet on account of the death of one of their chiefs named Burn, but he does not state his authority. He also tells us that out of the Rosicrucian Fraternity there was established in 1777 that association called "The Brothers of the Golden Cross," whose alchemical processes are described by Sigmund Richter. "This Society was very numerous in Germany, and even extended into other countries, especially into Sweden. A second schism from the Rosicrucians was the society of 'The Initiated Brothers of Asia,' which was organised in 1780, and whose pursuits, like those of the parent institution, were connected with alchemy and the natural sciences. In 1785, it attracted the attention of the police, and, two years later, received a fatal blow, in the revelation of all its secrets by one, Rolling, a treacherous member of the association."

These statements must be taken at their value, but even doubtful facts are of equal weight with hypotheses founded on assumptions of the most gratuitous kind, and supported by tortured quotations. It is, however, on the universal concensus of competent Masonic opinion that I should found the rejection of the Buhlean view. Mackey, in the "Synoptical Index" to his "Symbolism of Freemasonry," says that the Rosicrucian Society resembled the Masonic in its organization and in some of the subjects of its investigation, "but it was in no other way connected with Free Masonry." In the "Lexicon" he again tells us that "the Rosicrucians had no connection whatever with the Masonic fraternity," and that it is only malignant revilers, like Baruel in his "Memoirs of Jacobinism," who attempt to identify the two institutions. Other authorities are not less pronounced in their opinions.

It is to the institution of the Rose-Cross degree in Freemasonry that the confusion of opinion on this point is to be mainly traced. When ill-informed persons happen to hear that there are "Sovereign Princes of Rose-Croix," "Princes of Rose-Croix de Heroden," &c., among the Masonic Brethren, they naturally identify these splendid inanities of occult nomenclature with the mysterious and awe-inspiring Rosicrucians. The origin of the Rose-Cross degree is involved in the most profound mystery. Its foundation has been attributed to Johann Valentin Andreas, but this is an ignorant confusion, arising from the alleged connection of the theologian of Wirtemberg with the society of Christian Rosencreutz. There is no trace of its existence before the middle of the eighteenth century, though the "Dictionnaire Maçonnique" declares that it was created in Palestine by Godfrey de Bouillon in the year 1100, and that the Rose was emblematic of secrecy and the Cross of immortality. It professes to deal with the spiritual side of alchemy, and to seek that same mysterious Stone which was the object of Basil Valentin, Paracelsus, Khunrath, and the true *turba philosophorum* of psycho-chemical transmutations. But the shallow pretence has deceived no one, for the sublime tradition of the veritable *magnum opus* exclusively points to transcendent spiritual secrets, and not to the eternal commonplace of moral and masonic platitudinarians--that is to say, the illiterate initiations of Masonry, ignorantly adopting a garbled alchemical terminology, have fallen into the gross and porcine error of interpreting alchemical symbolism morally instead of pneumatically. Sovereign chapters and sovereign princes of Rose-Croix, Knight Princes of the Eagle and the Pelican, and Prince Perfect Masters, should continue to dine sumptuously; no one will dispute their proficiency as initiates of the gastronomical mystery, but, in the name of the Grand Architect, let them leave the morally unsearchable mystery of the philosophick gold to the true Sons of the Doctrine.

The Rose-Cross degree is represented by Carlile as the *ne plus ultra* of Masonry. It has three points, of which the two first are called Sovereign Chapters, and the third the Mystic Supper, which is held four times a year. The presiding officer is dignified with the sublime title of "Ever Most Perfect Sovereign;" the two Wardens are "Most Excellent and Perfect Brothers." There is also a Master of the Ceremonies, and the brethren are "Most Respectful Knights." The annual festival of the order is celebrated on Shrove Tuesday. The jewel is "a golden compass, extended on an arc to the sixteenth part of a circle, or twenty-two and a-half degrees," according to Mackey. Carlile describes it as a triangle formed by a compass and a quarter of a circle. "Between the legs of the compass is a cross resting on the arc of the circle; its centre is occupied by a full-blown rose, whose stem twines around the lower limb of the cross; at the foot of this cross, on the same side on which the rose is exhibited, is the figure of a pelican wounding its breast to feed its young, which are in a nest surrounding it; while on the other side of the jewel is the figure of an eagle, with wings displayed. On the arc of the circle the P∴ W∴ of the degree is engraved in the cipher of the Order." A triple crown surmounts the head of the Order. This symbolism is undoubtedly borrowed from the Rosicrucians, which is the whole extent of the connection supposed to subsist between the two Orders. The Rose-Cross degree in Freemasonry is admitted to be "a modern invention." The ritual of the receptions in the three points of this degree will be found in Carlile's "Ritual of Freemasonry," and in the first volume of Heckethorn's "Secret Societies of all Ages and Countries."

CHAPTER XVI. MODERN ROSICRUCIAN SOCIETIES.

IT is an opinion entertained by the elect in modern theosophical circles, that the true Rosicrucian Brotherhood migrated into India, and this notion is said to be countenanced by a Latin pamphlet of Henricus Neuhusius, published in 1618, under the title "Pia et utilissima Admonitio de Fratribus Rosæ Crucis," and which was afterwards translated into French. They have developed into Thibetan Brothers, have exchanged Protestant Christianity for esoteric Buddhism, and are no longer interested in the number of the beast. Their violent antipathy to the pope still remains: they have not yet torn him in pieces with nails, but probably expect to accomplish this long-cherished project about the period of the next general cataclysm.

This is an interesting theory which might be debated with profit. I have not personally discovered much trace of the Rosicrucians in India, but the absence of historical documents on this point affords a fine field for the imagination, which writers like Mr Hargrave Jennings should not allow to lie fallow. In my prosaic capacity as a historian, I have not been able to follow in the footsteps of the Fraternity further than the Island of Mauritius. Thanks to the late Mr Frederick Hockley, whose valuable library of books and manuscripts, treating of all branches of occultism, has been recently dispersed, I have discovered that a certain Comte de Chazal accomplished the *magnum opus* in that place at the close of the last century, and that he initiated another artist into the mysteries of the Rosicrucian Fraternity. The Comte de Chazal was possessed of vision at a distance, and witnessed the horrors of the French Revolution from a vast distance, with amazing perspicuity, by means of the mind's eye. The following curious document will be read with no ordinary interest:--

Copy of the Admission of Dr Bacstrom into the Society of the Rosa Croix by Le Comte de Ghazal at the Island of Mauritius, with the Seal of the Society.

ISLE OF MAURITIUS, DISTRICT OF PAMPELAVUSO,
12*th Sept.* 1794.

In the name of אלהזב יְהרָח the True and only God Manifested in Trinity.

I, Sigismund Bacstrom, do hereby promise, in the most sincere and solemn manner, faithfully to observe the following articles, during the whole course of my natural life, to the best of my knowledge and ability; which articles I hereby confirm by oath and by my proper signature hereunto annexed.

One of the worthy members of the august, most ancient, and most learned Society, the Investigators of Divine, Spiritual, and Natural Truth (which society more than two centuries and a half ago (*i.e.*, in 1490) did separate themselves from the Free-Masons, but were again united in one spirit among themselves under the denomination of *Fratres Rosæ Crucis*, Brethren of the Rosy Cross, *i.e.* the Brethren who believe in the Grand

Atonement made by Jesus Christ on the Rosy Cross, stained and marked with His blood, for the redemption of Spiritual Natures), having thought me worthy to be admitted into their august society, in quality of a Member Apprentice and Brother, and to partake of their sublime knowledge, I do hereby engage in the most solemn manner--

1. That I will always, to the utmost of my power, conduct myself as becomes a worthy member, with sobriety and piety, and to endeavour to prove myself grateful to the Society for so distinguished a favour as I now receive, during the whole course of my natural life.

2. That derision, insult, and persecution of this august society may be guarded against, I will never openly publish that I am a member, nor reveal the name or person of such members as I know at present or may know hereafter.

3. I solemnly promise that I will never during my whole life publicly reveal the secret knowledge I receive at present, or may receive at a future period from the Society, or from one of its members, nor even privately, but will keep our Secrets sacred.

4. I do hereby promise that I will instruct for the benefit of good men, before I depart this life, one person, or two persons at most, in our secret knowledge, and initiate and, receive such person (or persons) as a member or apprentice into our Society, in the same manner as I have been initiated and received; but such person only as I believe to be truly worthy and of an upright, well-meaning mind, blameless conduct, sober life, and desirous of knowledge. And as there is no distinction of sexes in the Spiritual World, neither among the Blessed Angels, nor among the rational immortal Spirits of the human race; and as we have had a Semiramis, Queen of Egypt; a Myriam, the prophetess; a Peronella, the wife of Flammel; and, lastly, a Leona Constantia, Abbess of Clermont, who was actually received as a practical member and master into our Society in the year 1736; which women are believed to have been all possessors of the Great Work, consequently *Sorores Roseæ Crucis*, and members of our Society by possession, as the possession of this our Art is the key to the most hidden knowledge; and, moreover, as redemption was manifested to mankind by means of a woman (the Blessed Virgin), and as Salvation, which is of infinitely more value than our whole Art, is granted to the female sex as well as to the male, our Society does not exclude a worthy woman from being initiated, God himself not having excluded women from partaking of every felicity in the next life. We will not hesitate to receive a worthy woman into our Society as a member apprentice (and even as a practical member, or master, if she does possess our work practically, and has herself accomplished it), provided she is found, like Peronella, Flammel's wife, to be sober, pious, discreet, prudent, and reserved, of an upright and blameless conduct, and desirous of knowledge.

5. I do hereby declare that I intend, with the permission of God, to commence our great work with mine own hands as soon as circumstances, health, opportunity, and time will permit; 1st, that I may do good therewith as a faithful steward; 2nd, that I may merit the continued confidence which the Society has placed in me in quality of a member apprentice.

6. I do further most solemnly promise that (should I accomplish the Great Work) I will not abuse the great power entrusted to me by appearing great and exalted, or seeking to appear in a public character in the world by hunting after vain titles of nobility and vain glory, which are all fleeting and vain, but will endeavour to live a sober and orderly life, as becomes every Christian, though not possessed of so great a temporal blessing; I will devote a considerable part of my abundance and superfluity (multipliable infinitely to work of private charity), to aged and deeply-afflicted people, to poor children, and, above all, to such as love God and act uprightly, and I will avoid encouraging laziness and the profession of public beggars.

7. I will communicate every new or useful discovery relating to our work to the nearest member of our Society, and hide nothing from him, seeing he cannot, as a worthy member, possibly abuse it, or prejudice me thereby; on the other hand, I will hide these secret discoveries from the world.

8. I do, moreover, solemnly promise (should I become a master and possessor) that I will not, on the one hand, assist, aid, or support with gold or with silver any government, King, or Sovereign, whatever, except by paying taxes, nor, on the other hand, any populace, or particular set of men, to enable them to revolt against the government; I will leave public affairs and arrangements to the government of God, who will bring about the events foretold in the revelation of St John, which are fast accomplishing; I will not interfere with affairs of government.

9. I will neither build churches, chapels, nor hospitals, and such public charities, as there is already a sufficient number of such public buildings and institutions, if they were only properly applied and regulated. I will not give any salary to a priest or churchman as such, to make him more proud and insolent than he is already. If I relieve a distressed worthy clergyman, I will consider him in the light of a private distressed individual only. I will give no charity with the view of making my name known to the world, but will give my alms privately and secretly.

10. I hereby promise that I will never be ungrateful to the worthy friend and brother who initiated and received me, but will respect and oblige him as far as lies in my power, in the same manner as he has been obliged to promise to his friend who received him.

11. Should I travel either by sea or by land, and meet with any person who may call himself a Brother of the Rosy Cross, I will examine him whether he can give me a proper explanation of The Universal Fire of Nature, and of our magnet for attracting and magnifying the same under

the form of a salt, whether he is well acquainted with our work, and whether he knows the universal dissolvent and its use. If I find him able to give satisfactory answers, I will acknowledge him as a member and brother of our Society. Should I find him superior in knowledge and experience to myself, I will honour and respect him as a master above me.

12. If it should please God to permit me to accomplish our Great Work with my own hands, I will give praise and thanks to God in humble prayer, and devote my time to the doing and promoting all the good that lies in my power, and to the pursuit of true and useful knowledge.

13. I do hereby solemnly promise that I will not encourage wickedness and debauchery, thereby offending God by administering the medicine for the human body, or the *aurum potabile*, to a patient, or patients, infected with the venereal disease.

14. I do promise that I will never give the Fermented Metallic Medecine for transmutation to any person living, no, not a single grain, unless the person is an initiated and received member and Brother of the Rosy Cross.

To keep faithfully the above articles as I now receive them from a worthy member of our Society, as he received them himself, I willingly agree, and sign this with my name, and affix my seal to the same. So help me God. Amen. S. BACSTROM, L.S.

I have initiated and received Mr Sigismund Bacstrom, Doctor of Physic, as a practical member and brother above an apprentice in consequence of his solid learning, which I certify by my name and seal.--Mauritius, 12 Sept. 1794. DU CHAZEL, F.R.C.

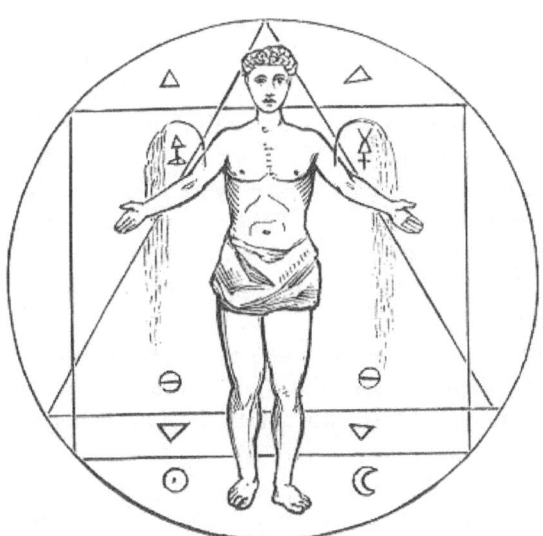

The Philosophic Seal of the Society of the Rosicrucians.

Among Mr Hockley's manuscripts there is also the "Diary of a Rosicrucian Philosopher" during the first period of the work. It describes the preparation of the first matter, and breaks off abruptly after a few leaves. Whether this unnamed philosopher was a true Rosicrucian, and whether the Comte de Chazal could lay claim to that distinction, are problems which cannot be solved. Individual pretenders and fraudulent associations have occasionally appeared ever since the publication of the "Fama" and "Confessio Fraternitatis."

It is certain that a pseudo-society existed in England before the year 1836, for in that year we find Godfrey Higgins saying that he had joined neither the Templars nor the Rosicrucians. "I have abstained from becoming a member of them, that I might not have my tongue tied or my pen restrained by the engagements I must have made on entering the chapter or encampment. But I have reason to believe that they have now become, in a very particular manner, what is called exclusively Christian Orders, and on this account are thought, by many persons, to be only a bastard kind of masons. They are real masons, and they ought to be of that . . . universal Christianity or Creestianity, which included Jews, Buddhists, Brahmins, Mohamedans." He identifies the Templars and Rosicrucians with Manichæan Buddhists, and asserts the Rosicrucians of Germany to be ignorant of their origin, "but, by tradition, they suppose themselves descendants of the ancient Egyptians, Chaldeans, Magi, and Gymnosophists; and this is probably true."

The present Rosicrucian Society of England, on its remodelling some thirty years ago, cut off by mutual consent its connection with the few ancient members then existing, who were probably representatives of the "Rosicrucians" referred to by Higgins, and established itself as a public body, in so far as the fact of its existence was not itself a secret. A previous initiation into Masonry is an indispensable qualification of candidates, as will be seen in the Ordinances of the Society. The reason for this regulation is that certain masonic secrets are revealed to the accepted, and it would otherwise be unfair to Masonry. Thus, on his admission as a novice, the postulant is required to repeat the Masonic arcana.

I am enabled to present to my readers, from sources hitherto unpublished, the--

Rules and Ordinances of the Rosicrucian Society of England.

The Society of Brethren of the Rosy Cross is totally independent, being established on its own basis, and as a body is no otherwise connected with the Masonic Order than by having its members selected from that fraternity.

I. That the meetings of the Society shall be held in London, at such house as the majority of members shall select, on the second Thursday in January, April, July, and October in each year. The brethren shall dine together once a year, at such time and place as the majority may select. The first meeting in the year shall be considered as the obligatory meeting, and any member unable to attend on that occasion, or at the banquet meeting, shall be required to send a written excuse to the Secretary-General. Each brother present at the banquet shall pay his quota towards the expenses thereof.

II. The Officers of the Society shall consist of the Three Magi, a Master-general for the first and second orders, a Deputy Master-general, a Treasurer-general, a Secretary-general, and seven Ancients, who shall form the Representative Council of the Brotherhood. The Assistant Officers shall be a Precentor, a Conductor of Novices, an Organist, a Torch Bearer, a Herald, a Guardian of the Temple, and a Medallist.

III, The Master-general and the Officers shall be elected annually at the obligatory meeting, and shall be inducted into their several offices on the same evening. The Master-general shall then appoint the Assistant Officers for the year.

IV. No brother shall be eligible for election to the office of Master-general or Deputy Master-general unless he shall have served one year as an Ancient, and have attained the third Order; and no brother shall be eligible for the offices of Treasurer-general, Secretary-general, or Ancient unless he be a member of the second Order.

V. The Society shall, in conformity with ancient usage, be composed of nine classes or grades; and the number of brethren in each class shall, in conformity with ancient usage, be restricted as follows:--

1st, or grade of Zelator   33
2nd, "   Theoricus   27
3rd, "   Practicus   21
4th, "   Philosophus <u>18</u>
      Total   99

The above shall form the First Order.

5th, or grade of Adeptus Junior   15
6th, "   Adeptus Major   12
7th, "   Adeptus Exemptus <u>9</u>
      Total   36

These brethren shall compose the Second Order.

8th, or grade of Magister Templi 6
9th, "   Magus   <u>3</u>
      Total   9

These shall be considered as the Third (or highest) Order, and shall be entitled to seats in the Council of the Society. The senior member of the ninth grade shall be designated "Supreme Magus," and the other two members Senior and Junior Substitutes respectively. The grand total of members shall thus be limited to 144, or the square of 12. The numbers of registered Novices or Aspirants shall not be restricted, but members only shall be permitted to be present at the *ceremonial* meetings of the Society.

VI. The distinction of Honorary Member may be conferred upon eminent brethren, provided that their election to such membership shall be unanimous, and that their number be strictly limited to 16, or the square of 4. An Honorary President, who must be a nobleman, and three Vice-Presidents, shall be elected from the honorary members. A Grand Patron may also be elected in like manner.

VII. No aspirant shall be admitted into the Society unless he be a Master Mason, and of good moral character, truthful, faithful, and intelligent. He must be a man of good abilities, so as to be capable of understanding the revelations of philosophy and science; possessing a mind free from prejudice and anxious for instruction. He must be a believer in the fundamental principles of the Christian doctrine, a true philanthropist, and a loyal subject, names of aspirants may be submitted by any member at the meetings of the Society, and if approved after the usual scrutiny, they shall be placed on the roll of Novices, and balloted for as vacancies occur in the list of members.

VIII. Every Novice on admission to the grade of Zelator shall adopt a Latin motto, to be appended to his signature in all communications relating to the Society. This motto cannot under any pretence be afterwards changed, and no two brethren shall be at liberty to adopt the same motto. IX. The fee for admission to each Order shall be ten shillings, and the annual subscription from every member to defray the contingent expenses of the society shall be five shillings. The registry fee for a novice or aspirant shall be seven shillings and sixpence.

X. As vacancies occur in each grade, by death, resignation, or otherwise, the members of such grade shall elect brethren from the next grade to supply the vacancies thus created.

XI. The Master-general shall have the superintendence and regulation of the ordinary affairs of the Society; subject, however, to the veto of the Magi in matters relating to the ritual. He shall be assisted in the discharge of his duties by the Council, and shall be empowered to arrange for the due performance of each ceremony, by appointing well-qualified brethren to assist as Celebrant, Suffragan, Cantor and Guards, in the various grades of the first and second Orders. The M. G. shall preside at the general meetings of the brotherhood, and shall at all times be received with the honours due to his important office.

XII. The Deputy Master-general shall, as the representative of the chief, preside at all meetings in his absence, and in the absence of any Past Master-general, and on such occasions shall be vested with equal authority for the time being; subject, however, to appeal being made from his decisions to the Master-general and his Council.

XIII. The Treasurer-general shall receive from the Secretary-general all moneys belonging to the Society, and shall keep an account of his receipts and disbursements, which shall be audited before the obligatory meeting in January, by the Ancients, under the supervision of the Master-general. No expenses shall be incurred without the knowledge of the chief or his deputy. The proceedings of the Society shall be printed quarterly, under the title of THE ROSICRUCIAN, and a copy shall be sent to every subscribing and honorary member by the Secretary-general. The record shall be conducted under the supervision of the Supreme Magus.

XIV.--The Secretary-general shall convene all meetings of the Council and general body; record the proceedings in the minute book, register the names, residences, and mottoes of all members, with dates of admission to each grade; collect all fees and subscriptions when due, and forthwith pay them over to the Treasurer.

XV. The Council of Ancients shall attend the meetings of the Society, and in the absence of the M. G., P. M. G., and D. M. G., the Senior Ancient present shall preside. They shall generally assist the Chief in the discharge of his duties, more especially with reference to the ceremonials of the several Orders.

XVI. The Precentor and Organist shall have the direction of all musical arrangements at the meetings of the Society.

XVII. The Conductor of Novices shall examine all aspirants, and report to the Council as to their qualifications for admission to the grade of Zelator; he shall also perform all the duties appertaining to his office in the G**** M***** C*****.

XVIII. The Torch Bearer shall discharge the peculiar duties allotted to him, more especially those which relate to the ceremonies in the first grade.

XIX. The Herald and Guardian shall defend the entrance of the Temple, and permit no one to enter without first acquainting the Conductor.

XX. The Jewels for the Magi, Officers, and Brethren, are to be worn at all ceremonial meetings. JEWELS OF THE ROSIE CROSS.

Jewel of the Supreme Magus.

An ebony Cross, with golden roses at its extremities and the jewel of the Rosie Cross in the centre. It is surmounted by a crown of gold for the Supreme Magus alone, as represented in the engraving below, and the jewel is to be worn round the neck, suspended by a crimson velvet ribbon.

Jewel of the two Junior Magi.

As above, but without the crown, and worn in the same manner.

Jewel of the Grand Officers.

A lozenge-shaped plate of gold enamelled white, with the Rosie Cross in the centre, surmounted by a golden mitre, on the rim of which is enamelled in rose-coloured characters LUX, and in its centre a small cross of the same colour. This jewel is worn suspended from the button-hole by a green ribbon an inch in width, and with a cross also embroidered on it in rose-coloured silk, as shown in the engraving below, which is as nearly as possible one-third of the actual size of the jewel.

Jewel of the Fraternity.

The lozenge-shaped jewel of the Rosie Cross, as above, without the mitre, suspended by a green ribbon an inch in width, and without the embroidered cross.

This information is transcribed from a secret record of the association, entitled "The Rosicrucian," which was first published in 1868, appearing as an infinitesimal quarterly of twelve small pages, and subsequently continued as a monthly magazine, which subsisted till the year 1879, when it accomplished another transformation, whose history I have failed to trace.

There is much curious material contained in the two series. An early number announces the objects of the society which it represents. It is "calculated to meet the requirements of those worthy Masons who wish to study the science and antiquities of the Craft, and trace it, through its successive developments, to the present time; also to cull information from all the records extant, of those mysterious societies which had their existence in the dark ages of the world when might meant right, when every man's hand was against his brother, and when such combinations were necessary to protect the weak against the strong."

These objects appear to have been fulfilled in a very desultory manner, so far, at least, as the organ of the association is concerned. Reports of Masonic meetings, long serial stories of an occult character, and somewhat feeble poetry by supreme magi and worthy fratres, permanently occupied a large proportion of an exceedingly limited space for a period of ten years.

In 1871 the society informed its members that it was entirely non-masonic in character, with the sole exception that every aspirant was required to belong to the masonic Brotherhood. The assigned reason is the numerous points of resemblance between the secrets of Rosicrucians and Freemasons. The object of the association was then stated to be purely literary and antiquarian, and the promulgation of a new masonic rite was by no means intended. "The society is at present composed of 144 Fratres, and is ruled over by three brethren, who have attained to the ninth degree, or Supreme Magus, Seventy-two of these compose the London College, and thirty-six is the statutory number of each of the two subordinate colleges" at Bristol and Manchester. Every College, excepting the Metropolitan, was restricted in 1877 to thirty-six subscribing members, exclusive of those of the ninth grade; the following numbers being permitted in each grade

1. Magister Templi or VIII°.
2. Adeptus Exemptus or VII°.
3. Adeptus Major   or VI°.
4. Adeptus Minor   or V°.
5. Philosophus   or IV°.
6. Practicus   or III°.
7. Thearicus   or II°.
8. Zelator   or I°.

The numbers were doubled in the Metropolitan College, but these arrangements were practically abrogated by the admission of supernumerary members until the occurrence of "substantive vacancies." A Yorkshire College was consecrated in 1877; a college in Edinburgh to represent the East of Scotland had been established some time previously.

The prime mover in this Association was Robert Wentworth Little, who died in the year 1878, at the age of thirty-eight; he was the Supreme Magus, and the actual revival of the Rosicrucian Order in England was owing to his instrumentality. The Honorary Presidentship has been conferred upon various noblemen, the late Lord Lytton was elected Grand Patron, and among the most important members must be reckoned the late Frederick Hockley, Kenneth Mackenzie, and Hargrave Jennings.

The most notable circumstance connected with this society is the complete ignorance which seems to have prevailed amongst its members generally concerning everything connected with Rosicrucianism. This is conspicuous in the magazine which they published. Frater William Carpenter complains that he has not obtained much light from the work of Frater Jennings, and that he himself is "an untaught speculator." Frater William Hughan is acknowledged as an adept, but he does not seem to have been aware that the "Fama" and "Confessio Fraternitatis" originally appeared in Germany. Frater Carpenter inclines to the opinion that the question had better be left to itself, as "an inquiry into the matter is destined to get every one who attempts it into an entanglement." He humbly confesses that it is too wonderful for him, too high, and that he cannot attain it. At the same time he hazards a new definition of the much-abused term Rosicrucian, which he believes to have been assumed by the Brotherhood not because they sought light by the assistance of *ros*, dew, but in *rus*, solitude, which is conclusive as to the philological abilities of this "untaught speculator." By the year 1872, the members seems to have discovered that their organ and indeed their society had scarcely borne out its original intention, for "the general body of members have done little to promote the elucidation of Rosicrucian lore;" but, in spite of resolutions to the contrary, matters continued in much the same condition, though glowing expectations were entertained on the initiation of one Frater Kenneth Mackenzie VI°., a burning and a shining light of occultism, somewhat concealed beneath the bushel of secresy. I gather from various casual statements that the balance of opinion in the camp of the "Rosicrucian Brotherhood in Anglia" is to the following effect--That Andreas was in some way connected with the authorship of the "Fama" and "Confessio Fraternitatis," that the fraternity of Christian Rosencreutz as described therein and in the "Chymical Marriage" had no tangible existence, but that they gave rise to the philosophic sect of Rosicrucianism, which name became, in the words of Thomas Vaughan, a generic term, embracing every species of mystical pretension.This harmless association deserves a mild sympathy at the hands of the students of occultism.

"It has not done much harm, nor yet much good;

It might have done much better if it would." Its character can hardly have deceived the most credulous of its postulants. Some of its members wrap themselves in darkness and mystery, proclaiming themselves Rosicrucians with intent to deceive. These persons find a few--very few--feeble--in truth very feeble--believers and admirers. Others assert that the

Society is a mask to something else--the last resource of cornered credulity and exposed imposture. There are similar associations in other parts of Europe and also in America, *e.g.*, the Societas Rosicruciana of Boston. In concluding this notice of modern Rosicrucian associations, I beg leave to warn my readers that all persons, whether within or without the magic circles of public libraries, who proclaim themselves to be Rosicrucians are simply members of pseudo-fraternities, and that there is that difference between their assertion and the facts of the case "in which the essence of a lie consists."

Though the true Rosicrucians, supposing such a society to have had at any period a tangible and corporate existence, disappeared very suddenly from the historical plane, the glamour of the mystery which surrounded them proved a prolific *prima materia* for the alchemical transfigurations of romance and poetry, and insured them a place in legend. Two curious traditions are noticed by Hargrave Jennings, but his mental tortuosity has, in both cases, induced him to pervert the story which be recounts by the introduction of worthless and untruthful details manufactured by his own imagination, and prudently ascribed to other, of course unnamed, sources of information. One of these is the alleged discovery of the tomb of Rosicrucius. Mr Jennings cites Plot's "History of Staffordshire" as his authority for this legend; I have carefully looked through the large folio volume of this "painstaking antiquary," but have failed to verify the reference; the *Spectator* for May 15, 1712, cites the story in the words of the original narrator, and this version I present, for comparison, to the students of the "distinguished esoteric *littérateur's*" pseudo-history. Mr Hargrave Jennings says that it is "poor and ineffective," an opinion not uncommon to other interpreters of history who manipulate their materials in the interests of their private opinions.

"A certain person having occasion to dig somewhat deep in the ground, where this philosopher lay interred, met with a small door, having a wall on each side of it. His curiosity, and the hopes of finding some hidden treasure, soon prompted him to force open the door. He was immediately surprised by a sudden blaze of light, and discovered a very fair vault. At the upper end of it was a statue of a man in armour, sitting by a table, and leaning on his left arm. He held a truncheon in his right hand, and had a lamp burning before him. The man had no sooner set one foot within the vault, than the statue, erecting itself from its leaning posture, stood bolt upright; and, upon the fellow's advancing another step, lifted up the truncheon in its right hand. The man still ventured a third step, when the statue, with a furious blow, broke the lamp into a thousand pieces, and left his guest in a sudden darkness.

"Upon the report of this adventure, the country people soon came with lights to the sepulchre, and discovered that the statue, which was made of

247

brass, was nothing more than a piece of clock-work; that the floor of the vault was all loose, and underlaid with several springs, which, upon any man's entering, naturally produced that which had happened. "Rosicrucius, say his disciples, made use of this method to show the world that he had re-invented the ever-burning lamps of the ancients, though he was resolved no one should reap any advantage from the discovery."

The second story has suffered still further outrage. Mr Hargrave Jennings asserts that it is related upon "excellent authority." This authority is a work by Dr John Campbel, entitled "Hermippus Redivivus; or, the Sage's Triumph over Old Age and the Grave," and the reference therein is "Les Memoires Historiques" for the year 1 687, tome i. p. 365, which no one has been able to identify, and which, according to William Godwin, had perhaps no other existence than in the fertile brain of the compiler.

"There happened in the year 1687, an odd accident at Venice, that made a very great stir then, and which I think deserves to be rescued from oblivion. The great freedom and ease with which all persons, who make a good appearance, live in that city, is known sufficiently to all who are acquainted with it; such, therefore, will not be surprised that a stranger who went by the name of Signor Gualdi, and who made a considerable figure there, was admitted into the best company, though nobody knew who or what he was. He remained at Venice some months, and three things were remarked in his conduct. The first was, that he had a small collection of fine pictures, which he readily showed to anybody that desired it; the next, that he was perfectly versed in all arts and sciences, and spoke on every subject with such readiness and sagacity, as astonished all who heard him; and it was in the third place observed, that he never wrote or received any letter; never desired any credit, or made use of bills of exchange, but paid for every thing in ready-money, and lived decently, though not in splendour. "This gentleman met one day at the coffee-house with a Venetian nobleman, who was an extraordinary good judge of pictures: he had heard of Signor Gualdi's collection, and in a very polite manner desired to see them, to which the other very readily consented. After the Venetian had viewed Signor Gualdi's collection, and expressed his satisfaction, by telling him that he had never seen a finer, considering the number of pieces of which it consisted, he cast his eyes by chance over the chamber-door, where hung a picture of this stranger, The Venetian looked upon it, and then upon him. 'This picture was drawn for you, sir,' says he to Signor Gualdi; to which the other made no answer but by a low bow. 'You look,' continued the Venetian, 'like a man of fifty, and yet I know this picture to be of the hand of Titian, who has been dead one hundred and thirty years, how is this possible?' 'It is not easy,' said Signor Gualdi gravely, 'to know all things that are possible, but there is certainly no crime in my being like a picture drawn

248

by Titian.' The Venetian easily perceived, by his manner of speaking, that he had given the stranger offence, and therefore took his leave.

"He could not forbear speaking of this in the evening to some of his friends, who resolved to satisfy themselves by looking upon the picture the next day. In order to have an opportunity of doing so, they went to the coffee-house about the time that Signor Gualdi was wont to come thither; and not meeting him, one of them, who had often conversed with him, went to his lodgings to enquire after him, where he heard that he had set out an hour before for Vienna. This affair made a great noise, and found a place in all the newspapers of that time."

The mysterious Signor Gualdi was "suspected to be a Rosicrucian." The acknowledged fictions of a later period occasionally introduce the Society to the novel-reading public. Among these may be mentioned the incoherent and worthless romance, entitled "St Irvyne; or, The Rosicrucian," which was written by Shelley at the age of seventeen; Lord Lytton's "Zanoni;" "The Rosicrucian's Story," by Paschal R. Randolph, an American half-breed of no inconsiderable talent, who translated the "Divine Pomiander," formed an ephemeral Rosicrucian publishing company, and crowning a chequered existence with a sudden suicide, is still much respected among certain spiritual circles, occasionally "communicating" with quite the average veracity of other "controls" performed by the "choir invisible." The official organ of the English *Societas Rosicruciana* has also provided its select and esoteric circle of "antiquarian" illuminati with "Leaves from the Diary of a Rosicrucian," a romance of considerable ability by Kenneth Mackenzie, F. R. C., IX°.

CONCLUSION.

"THERE is a point," quoth a grandiloquent pseudo-Rosicrucian in an impressive and tragedy voice, "there is a point," he repeated in the conventional whisper of the unexplainable mystic, "beyond which we inevitably must keep silence. We are driven to take refuge in portentous darkness and in irretrievable mystery." The godless and incorrigible scepticism of a coarse, unsubdued intelligence, surrendered to a reprobate sense, and basely and wilfully grovelling in the blind alleys of natural causes, begs leave to believe that this is because extremes meet, that the heights of the inexpressible are closely approximate to the abysmal depths of bathos. But the unsubdued intelligence is known to have covered the shame of its naked ignorance with the "filthy rags" of *a posteriori* methods. Anathema maranatha. Let it have no part in the life to come! Nevertheless, I have found it superfluous to "keep guard over" the secrets of the Rosicrucians, or to veil their mysteries in inviolable silence, and this is for a simple reason, namely, that they have never revealed any. If the manifestoes I have published emanated in reality from a secret society, it has stood guard over its own treasures, and as neither Mr Hargrave Jennings nor myself can "boast of having--really and in fact--seen or known any supposed (or suspected) member in the flesh," we have nothing to reveal or to withhold. "The recondite systems connected with the illustrious Rosicrucians" are, of course, enveloped in darkness, and, in common with other students of esoteric lore, I am inclined to consider that this darkness does cover a real and, possibly, a recoverable knowledge. But it is not of our making and in our age, which has nothing to fear from the rack or the faggot, and but little from the milder agonies of eternal Coventry, it is no longer worth preserving. *Nihil est opertum quod non revelabitur, et occultum quod non scietur.* The time has come when that which was muttered in darkness may be declared plainly in the full face of day, and when that which was whispered in the ear can be proclaimed on the house-top. The tremendous secrets of spiritual alchemy are about to surrender at discretion to the searching investigations of the sympathetic and impartial student at work in the cause of truth. On the faith of a follower of Honnes, I can promise that nothing shall be held back from those true Sons of the Doctrine, the sincere seekers after light who are prepared to approach the supreme arcana of the psychic world with a clean heart and an earnest aim. True Rosicrucians and true alchemical adepts, if there be any in existence at this day, will not resent a new procedure when circumstances have been radically changed. The pontiffs of darkness and mystery will probably discover that it is too late to make use of that policy of assassination which is supposed to have been applied in the case of the Abbé de Villars. I appeal, therefore, to those students of occultism who are men of method as well as of imagination, of

250

reason as well as of intuition, to assist me in clearing away the dust and rubbish which have accumulated during centuries of oblivion, misrepresentation, and calumny in the silent sanctuaries of the transcendental sciences, that the traditionary secrets of Nature unencumbered by evasive veils, which preserved them perhaps in the past from the violence of tyrants and intellectual task-masters in the high places of religion and science, but which are rent on every side, and "execrable from the moment that they are useless," may shine forth in the darkness of doubt and uncertainty, to illuminate the strait and narrow avenues which communicate between the seen and the unseen.

While this work was passing through the press, Mr Hargrave Jennings has issued the third edition of "The Rosicrucians, their Rites and Mysteries." It is spread over the space of two large volumes of an imposing and handsome appearance. It embodies some new but wholly irrelevant materials, and does not contain one syllable of additional information on its ostensible subject. The additional illustrations are quite beside the question, having no reference, however esoteric and remote, to the Rosicrucian mystery. This edition, in fact, justifies still further the severe criticism which I have been forced to make on the purposeless and rambling speculations of its eccentric author.

ADDITIONAL NOTES.

NUMBER I.

ACCORDING to the "Kabbala Denudata" of the Baron Knorr de Rosenroth, the Rose signifies the Shecinah. The reason is given in the Zohar, sect. Æmor., "*Quod sicut Rosa crescit ad aquas, et emiitit odorem bonum, sic Malchuth hoc gaudet nomine, cum influxum assugit a Binah, quæ bonum elevat odorem.*"

The definition of John Heydon concerning the letters R. C. comes too late to be of much value on historical grounds. But some may ask what I mean by R. C. The ceremony is an Ebony Cross, flourisht and decked with Roses of Gold. The Cross typifies Christ's sufferings upon the Cross for our sins; the Roses of Gold shew the glory and beauty of his resurrection from death to life. This is carried to Mesque, Cascle, Apamia, Chaulatean, Virissa Caumich, Mount Calvery, Haran, and Mount Sinai, where they meet when they please and make resolution of all their actions, then disperse themselves abroad, taking their pleasure always in one of these places, where they resolve also all questions of whatsoever hath been done, is done, or shall be done in the world, from the beginning to the end thereof. And these are the men called Rosicrucians."

NUMBER II.

It is the sign of Mercury, but its position in the twelfth clavis of Basil Valentine indicates a further and more arcane importance. "The vivific gold, the vivific sulphur, or the true fire of the philosophers, is to be sought in the house of Mercury," says Eliphas Lévi ("Mysteries of Magic," p. 202). The "sulphur, mercury, and salt of the philosophers," says the same adept, "condensed and volatilized by turns, compose the azoth of the philosophers." The alchemical "balm of sulphur," according to the Baron Tschoudy's "Catechism for the Grade of Adept, or Sublime and Unknown apprentice Philosopher" (see "L'Etoile Flamboyante"), is identical with the "radical moisture," which is also the mercury of the philosophers, the base of every species in the three kingdoms of Nature, but more particularly the seed and base of metals when it is prepared philosophically by the extraction of what is superfluous and the addition of what is wanting for the performance of the Hermetic opus. On this point, see Pernetz, "Dictionnaire Mytho-Hermétique."

NUMBER III.

This is a common and significant superstition. Perhaps it originated in the Phœnix legend; it is dear to mystical writers, at any rate, and has prompted some curious and abstruse reasoning. The bee is especially a subject of folklore, and is a symbol of the ungenerating and sexless spirit of man, which yet presents itself to the mind under a male aspect.

NUMBER IV.

The symbolical representation of the tetrad under the figure of a four-square garden, enclosure, house, or city is very common among mystical writers. A familiar instance is found in the Apocalypse, where the New Jerusalem is represented as a perfect square descending out of heaven. Compare the "Roman de la Rose"--

"Haut fut li mur et *tous quarrés*
Si en fu bien clos et barrés,
En leu de haies, uns vergiers,
Où onc n'avoit entré bergiers."

This passage is rendered by Chaucer in the following manner:--

"Square was the wall, and high somedele
Enclosed, and ybarred wele,
In stead of hedge, was that gardin,
Come never shepherde therein."

NUMBER V.

The appendix to a series of epistles, entitled "Selenia Augustalia," and written by Johann Valentin Andreas, contains an account, thus arranged, of the offspring of this marriage:--

JOH. VALENTINI ANDREÆ.

Propago.

Johann Valentin Andreæ, *natus* 1586, 17 *Aug.*, et Agnes Elisabeth Grüningeren, *n.* 1592, 29 Mart.; nuptias habent 1614, 2 Augusti.

Unde liberi.

I. Maria, nat. 1616, 26 Mart; nubit Petro Waltero, 1636, 20 Jun., Unde. 1. Maria Elisabeth, nat. 1637, 21 Nov.; obiit 1637, 30 Novemb.

2. Maria Barbara, nat. 1638, 28 Nov.

3. Anna Maria, nat. 1640, 1 April; obiit 1640, 23 Junii.

4. Augustus, nat. 1643, 3 Octob.; obiit 1646, 25 Mart.

5. Maria Margareth, nat. 1647, 19 Jul.

II. Concordia, nat. 1617, 29 Junii; obiit. 1617, 27 Julii.

III. Agnes Elisabeth, nat. 1618, 10 Sept.; obiit. 1618, 10 Sept.

IV. Agnes Elisabeth, nat. 1620, 4 Decemb.; nubit Johanni Rühlino, 1630, 7 Octob.

Unde.

1. Maria Elisabeth, nat. 1640, 25 Mali; obiit 1640, 9 Junii.

2. Johann Valentin, nat. 1641, 4 Aug.

3. Anna Maria, nat. 1642, 16 Julii.

4. Johann Ludovicus, nat. 1643, 25 Aug.; obiit 1643, 29 Octob.

5. Margaretha, nat. 1644, 29 Septemb.; obiit 1650, 15 Junii.

6. Rudolph Augustus, nat. 1645, 8 Octob.

7. Anna Catharina, nat. 1647, 12 April; obiit 1647, 20 Junii.

8. Joh. Ludovicus, nat. 1648, 18 Maui; obiit 1649, 11 Mart.

9. Johann Georgius, nat. 1649, 25 Mail; obiit 1649, 17 Julii.

10. Joh. Eberhardt, nat. 1650, 23 Junii.

11. Anna Margareth, nat. 1651, 5 Aug.

12. Maria Barbara, nat. 1652, 11 Aug.

V. Gottlieb, nat. 1622, 19 Sept.; ducit Barbaram Sanbertinam, 1643, 19 Junii. Uncle.

1. Christina Patientia, nat. 1644, 24 Decem.; obiit 1645, 3 Jan.

2. Joh. Valentin, nat. 1646, 17 Mart.

3. Gottliebin, nat. 1647, 3 Nov.

4. Augustus Gottlieb, natus 1649, 16 Jan.

5. Jacob Erasmus, nat. 1650, 3 August; obiit 1651, 27 Mart.

6. Maria Barb. Elisab., nat. 1652, 13 Apr.

VI. Ehrenreich, nat. 1624, 10 Julii; obiit 1634, 21 Septemb.

VII. Wahrermund, nat. 1627, 27 Nov.; obiit 1629, 6 Febr.

VIII. Johan Valentin, nat. 1631, 9 Aug.; obiit 1632, 5 Sept.

IX. Patientia, nat. 1632, 25 Octob.; obiit 1632; 6 Decemb.

NUMBER VI.

In the first volume of his "Philosophical Dictionary" Voltaire, however, recounts what he considered to be the best exploit ever performed in alchemy, and which was that of a Rosicrucian, who, as early as the year 1620, paid a visit to Henri I., duc de Bouillon, of the house of Turenne, and the sovereign prince of Sédan, with the object of informing him that his power and dominion were in no way proportioned to his valour, and that he, the stranger in question, was fired with the disinterested design of making him as wealthy as an Emperor. "I can remain no longer than two days on your estate," said the impostor; I must then proceed to Venice and be present at the grand assembly of my brethren. In the first place, you must keep my secret inviolable; in the second, send to the first apothecary in the town and purchase a quantity of litharge; cast but one grain of this red powder therein, and in less than a quarter of an hour it will be transformed into gold."

The prince performed the operation, and repeated it three times in the presence of the virtuoso. This personage had previously purchased all the litharge which was to be found at the apothecaries in Sédan, and had resold it to them, tinctured with several ounces of gold. The adept on departing presented all his powder of projection to the duc de Bouillon, who did not doubt for a moment that, having manufactured three ounces of gold with three grains, he would make one hundred thousand ounces with a proportionate quantity of this priceless and mysterious powder. The philosopher was in haste to quit the town; he declared that he had given all his powder to the prince, and that he needed some coin of the realm to repair to Venice for the inauguration of the assembly of Hermetics. A man of moderate tastes, he asked simply for twenty thousand crowns, but was forced by his princely disciple to accept twice that sum; but when the unfortunate duke had exhausted all the litharge in Sédan he could no longer manufacture gold, nor could he anywhere discover his philosopher.

APPENDIX OF ADDITIONAL DOCUMENTS.

By an error of transcription the preface to the "Fama Fraternitatis" was omitted from the text of the present revised version. It is addressed to "the wise and understanding reader."

Wisdome (sayeth Solomon) is a treasure unto men that never faileth, for she is the breth of the power of God and an inherence flowing from the glory of the Almighty; she is the brightness of the everlasting light, the unspotted mirror of the power of God, and the image of His goodness. She teacheth civility with righteousness and strength, she knoweth things of old, and conjectureth aright what is to come; she knoweth the subtleties of speaches and can expound darke sentences; she foreseeth signes and wonders, with the advent of seasons and times. With this treasure was our first father Adam before his fall fully indued; hence it doth appear that after God had brought before him all the creatures of the field and the fowls under the heavens, he gave to everyone of them theyr proper name, accordinge to their Nature.

Although now, through the sorrowful fall into sinn, this excellent jewell wisdome hath bene lost, and mere darkness and ignorance is come into the world, yet, notwithstanding, the Lord God hath sometimes hetherto bestowed and made manifest the same to some of his friends; the wise Kinge Solomon Both testifie of himself that he upon his earnest prayer and desire obtained such wisdome of God that thereby he knew how the world was made, understood the operation of the elements, the beginninge, endinge, and middest of the times, the alterations, the dayes of the turning of the sunne, the change of seasons, the circuits of yeres and the positions of stars, the natures of livinge creatures and the furies of wild beasts, the violence of winds, the reasonings of men, the diversities of plants, the vertues of roots, and all such things as are either secret or manifest, them he knewe.

Now, I doe not think that there can be found anyone whoe would not wish and desire with all his heart to be partaker of this noble treasure, but seinge the same felicity canne happen to none except God Himself give wisdome and send His Holy Spirit from above, we have sett forth in print this little treaty, to wit, the *Famam* and *Confessionem* of the Laudable Fraternity of the Rosy Cross, to be read by every one, because in them is clearly shewn and discovered what concerning it the world hath hereafter to expect. Although now these things may seem somewhat strange, and many might esteme it to be a philosophical showe and no true historie which is published and spoken of the Fraternity of the Rosy Cross, it shall therefore sufficiently appear by our Confession that there is more *in recessu* then may be imagined, and it shall also be easily understood and observed by everyone, (yf he be not altogether void of understandinge) what now adayes is meant thereby.

Those who are true disciples of wisdome and true followers of the spirituall arte will consider better of these things, and have them in greater estimation, as also judge farr otherwise of them, as hath been done of some principall persons but espetially of Adam Haselmeyer, *Notarius Publicus* to the Archduke Maximilian, whoe likewise hath made an extract *ex scriptis Theologicis Theophrasti*, and written a treatise under the title Jesuits, wherein he willeth that every Christian should be a true Jesuite, that is, should walke, live, and be in Jesus. He was but ill rewarded of the Jesuites, because in his answer written upon the *Famam* he did name those of the Fraternity of the Rosy Cross, "the highly illuminated men and undeceiving Jesuites," for they, not able to brook this, layde hands on him and put him into the gallies, for which they likewise are to expect theyr reward.

Blessed Aurora will now begin to appeare, whoe (after the passing away of the darke night of Saturne) with her brightness altogether extinguished the shinninge of the moon, or the small sparkles of the heavenly wisdome which yet remaines with men, and is a fore runner of pleasant Phœbus, whoe, with her cleare and fiery glisteninge beames, brings forth that blessed day, long wished for of many true-hearted, by which daylight then shall truely be knowne and seene, all heavenly treasures of godly wisdome, as also the secrets of all hidden and invisible things in the world, according to the doctrine of our forefathers and auncient wise men.

This will be the right Kingly Rubie, most excellent shining Carbuncle, of the which it is sayd that he doth shine and give light in darkenes, and is a perfect medecine of all imperfect metaline bodyes, to change them into the best gould and to cure all diseases of men, easing them of theyr paynes and miseries.

Be therefore gentle reader admonished, that with me you doe earnestly pray to God, that it may please Him to open the harts and eares of all ill-hearing people, and to grant unto them His blessing, that they may be able to know Him in His omnipotency, with admiring contemplation of Nature, to His honor and praise, and to the love, helpe, comfort, and strengthening of our neighbours,, and to the restoring of health of all the diseased. Amen.

A ROSICRUCIAN ALLEGORY. There is a mountain situated in the midst of the *earth* or *centre* of the *world*, which is both *small* and *great*. It is soft also above measure, hard and strong. It is *far off and near at hand;* but, by the Providence of God, it is invisible. In it are hidden most ample treasures, which the world is not able to value. This mountain, by the envy of the devil, is compassed about with very cruel beasts and ravenous birds, which make the way thither both difficult and dangerous; and, therefore, hitherto, because the time is not yet come, the way thither could not be sought after by all, but only by the worthy man's self-labour and investigation.

257

To this *mountain* you shall go in a *certain night*, when it comes most long and dark, and see that you *prepare* yourself by *prayer*. *Insist* upon the *way* that leads to the *mountain*, but ask not of any man where it lies; only follow your *guide*, who will *offer* himself to you, and will meet you in the way.

This guide will bring you to the mountain at *midnight*, when all things are silent and dark. It is necessary that you arm yourself with a resolute, heroic courage, lest you fear those things that will happen, and fall back. You need no sword or other bodily weapon, only call upon your God, *sincerely and heartily seeking Him.*

When you have discovered the mountain, the first miracle that will appear is this--a most vehement and very great wind will *shake* the whole *mountain* and shatter the *rocks* to pieces. You will be encountered by lions, dragons, and other terrible wild beasts; but fear not any of these things. Be resolute and take heed that you return not, for your guide who brought you thither will not suffer any evil to befall you. As for the *treasure*, it is not yet discovered, but it is very near. After this wind will come an earthquake, which will overthrow those things which the wind had left. Be sure you fall not off. The *earthquake* being passed, there shall follow a *fire* that will consume the earthly rubbish and discover the treasure, but as yet you cannot see it. After all these things, and near daybreak, there shall be a great *calm*, and you shall see the *day-star* arise, and the darkness will disappear. You will *conceive* a great treasure; the chiefest thing and the most perfect is a certain exalted tincture, with which the world, if it served God and were worthy of such gifts, might be tinged and turned into most pure gold.

THE ROSIE CRUCIAN PRAYER TO GOD.

Jesus Mihi Omnia.

Oh Thou everywhere and good of all, whatsoever I do remember, I beseech Thee, that I am but dust, but as a vapour sprung from earth, which even Thy smallest breath can scatter. Thou hast given me a soul and laws to govern it; let that fraternal rule which Thou didst first appoint to sway man order me; make me careful to point at Thy glory in all my wayes, and where I cannot rightly know Thee, that not only my understanding but my ignorance may honour Thee. Thou art all that can be perfect; Thy revelation hath made me happy. Be not angry, O Divine One, O God the most high Creator! If it please Thee, suffer these revealed secrets, Thy gifts alone, not for my praise but to Thy glory, to manifest themselves. I beseech Thee, most gracious God, they may not fall into the hands of ignorant envious persons that cloud these truths to Thy disgrace, saying they are not lawful to be published because what God reveals is to be kept secret. But Rosie Crucian philosophers lay up this secret into the bosome of God which I have presumed to manifest clearly and plainly. I beseech the Trinity it may be printed as I have written it that the truth may no more be darkened with ambiguous language. Good God, besides Thee nothing is! O stream Thyself into my soul, and flow it with Thy grace, illumination and revelation! Make me to depend on Thee. Thou delightest that man should account Thee as his King, and not hide what honey of knowledge he hath revealed. I cast myself as an honourer of Thee at Thy feet, and because I cannot be defended by Thee unless I believe after Thy laws, keep me, O my soul's Soveraign, in the obedience of Thy will, and that I wound not my conscience with vice and hiding Thy gifts and graces bestowed upon me, for this, I know, will destroy me within, and make Thy illuminating Spirit leave me. I am afraid I have already infinitely swerved from the revelations of that Divine Guide which Thou hast commanded to direct me to the truth, and for this I am a sad prostrate and penitent at the foot of Thy throne. I appeal only to the abundance of Thy remissions, O God, my God. I know it is a mysterie beyond the vast soul's apprehension, and therefore deep enough for man to rest in safety in! O Thou Being of all beings, cause me to work myself to Thee, and into the receiving arms of Thy paternal mercies throw myself. For outward things I thank Thee, and such as I have I give unto others, in the name of the Trinity, freely and faithfully, without hiding anything of what was revealed to me and experienced to be no diabolical delusion or dream, but the *Adjectamenta* of Thy richer graces--the mines and deprivation are both in Thy hands. In what Thou hast given me I am content. Good God, ray Thyself into my soul! Give me but a heart to please Thee, I beg no more then Thou hast given, and that to continue me uncontemnedly and unpittiedly honest. Save me from the devil, lusts, and men, and from those fond dotages of mortality which would weigh down my soul to lowness and debauchment. Let it be my glory (planting myself in a noble height above them) to contemn them. Take me from myself and fill me but with Thee. Sum up Thy blessings in these two, that I may be rightly good and wise, and these, for Thy eternal truth's sake, grant and make grateful.

Made in United States
Cleveland, OH
01 August 2025

18969251R00148